Cultivating the Spirit on One Acre of Red Clay

Kirk H. Neely
Illustrations by Krista Redding
Paintings by author

Parson's Porch Books

Cultivating the Spirit on One Acre of Red Clay
ISBN: Softcover 978-1-960326-26-3
Copyright © 2025 by Kirk H. Neely

All Scriptures if found in the New International Version (NIV)) unless otherwise noted.

Parson's Porch Books is an imprint of Parson's Porch *&* Company (PP*&*C) in Cleveland, Tennessee. PP*&*C is a self-funded charity which earns money by publishing books of noted authors, representing all genres. Its face and voice is **David Russell Tullock** (dtullock@parsonsporch.com).

Parson's Porch *&* Company *turns books into bread & milk* by sharing its profits with the poor.

www.parsonsporch.com

*Cultivating the Spirit on
One Acre of Red Clay*

Write what you have seen…

Revelation 1:19 (NIV)

Dedication

To my paternal grandparents,
Kreswell Edward Neely, Sr.
and Mamie Lawton Neely,

To my parents,
Kirk and Louise Hudson Neely,

To my father and mother-in-law,
Jackson S. and Elizabeth Mitchell Long,

And to all who till, plant, and tend the good earth.

Contents

One Acre of Red Clay

"See, I have given you this land."
-Deuteronomy 1:8, NIV

What is the world's oldest profession? Not so fast. What you have always heard from sociologists may not be the correct answer. According to the Biblical account, the oldest profession existed before the concept of sin. Genesis 2:15 reads, "The Lord God took the man and put him in the Garden of Eden to work it and take care of it" (NIV). May I suggest that the oldest profession is gardening, the care of the earth?

Genesis 1:29 introduces this story of creation. God said, "I give you every seed-bearing plant on the face of the whole earth and every tree that has fruit with seed in it. They will be yours for food" (NIV).

I was born on August 21, 1944. It was near the end of World War II. On the day I was born, my grandfather had been working in the lumberyard all day long. When he got home, he started tilling his garden with a one-wheeled plow with a single turn blade and oak handles. When the call came that my mother was in labor, Pappy came in from the garden and told my grandmother that he was headed to the hospital.

She told him, "Ed, you can't go like that."

Pappy said, "Them who know me know I can do better them who don't, it don't matter."

When Clare and I examine our heritage, we discover a long line of farmers and gardeners in each of our family trees all with similar sentiments to Pappy, such as Clare's father, Mr. Jack.

At birth, he was named Stonewall Jackson Long. Before enlisting in the United States Marine Corps, he changed his name to Jackson S. Long because he said he would rather be known as Jackson S. than Stonewall J. He was Clare's father, my father-in-law, whom I called Mr. Jack.

Mr. Jack was the fifth of nine children raised on a dirt farm in Saluda County, South Carolina. He dropped out of high school just a few weeks before graduation to help his father do the spring planting. He later became an executive with Southern Cotton Oil Company and eventually retired as President of the company.

Mr. Jack drank Kentucky bourbon and smoked unfiltered cigarettes, which he lit with kitchen matches. While he was aware that smoking caused cancer, he thought that either the filters or the lighters contained carcinogens. Mr. Jack was sure that tobacco did not cause cancer because it grew in the good earth.

In retirement, Mr. Jack returned to his roots. He purchased a Troy-Bilt tiller and grew a half-acre garden. His plot was pristine. He grew beautiful vegetables in uniform rows. Mr. Jack's garden was almost pest-free and weed-free. Best of all, he loved sharing the abundance of his tender loving care with family, friends, and neighbors.

My dad, too, grew a big garden. It was about the same size as Mr. Jack's garden, tilled with a small Ford tractor. Dad's plot was a family project. All eight of the children worked in the red soil. The garden was bountiful. The harvest was abundant, with enough to share, can, and freeze.

Mr. Jack and Dad came by their gardening skills honestly. They learned by necessity and the examples set by their parents and grandparents. Both had lived through the Great Depression.

In 1807, a fellow named Anthony Foster, a planter and a businessman, built a large home on what is now South Carolina Highway 56 in Spartanburg. Eventually, Mr. Foster turned his home into a tavern that included rooms for rent. Because his house was located at the crossroads of Charleston Road and the Old Georgia Road, the home became, in 1830, the last stagecoach stop at the nearby Glen Springs Resort and Hotel.

The stately building had several renovations over the years, including tall columns on the front, which were added in 1845 in the Antebellum Period. Today, the home has twenty rooms. One of those rooms is designated as the "John C. Calhoun Suite" because of his many stays there during his political career. The former vice president enjoyed the hospitality of Foster's Tavern. Foster's Tavern is constructed entirely of hand-thrown red brick made from clay dug from a nearby clay pit.

In 1923, my grandfather and grandmother moved their family from Greenville to Spartanburg in the Upstate of South Carolina. Pappy had been working for his brother-in-law, Asbury Lawton, managing Lawton Lumber Company in Greenville. Pappy decided he wanted to own his own business. So, to avoid competing with his brother-in-law, he and the family moved to

Spartanburg, where he purchased and operated Standard Lumber Company. Pappy called the business a one-horse lumberyard. He had one employee, Charlie Norman. The lone draft horse's name was Old Dan.

Pappy was able to earn a good living to support his growing family. He built a fine home on the Greenville highway just on the outskirts of Spartanburg, where the pavement ended.

In February 1928, the eighth child was born. The business and the family were thriving.

In October 1929, the dark cloud of the Great Depression descended. Homebuilding was at a standstill. Home repairs diminished. People had no extra money to spend. The lumber business dried up. Pappy mortgaged the lumberyard in an attempt to keep it afloat. Prosperity was just around the corner, or so the politicians declared. Pappy mortgaged his beautiful home and sank the money into his business. Despite his efforts, Pappy lost both his business and his home.

After that, the family moved to a rental house in Cedar Springs. Pappy bought a mule at a chain gang auction and farmed acreage adjacent to the rented home. He tilled and planted a large vegetable garden to feed his family. They had one cow and one goat to provide dairy products. They raised turkeys and sweet potatoes to provide a meager income. In 1932, the youngest, ninth, and last child was born. Through grit, determination, and faith, the family survived, as did many others.

In 1937, Pappy bought a parcel of land with a railroad siding along the Southern Railway Line between Spartanburg and Columbia. He had no collateral. The bank loaned him the money on his word. He built a lumber shed on one end of the property and reopened Neely Lumber Company. On the other end of the property, he cut off a one-acre wedged-shaped lot on which to build his home.

Some folks cautioned Pappy against building on the land. It was the same old red dirt pit that had been the source of clay for the hand-thrown brick used to construct Foster's Tavern in 1807. Some thought the soil composition made the land unstable and unsuitable for building. "If you build there, you're asking for trouble. Every time a train goes past, the house will shake so badly that the windows will break out."

Pappy took the comments seriously. When the footings for the home were dug, he brought in a fellow who had the equipment to drill holes for electric power poles. The deep holes were spaced several feet apart along the footing trench. When the concrete was poured, and the footings filled up, those holes created pilings supporting the house in the unstable clay.

The family called it the "big house" and that is where Mammy and Pappy lived until 1961. By then, Pappy had suffered two heart attacks and a stroke. Mammy suffered from asthma. They moved to a new home in Duncan Park built by their third son, Asbury Neely. In exchange, Uncle Bury, as we called him, received the deed to the one-acre parcel of land and the big house.

For the next twenty years, the house was occasionally rented, served as a place of worship for three start-up churches, and was finally converted to office space. When Clare and I moved to Spartanburg in 1980 with our four sons, the old home was vacant.

After a futile search to find a home we could afford, Clare saw the big house. "Why can't we live there?" she asked. I asked Uncle Bury if we could rent the house. He was delighted to have occupants. We moved in, eventually purchasing the home and making improvements along the way. The old home place, the big house, has been our home for the last forty-three years. This slice of land, shaped like a piece of Mammy's sweet potato pie, has become our garden.

One acre of red clay has gradually become holy ground, an unlikely sanctuary wedged between a railroad track and a four-lane highway. We are surrounded on every side by commercial property. Until recently, a pawn shop was across the street. A landscape company and wood yard were located next door on Uncle Bury's old real estate property. Littlejohn Trucks specializing in eighteen-wheel tankers sprawls down the street. My nephew, Kam, has started a business at the old lumber yard and our neighbors on the other side are living in a mobile home. Once out in the country on a tar and gravel road, the old home place has been surrounded by commerce. Yet, this is our sanctuary, and we love every square inch of it.

When we first moved into the big house, a well-meaning church member asked, "That is just temporary, isn't it?" Of course, it is just temporary. We have only lived here for forty-three years. At some point, we will be gone.

My son-in-law and I were sitting together on our back porch recently. Jay is a well-educated farm boy from Illinois. His Dutch family roots grow deep in the black earth of the Great Plains. From our vantage point on the porch, Jay looked out at the garden.

"You know," he started. "When you're gone, it won't take long for all of this to go to briars and bramble." I agreed. "It won't take long." I paused before adding, "Somebody else may want to take it over or not. For now, it is mine to tend. I'll do that as long as I continue to enjoy doing so and as long as my physical health will allow me to do so. After that, I'll give it back to the Lord."

Then I said, "Jay, you should have seen it when the Lord had it all by himself."

I am grateful that Jay and his family have moved in with us. He has taken great interest in this old home place. Already, Jay and Betsy and their daughters have made this one acre their own. Jay and Betsy both come from long lines of farmers and gardeners who love and cherish the good earth.

When Moses saw a bush that was burning but not consumed, his curiosity got the best of him. He moved closer to the unusual sight, and a voice spoke to him from the flaming shrub. "Come no closer! Remove the sandals from your feet, for the place on which you are standing is holy ground" (Exodus 3:5).

There in the sand, Moses stood barefooted and stammering before an ordinary bush with an extraordinary message. It was a theophany, an encounter with the Almighty. It was a sacred moment, a divine engagement, and a declaration of holiness. If that hot, dry, desolate place can become holy ground, then this one acre of red clay can also become a sacred space. So, too, can your garden be sanctified and made holy.

You may want to add a burning bush to your garden. *Euonymus alatus* is a readily available compact variety. The shrub makes a suitable specimen plant in almost any soil condition as long as it is not boggy. The burning bush earns its name from the brilliant fall foliage which may be the brightest red in the fall garden. If you have a burning bush, you are bound to have holy ground.

Garden Tools

What are the tools you need for a garden? You might expect me to mention the standard assortment of long and short tools. I have an interesting collection of antique garden tools. Many of those tools were homemade. The ones I use in my garden are typically made of high tempered steel which require annual maintenance such as cleaning, sharpening, and handle replacement. But what are the tools we need to cultivate the spirit?

My list includes an inexpensive Bible with large print font and a laminated cover. Choose the translation you prefer. The second thing? I suggest you have a holding cross, also known as a palm cross, which is a simple cross to hold as you pray. Third is a spiral notebook paired with a good pencil, one you can sharpen with a pocketknife. The notebook can be used as a place to jot down gardening ideas.

Many years ago, Ruth Stout wrote a book called *No Work Gardening*. Her method was simply to employ a lot of straw: used to mulch for moisture preservation, to smother weeds, and to enrich the soil. Mulching is always a great idea, but _no_ work? I don't think so. One of the ways I enjoy gardening is by working, but the garden is also a space to play.

In my garden, I have tried to add some whimsical touches. I have a windmill that I oil with WD-40 that accomplishes absolutely nothing. It spins when the wind blows and fascinates our grandchildren, but there is no grand purpose for its being in my garden aside from bringing playfulness.

I have a space I call the friendly woods where I have put ceramic faces representing each of our children on oak trees. I have a gazing ball that reflects light and is said to keep witches away. As far as I know, it works. But beyond work and play, the garden is truly a place to reflect and to ponder.

Cultivating the Spirit requires that we use the one tool that is more important than all the rest. That tool is our personal relationship with God.

Scattered throughout the Psalms, we find the word *selah*. This word is actually a musical notation which means "to pause." Near the back of our property, there is a railroad crossing. The only marking there for years was the familiar sign "stop, look, listen." Traditionally, the sign was shaped like St. Andrew's Cross. Now the crossing is equipped with an automated barrier and flashing lights, but the old St. Andrew's Cross reading "stop, look, listen" is appropriate for the garden, a reminder of *selah*.

Gardening rarely calls for quick decisions. We usually need to stop and think before we act. This is true when we are purchasing plants, shopping in catalogs, planning for new areas in the garden.The wisdom of the Hebrew scriptures as well as the tradition of our elders is that haste makes waste. If there is a fire or a person is drowning, a person is injured or a child is in danger, quick decisions are called for. But in the garden, it is more important to stop and reflect. To ponder what we see. As Psalm 46:10 puts it, "Be still and know that I am God" (NIV). *Selah.*

Do not wait; the time will never be 'just right.' Start where you stand, and work with whatever tools you may have at your command, and better tools will be found as you go along.

George Herbert

The expectations of life depend upon diligence; the (gardener) that would perfect his work must first sharpen his tools.

Confucius

For the Contemplative Gardener

Whatever is true, whatever is noble, whatever is right, whatever is pure, whatever is lovely, whatever is admirable—

if anything is excellent or praiseworthy—
think about such things.

(Philippians 4:8)

A Divine Plan

"Now the Lord God had planted a garden…"
-Genesis 2:8a, NIV

Almost every culture and all of the great religions of the world have a garden story. One Hindu creation story finds Vishnu on a vast ocean nestled in the coils of a giant seven-headed cobra. From the depths of the sea came the primordial voice of creation, the sound that to this day begins every Hindu chant, and every prayer. *Ohm* rose to the surface. *Ohm*, the sound of creation, signaled the beginning. From Vishnu's navel, a lotus flower bloomed. From the lotus flower emerged Brahma with four faces and four arms. Brahma plucked the petals from the lotus flower and created all parts of the universe.

In the Buddhist tradition, Siddhartha Gautama sat under a Bodhi tree for forty-nine days until he found enlightenment through the middle way. This state of enlightenment is called nirvana. Under the tree, also known as the holy fig (*Ficus religiosa*), Siddhartha became the Buddha, the enlightened one.

The three best-known monotheistic religions, Judaism, Christianity, and Islam, all share a similar creation story. It all begins in a beautiful garden.

"And the Lord God planted a garden in Eden, in the east; and there he put the man whom he had formed. Out of the ground the Lord God made to grow every tree that is pleasant to the sight and good for food, the tree of life also amid the garden, and the tree of the knowledge of good and evil…. The Lord God took the man and put him in the garden of Eden to till it and keep it" (Genesis 2:8-9, 15, NIV).

Notice that even before sin came into the world, humans were given work to do. According to this Biblical account, the first job was gardening.

Ficus religiosa, the sacred fig tree, is associated with Buddhism as the Bodhi tree, the tree under which Buddha became enlightened. The leaves have a distinctive heart shape. Leaves that fall are regarded as good luck tokens. The sacred fig tree is hardy in zones 10-11. In cooler regions, it is best grown as a house plant, patio plant, or a bonsai.

The Tree of Life

"In the middle of the garden was the tree of life…"
-Genesis 2:9, NIV

Notice, too, that in this scripture the tree of life is mentioned. The tree of life is a concept rooted in many religious traditions. It is usually associated with wisdom and with serenity. I contend that every garden needs a designated tree of life.

Stud Goings was a tobacco farmer in Monticello, Kentucky, in the mountains near Lake Cumberland. He had a small tobacco allotment and raised Kentucky Burley. His beagle dog, Luther, was constantly by his side. Stud's backyard featured an old Ford pickup truck propped on concrete blocks. A bare dirt path meandered to his dilapidated barn.

Along the way, a small vegetable garden flourished in the sunshine. Two dozen or so free-range chickens and a covey of Guinea hens skittered to and fro. Under a white pine tree (*Pinus strobus*) oozing sap were two oak nail kegs, turned upside down, intended for sitting.

"When things become too burdensome," he explained, "I just sit here in the shade. I call this white pine 'the tree of life.'"

It was in that shady spot that Stud rested after he had worked his garden or stripped tobacco. There he swapped stories with his neighbors.

The only time I ever worked with a tobacco crop was when Stud was short of help. I happened by his place one Saturday afternoon when a thunderstorm threatened. I was chaplain at Lake Cumberland Boys Camp for juvenile delinquents. It was about a mile from Stud's farm meaning I could pop by on short notice. He was in a big hurry to strip burley leaves and get them on racks in his tobacco barn. I rolled up my sleeves and gave him a hand.

When we finished the work and the storm passed, we sat on the nail kegs beneath the tree of life. We drank refreshments from Mason jars. My jar was filled with cool well water. I suspect Stud's jar contained something stiffer. Stud smoked a cigar. "This is where my tired body and my weary soul catch up with each other."

That is a perfect description of the importance of having a tree of life in the garden. My particular tree of life is a large water oak (*Quercus nigra*). This massive tree was planted as a sapling by my grandfather in 1937 to provide shade on the west side of the big house. A swing made from a worn-out truck tire hangs from the branches. Our children and now our grandchildren have played for hours on that tire swing. It is, indeed, a tree of life.

> *Quercus nigra*, the water oak, is in the red oak family. It is native to the eastern and south-central United States. The water oak serves the same ecological role as weeping willow and other wetland trees. It is adapted to wet, swampy areas, such as along ponds and stream banks, but can also tolerate well-drained sites and heavy, compacted soils. The water oak is often the most abundant species in a stand of trees.

The Master Gardener

"Who is it you are looking for?" Thinking he was the gardener, she said,
"Sir, if you have carried him away, tell me where you have put him,
and I will get him."
-John 20:15, NIV

The hills, gardens, and even the deserts of the Bible are more than just a backdrop of the events related to scripture. They are an illustration of the way that God's word intertwined with His revelation in scripture. They are an important part of our spiritual pilgrimage.

For example, Jesus referred to the lilies of the field to tell us of God's generosity toward us. Jesus warned of false prophets. He raised the question, "Are grapes gathered from thorns, or figs from thistle?" (Matthew 7:16, ESV). As Jesus entered Jerusalem, people took branches of palm trees (*Arecaceae*) and myrtle (*Myrtaceae myrtoideae*) to wave before Him. These branches were symbols of victory and triumph.

During the Passover meal with His disciples, Jesus broke bread made from local grain and drank wine made from local vineyards. Because it was a Passover meal, it was eaten with bitter herbs.

Following the Last Supper, Jesus crossed the Kedron Valley and went to a large grove of olive trees (*Olea europaea*) on a mountainside to pray. The very word Gethsemane means olive press.

As Jesus died on the cross, He was offered a sponge soaked with vinegar. It was lifted to His lips on a branch of hyssop (*Hyssopus officinalis*).

There are more than 125 plants mentioned in the Bible. They symbolize God's mercy and judgment, God's bounty, and blessing. They were used for physical and spiritual healing.

As the people of Israel prepared to enter the land of promise, they left the wilderness to enter a fruitful land. "For the Lord your God is bringing you into a good land – a land with streams and pools of water, with springs flowing in the valleys and hills; a land with wheat and barley, vines and fig trees, pomegranates, olive oil, and honey..." (Deut. 8:7-8, NIV).

The following is a list of some of the plants mentioned in the Bible.

Almond	Genesis 43:11
Aloe	Proverbs 7:17
Anemone	Matthew 6:28
Anise (Dill)	Exodus 30:34
Apple	Genesis 2:7; Job 31:39; Jeremiah 15:9; Proverbs 25:11
Barley	Numbers 5:15
Bulrushes	Exodus 2:3
Burning Bush	Exodus 3:1, 2
Carob or Locust	Luke 15:16; Matthew 3:1
Castor Oil Tree	Jonah 4
Cedar of Lebanon	I Kings 5:10; II King 19:23
Chestnut	Luke 17:5
Cinnamon	Proverbs 7:17
Crown of Thorns	Mark 15:15
Date Palm	John 12:13
Frankincense	Matthew 2:10, 11
Galbanum (Fennel)	Matthew 23:23
Grapevine	Genesis 9:20
Judas tree	Matthew 27:3
Jujube	Matthew 27:30
Mint	Matthew 23:23
Mulberry	Luke 17:5
Mustard	Matthew 13:31
Rue	Luke 11:42
Tares	Matthew 13:24
Thymine Wood	Revelation 18:12
Wormwood	Revelation 8:10

Gardens of the Bible

"Though it is the smallest of all seeds, yet when it grows,
it is the largest of garden plants."
-Matthew 13:32, NIV

T he Bible traces the importance of gardens throughout its pages. The Persian word Paradise means beautiful walled garden. There are more than fifty references to gardens in the Old Testament. Here are a few examples:

- The Garden of Eden is described as a sacred enclosure. (Genesis 2)
- It all began in a garden. (Genesis 2:8-17)
- The Promised Land was described as a garden. (Deuteronomy 11:8-12)
- King Solomon was a master gardener. (I Kings 4:33; Ecclesiastes 2:4-7)
- Israelites in exile were told to plant gardens. (Jeremiah 29:5, 28)
- Babylon was the site of the famous hanging gardens. (Esther 1:4-6)

Gardens were also important in the New Testament, especially in the life and ministry of Jesus.

- Jesus used gardens in His parables and His teaching. (Matthew 13:32; Luke 11:42; John 15:1-8)
- Jesus referred to God as a gardener. (John 15:1)
- Jesus made His most important decision in a garden. (Mark 14:32)
- After the crucifixion, Jesus was buried in a garden. (John 19:41)
- After His resurrection, Jesus was identified as a gardener. (John 20:15)

I would encourage you to keep a Bible close by somewhere in your garden. I keep my own tattered and faded garden Bible on our screened back porch. Reading these passages and others makes me more mindful of the presence of God in the garden.

God's Domain

"The earth is the Lord's, and everything in it."
-Psalm 24:1a, NIV

The contemplative gardener begins by relinquishing control. Weed control and pest control are a constant struggle. It is tempting to resort to high-powered herbicides and pesticides to combat these enemies. Danger, danger! To use such chemicals is to commit environmental genocide. Remember, our garden is God's domain. We are the caretakers. Whatever action or inaction we take must be done in keeping with a divine plan.

We have much to learn from indigenous peoples. To many indigenous peoples, individual ownership of the land is unthinkable. For them, the land belongs to everyone. All the animals have as much right to the good earth as people do.

A negligence in using pesticides has caused serious issues. Bluebirds and bald eagles have fallen victim to the use of DDT, a powerful pesticide. Rachel Carson, in her book titled *Silent Spring*, forewarned us.

When bluebirds eat an insect contaminated by DDT, the shell of their eggs are so fragile that when the mother bird sits on the nest, she crushes the eggs beneath her. The same is true for the bald eagle. When run-off from farmland drains into rivers, the fish become contaminated. The bald eagle, our national bird, is a fish lover. DDT enters the bloodstream of a bald eagle through these fish. Again, when a mother bird sits on her nest, her eggs are destroyed under her own weight.

No walls are high enough to keep out the many pests that threaten to invade. English ivy (*Hedera helix*), Chinese wisteria (*Wisteria sinensis*), and greenbrier (*Smilax rotundifolia*) can come right through a chain link fence. Crabgrass (*Digitaria sanguinalis*), Johnson grass (*Sorghum halepense*), and Bermuda grass (*Cynodon dactylon*) do not hesitate to make themselves right at home in cultivated ground. Aphids, Japanese beetles, and fire ants are unwelcome visitors. Starlings, grackles, and house sparrows wing their way into our garden uninvited. Like every other aspect of life, there is no permanent way to keep trouble out.

The Cherokee people have a poignant way of viewing weeds. They say that a weed is just a plant in the wrong place. They also say that weeds are plants for which the purpose is yet to be discovered. They believe that all plants can be responsibly used in some way and that it is up to us to discover each plant's unique purpose.

The bane of the southland, kudzu, is an invasive species brought to this country in 1876. At the World's Fair Centennial Exhibition in Philadelphia that year, the Japanese delegation brought two potted kudzu plants (*Pueraria montana*). They were placed on either side of the entryway to the fair. The plants were beautiful with lush green leaves and delicate purple flowers.

A visitor from Chipley, Florida, Charles Pleas took several cuttings from the branches. He wrapped them in moist paper. He then took them back to his greenhouse in Florida. Once home, he divided the cuttings and began growing kudzu. He advertised it as a new plant from Japan, perfect as a front porch vine.

Channing Cope, writer for *The Atlanta Journal-Constitution*, advocated for the use of kudzu as a method of preventing erosion and trouble. The United States Department of Agriculture quickly jumped on the bandwagon. They began encouraging farmers to plant kudzu, which quickly became an invasive plant. The Cherokee people would say it is simply a plant in the wrong place. A drive down any rural road, any interstate, or US highway, crisscrossing the South reveals the truth and consequences of taking matters into our own hands.

There are many such examples. In recent years, the Bradford pear (*Pyrus calleryana*), a beautiful plant in the springtime, has become invasive due to cities including them in their landscaping.

Incidentally, the Cherokee people have tried to find a use for kudzu. The blossoms of kudzu have been used to flavor jellies. Kudzu vines have been woven into baskets.

My friend, Newt Hardy, spent his retirement years planting Yoshino cherry trees (*Prunus yedoensis*). This tree is a beautiful import from Japan and a feature of springtime in our nation's capital. Newt also worked to combat kudzu. He told me that kudzu grows like strawberries - each kudzu plant has a central crown which sends out multiple vines in all directions. Everywhere the vine touches the earth, it puts out roots and creates a new crown. He went on to say that the only way to kill kudzu was to take a backhoe and dig up every crown. At a civic club meeting, Newt brought a clean kudzu crown for us to see. It was as large as the stump of a mature yellow pine tree (*Pinus ponderosa*). In the chapter on greenbriers, I give another example of a good use of a plant often considered a weed.

Near the conclusion of Genesis 1, we read a clear direction from God in verse 28: "Be fruitful and increase in number; fill the earth and subdue it" (NIV). The human race has certainly multiplied. There are now more than seven billion of us on this third planet from the sun. It's a rather small planet compared to the others, but it is our home. We share this big blue marble, which is hurtling through space, with all the people of the world, all of whom are created in the image of God.

Even so, it's too easy for us to adopt the policy of the early settlers in this country. Manifest destiny was the idea that if we want land, we could take it, no matter who else lived on it at the time.

The history of our country includes the severe mistreatment of people of color. When I was growing up, we sang a song: "Red, yellow, black and white, / They are precious in His sight." That simple childhood song is a point of view that manifest destiny crushes underfoot. The truth is that the earth is God's domain and the God of true justice and true mercy expects us, His children, to treat each other with respect.

The concept of subduing the earth is terribly misunderstood. Rather than suggesting an attitude of powerful oppression, the wisdom of the Hebrew Bible suggests that we be good stewards of this planet. Subduing the earth does not mean hunting humpback whales, gray wolves, or the blue-footed booby to the point of extinction. We share this orb, not only with over seven billion people, but also with a rich, wonderous variety of plant and animal life.

From the moment of creation, God gave us plants to enjoy. After the flood, God included animals among the things that we might incorporate into our diet. I'm not opposed to hunting, it is a time-honored tradition of the human race, used for food and balancing the ecosystem.

We read the story of Cain and Abel in Genesis 4. Perhaps you have asked the question as I have, "Why did God accept Abel's offering, but not Cain's?" At least part of the answer is that Abel offered plants as his sacrifice to God. Cain, on the other hand, offered an animal. After the flood, that would have been perfectly acceptable. But, soon after Creation, it was not. I am not a vegetarian. However, I believe that the food we eat should be pleasing to God.

This good earth gives us enough food to feed all seven billion people. The problem is one of allocation. A small percentage of the world's population consumes the majority of the food produced. I certainly have been a part of the majority. I have also been obese, I am a diabetic, I have renal failure, and am on dialysis three times a week. I ate all my dessert in the first 40 years of my life. That's the truth and now I'm living with the consequences.

Please, dear readers, let's find ways to address the problem of world hunger and famine. If grain were used to make bread, instead of to fatten cattle so that our steaks would be marbled, a lot of that grain could be baked into nutritious bread or cereal. If we learned to share water, plain, pure water, as God intended, we would go a long way in addressing drought and hunger. If we learned to recycle paper, plastic, and metals, we would be better stewards of the resources on this planet, just as God intended.

My view is that the stewardship of the earth, and its resources, is what God expects of us. We all need to become more aware and we all need to do better. It is one of the best reasons to cultivate a garden. In doing so, we cultivate our own spirit.

The garden is a natural habitat, an ecosystem where nature seeks a comfortable home. We will never be able to finally conquer the invasive plants and critters that seek entry. Putting aside books, tools, chemicals, hybrids, and almost all of our unrealistic expectations, the contented gardener comes to the realization and the acceptance that our garden is forever a work in progress, never a completed project that looks like the picture we have seen or imagined.

God Almighty first planted a garden.
Francis Bacon

We must cultivate our own garden. When man was put in the garden of Eden, he was put there so that he should work, which proves that man was not born to rest.

Voltaire

A Garden Walk

"…the Lord God was walking in the garden in the cool of the day."
-Genesis 3:8, NIV

I n our area, there are many beautiful gardens within easy driving distance of my home. Some of my favorites include Hatcher Garden and Woodland Preserve. The garden is on property donated by Harold and Josephine Hatcher, land that they developed privately before donating it as a public garden. The garden affords a wonderful array of plantings suitable for my soil and climate. The garden includes magnificent water features. It is home to a wide variety of birds and other critters.

On my visits there, I have seen many impressive creatures including a magnificent Red-Tailed Hawk, and many kinds of snakes, including a Northern Banded Water Snake. In this beautiful garden, I have conducted several weddings and one funeral service which included the scattering of the ashes of the deceased.

North Carolina features many wonderful gardens. I have had the privilege to visit each one many times. The Botanical Gardens of Asheville is located on Weaver Blvd in the wondrous mountain city. Another one nearby, the Biltmore Gardens, is a collection of themed plantings on the Biltmore Estate property.

The North Carolina Arboretum, located at the intersection of the Blue Ridge Parkway and Olmstead Way, makes a wonderful day trip, but be prepared to pay a small entrance fee. The main gardens of the arboretum are beautiful in every season of the year. One of my favorite parts of this visit is to view the amazing collection of bonsai trees, some as old as 75 years. Take lunch when you go as there are many excellent places to enjoy a picnic.

Near Gastonia, North Carolina, the Daniel Stowe Botanical Gardens are a wonder to behold. This is located on 380 acres of rolling meadows, woodlands, and lakefront property. It is on New Hope Road, in Belmont, North Carolina, Again, take a lunch and plan to spend the day.

Walking in a garden can be a spiritual experience. I suggest that when you take a garden stroll, go at a slow pace. It is a rich visual experience often accompanied by a symphony of birds, cicadas, and the wind. Let this walk through a garden become a study session. With a notebook in hand, you can record the names of plants that inspire your own efforts in cultivation.

One time, I saw a man at the Daniel Stowe Garden using a dictation device to take notes. Another time, I saw an art student at the NC Arboretum with a sketch pad and colored pencils trying so hard to capture on paper the beauty before her. Of course, now you see many people taking pictures with their cellphones, so they remember what they saw growing during their visit.

I don't know about you, but when I come home from a trip to one of these beautiful gardens maintained by a well-paid staff, it's easy for me to be disappointed in the way my garden looks. I learned a long time ago to let visits to other well-manicured gardens become a source of inspiration and not a reason for discouragement.

I have a secret for you: my garden and your garden will never look like the pictures in fine gardening or *Southern Living*. Here's another secret: people whose gardens are featured in those magazines know that the photographers and the editors have many ways to make a garden look better than it is. Friends here in my hometown had their beautiful garden featured in a glossy gardening magazine. On the day of the photo shoot, they got up early to deadhead mulch. Their garden was as pretty as it had ever been. However, the director of the shoot still brought in potted trees, shrubs, and blooming flowers to place around their garden, staging it to a beauty beyond reality. Later, my friend said, "We were honored to have our garden featured, but the truth is it didn't look a thing like our garden."

In my mind, my garden looks a whole lot better than it does in reality. I think that may be true for all who love to garden. We have an idea about how our space can look but knowing that to be true, I want to take you on a walk through my garden. Remember please that we live on one acre of red clay. The house, the barn, and a few other structures take up much of that space. Our garden wraps around these buildings. Take a walk with me now through the garden in my mind.

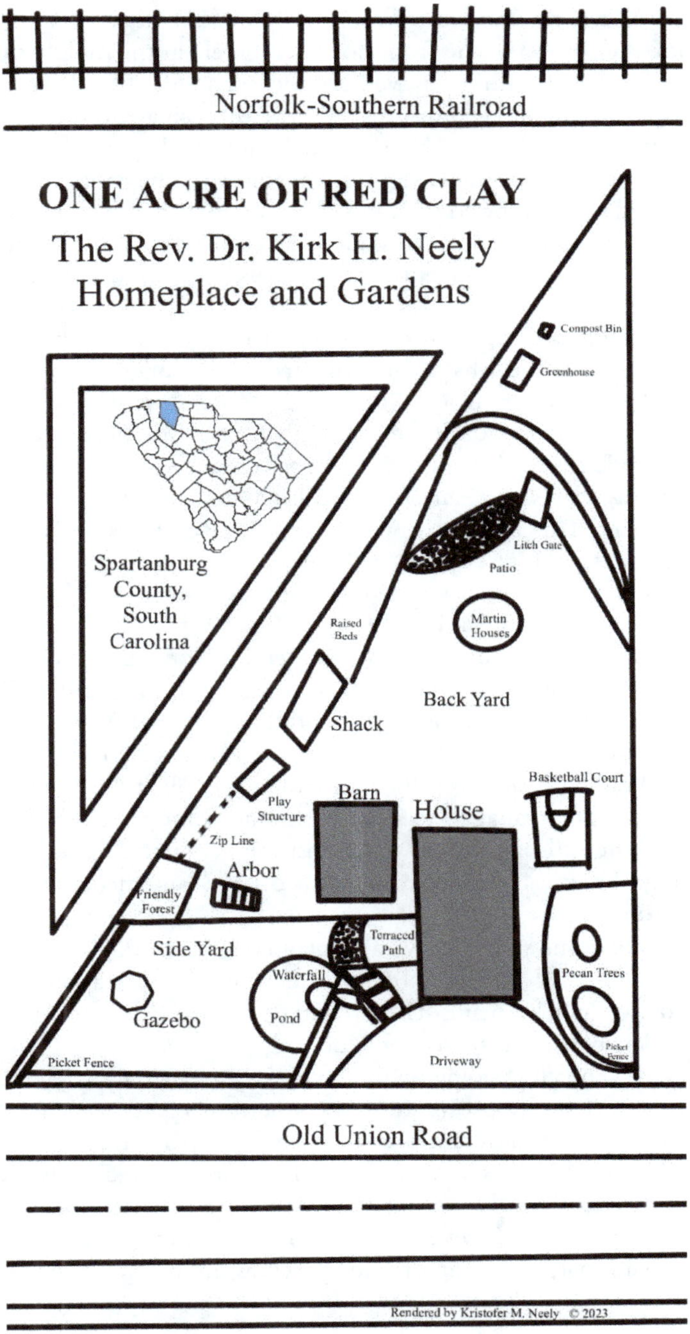

Norfolk-Southern Railroad

ONE ACRE OF RED CLAY
The Rev. Dr. Kirk H. Neely
Homeplace and Gardens

Compost Bin

Greenhouse

Litch Gate

Patio

Spartanburg
County,
South
Carolina

Raised
Beds

Martin
Houses

Back Yard

Shack

Basketball Court

Barn

House

Play
Structure

Zip Line

Arbor

Friendly
Forest

Terraced
Path

Pecan Trees

Side Yard

Waterfall

Gazebo

Pond

Picket Fence

Driveway

Picket Fence

Old Union Road

Rendered by Kristofer M. Neely © 2023

First, we stand in front of our home, the house built by my grandfather in 1937. The front door is squarely in the middle of the house's exterior with a bay window on each side. On the second floor, there are three transoms, each with a single window. The windows are lined by red shutters, including the bay windows. The front door is also painted bright fire engine red. The roof is also this bright red to correspond with the door. Some of our friends say our house looks like a Lutheran church as many traditional Lutheran churches have a red front entrance. There is a reason that we decided on this color.

Our signature flower is a bright red geranium (*Pelargonium hortorum*). Clare and I have them planted in containers on each side of the front door from April until September. On our first anniversary, I was working as a chaplain at a Boy Scout camp in Indiana. Clare and I lived in a tent for three weeks. We went to a restaurant in New Harmony, Indiana to celebrate our first anniversary. This restaurant was called The Red Geranium. It was that night that I discovered red geraniums were Clare's favorite flowers. Since then, I have tried to plant them everywhere we have lived. Now our yard features them.

Geraniums thrive in hot weather and don't like getting their feet wet. They are best watered from the root up. By simply filling the reservoir below the plant, they are happy to self-water as they feel the need. While the soil on top often feels dry, they are well watered underneath. Keep this in mind as you plant them. In some years, we have managed to customize our home as a nod to our flower. The red paint everywhere and the geraniums all add to an inviting Christmas feeling which guests often compliment when they come to visit us.

In some years, I have also planted a winter daphne (*Daphne odora*) in one of the pots beside the front door. Daphne is an incredibly finnicky plant. They require just enough water, but no more. Again, these reservoir pots do well.

The vinyl siding on the house is Cape Cod Gray. Standing in front of the house there are symmetrical plantings. There are shrubs of several different ilex varieties which frame the flower beds.

On closer examination, the beds are planted with bright yellow daffodils (*Narcissus pseudonarcissus*) in the spring, purple fountain grass (*Pennisetum setaceum rubrum*) and zinnia (*Zinnia violacea*) in the summer, a border of cheery yellow mums (*Chrysanthemum morifolium*) in the fall, and a variety of creeping Jenny (*Lysimachia nummularia*) as a ground cover. There are two boxes on either side of the porch planted with pansies (*Viola pedunculata*) from October until Good Friday. Then, those flowers are traded for bronze-leaf begonias (*Begonia interspecific*) and cascading white petunias (*Petunia axillaris*). As summer takes its toll, especially in dry weather, we plant a few coleuses (*Coleus scutellarioides*) to fill in. There are six hanging baskets on the porch, three on each side. They are planted to match the boxes. When the hot dry weather of summer encroaches, we plant sprigs of purple creeper (*Parthenocissus quinquefolia*), which does very well in the hot dry weather.

If we look down the hill to right, we see a large pecan tree (*Carya illinoinensis*) with a bench constructed around the base. From one sturdy limb, on the side near the road, there is a swing for our grandchildren. On the other side of this large tree, there is a domed bird feeder, filled with seed. The sideyard is surrounded by a white picket fence. In the lower part of the sideyard, we have an old, Charleston-style joggling board.

We have a white metal wrought iron swing inherited from Clare's mother and two black Charleston-style benches. This sitting area backs up to a chain link fence that supports a variety of vines including honeysuckle (*Lonicera sempervirens*), Virginia creeper (*Parthenocissus quinquefolia*), and a large Cherokee rose (*Rosa laevigata*).

There is a single bluebird house positioned about halfway up the picket fence on the opposite corner of this side yard. Around the base of a larger pecan tree is a garden that features Lenten roses (*Helleborus orientalis*) of several different colors and two variegated aucuba plants (*Aucuba japonica*) whose leaves often contribute to floral arrangements inside the house. Some of the flowers in our garden can be cut to make beautiful arrangements.

As I stand in front of the house and look to the left, we see a white picket fence. Near the street, this fence has a wide gate that will accommodate a small pickup truck. This is the gate for lawnmowers, blowers, and weed eaters. Closer to the house, there is an arched garden gate. Two small seats are facing each other inside this gate. The gate opens to allow passage. There is a stepping stone with the inscription "The Neely Garden."

On either side of this arched gate, there is a latticework trellis. These trellises support a Zéphirine Drouhin rose and a Henryi clematis. The Zéphirine Drouhin rose has very few thorns and small fragrant blossoms which bloom throughout the summer. The clematis has large white blooms which make an appearance only in the spring. Just outside of this gate to the right is a variegated yucca plant (*Yucca filamentosa*).

To the left, outside the fence, three large golden Miss Huff lantana flowers (*Lantana camara 'Miss Huff'*). These hardy perennials bloom profusely in the late spring until fall and attract pollinators such as bees, butterflies, and hummingbirds throughout the season. In between the lantanas are pink fringe plants (*Loropetalum chinense*) that bloom early in the spring and one specimen burning bush. Inside the gate to the left, there is a stone path that leads to an outdoor water spigot with a long garden hose for easy watering.

Above the path and next to the fence, there is a planting of deep purple Siberian iris (*Iris sibirica*) and two camellia plants (*Camellia japonica*) given to us by my stepmother, Ruth Neely. Down the hill, below this path, there is a propane tank that supplies fire logs inside our parlor. The hill is covered with *Vinca minor*, a type of dogbane, one of my favorite ground covers. Most often referred to as periwinkle or myrtle, the deep purple-blue flowers bloom in the early spring.

There is also an understory sassafras tree (*Sassafras albidum*) which opens each spring with bright chartreuse buds. Nearby there is a pink rhododendron (*Rhododendron elegans*). On the left side of the inner garden gate, there is an old redbud tree (*Cercis canadensis*), bent with age, along with a companion dogwood (*Cornus florida*), both transplanted in this place from our old home in North Carolina. Beyond the white dogwood, there is a pink Cherokee dogwood (*Cornus florida 'Rubra'*), given to us by a dear friend. Standing beneath the dogwood tree is a statue of Saint Augustine.

As we walk into the garden, we see around the Redbud tree, a planting of Lenten roses, blue woodland scilla (*Scilla siberica*), and lily of the valley (*Convallaria majalis*) which came from my mother. There is a moss-covered bird bath also inherited from my mother. On the other side of the redbud tree, there is a Charleston bench positioned at the top of a circulating waterfall. If we walk down the hill, on steps made from railroad ties, we descend by the waterfall.

This waterfall is a feature I built with stones gathered with permission from a scout camp in Saluda, NC. At the bottom of the waterfall, there is a small pool which, at one time, accommodated a nice collection of goldfish. But one afternoon, a large blue heron came and stood on one leg and decimated our collection of goldfish. I was not concerned as the goldfish were there primarily to eat the mosquito larvae. Feeding the large blue heron was worth a few goldfish. The blue heron was one of the amazing visitors to our garden.

That same garden pool now features a large collection of bullfrogs, whose tadpoles now do the work of the goldfish. Visitors to the pond have included a great variety of birds looking for a sip of water. We have had one small snapping turtle and three or four northern banded water snakes. At the bottom of the steps on the right side, there are two large hemlock trees (*Tsuga canadensis*) with a stone bench that will perfectly accommodate two people. On one of the rocks beside the waterfall is a statue of St Patrick kneeling.

At the base of the large oak tree (*Quercus*), on the left, is a statue of St Benedict of Nursia. This larger side yard is surrounded by a white picket fence and a chain link fence. At the back of this space, there is an 8-sided gazebo. My good friend and fellow pastor, Mike McGee, and I built this gazebo together. He supplied the design and the skill; I supplied the lumber and labor. It is a favorite resting spot for children and adults alike. Along the chain link fence, there are oak-leaf hydrangeas (*Hydrangea quercifolia*) and a volunteer wild Irish rose (*Iris germanica*). There's a small ground cover rose (*Rosa*), also known as a carpet rose, near the gazebo and a dwarf magnolia (*Magnolia grandiflora*) planted next to the gazebo.

On the picket fence that goes up toward the street, there is a climbing Don Juan rose (*Rosa 'Don Juan'*). The hill above this side yard supports three tall pecan trees (*Carya illinoinensis*). Orange-sided daylilies (*Hemerocallis fulva*) are planted along the fence and bloom on the street side. There are also two climbing roses (*Rosa setigera*) on the street side which bloom virtually all summer long. There are bluebird boxes on each side of this side yard. On the upper end of the yard, between the gazebo and the waterfall, I planted two Japanese maples (*Acer palmatum*).

One of the projects that is still in my mind is to make a small Japanese Zen garden between these two maples. This garden would be surrounded by decorative grass and would include a large specimen boulder surrounded by pea gravel that could be raked into interesting patterns. As we move back towards the pond at the base of the waterfall, we can see how the water spills over the side of the hill, split by rocks, creating small falls down the hill. There are two benches at the base with creeping Jenny (*Lysimachia nummularia*) planted which leads to the pond.

At the base of the hill on the right side of the falls, there is a nice growth of mondo grass (*Ophiopogon japonicus*). Within the crevices along the waterfall, there are perennial ferns. The rocks are covered with green moss, the entire hillside is planted with naturalized flowers. The bulbs were given to me by a dear friend and church member. We have a small collection of Virginia bluebells (*Mertensia virginica*) that have been in Clare's family since her great-grandmother. As we approach the gate in the chain link fence that leads into our backyard, we pass another redbud tree (*Cercis canadensis*) leaning over the pathway to the gazebo. At the top of the waterfall, there is a volunteer winged elm (*Ulmus alata*). From its branches, we have hung six candle lanterns which we light on special occasions.

As we go through the gate, there is a chain link fence that leads into the backyard. We see to the left and the right an assortment of hostas, sometimes called plantain lilies, (*Hosta plantaginea*); these plants are low maintenance and beautiful from late spring until fall. They have small flower sprigs with fragrant perfume, but the real attraction to hostas are the brilliant green leaves with their magnificent foliage. Last I checked, there were over four hundred varieties of hostas. I have nowhere near that many. I only have 20-30 varieties.

As we walk down the gravel path, we see an arbor. When we first moved to our new home in 1980, there was a huge structure there with a broken-down tree limb lying on top. Clare and I built an arbor, in an attempt to lift large tree limbs and save them. However, when the plant died, I decided to start over with the arbor. We used paving stones and sturdy lumber. Now the arbor supports yellow jasmine (*Gelsemium sempervirens*) on each front corner, star jasmine, formerly known as Confederate jasmine, (*Trachelospermum jasminoides*) on the middle post on either side, and one wisteria (*Wisteria frutescens*) on the back right corner. I have tried to keep the wisteria trained on the arbor but it has wandered out of bounds – as it tends to do. Still, the wisteria blooms beautifully every spring.

Behind the back of the arbor, we have a cast iron chiminea. This is the best place to build a fire and sit and ponder in the cooler months.

Between the arbor and the house is my grandfather's old barn, painted gray like the house. This barn is desperately in need of a new roof and many other repairs, but it's also a place where I have invited many flowers. On each side of the barn, I have plantings suitable for these small micro-climates. The perimeter of the barn is host to many specimen plants. On the front south face of the barn, there is a front door, painted white, with a window on each side. These windows are painted with silver paint from the inside, making them a reflective mirror for the flowerbox plantings beneath each window.

On the left side of the barn's front door is a variegated weigelia plant (*Weigela florida 'variegata'*). On the right side of the door are a lantana and a large oak-leaf hydrangea (*Hydrangea quercifolia*). On either side of the windows, I have used a vinyl lattice material to make shutters. Beside the left window, I have a miniature climbing rose (*Rosa setigera*) and purple clematis (*Clematis occidentalis*). On the right-hand side window, I have planted scarlet honeysuckle (*Lonicera sempervirens*). Around the barn on the left, there is a large bed bordered by railroad ties. This area is in constant shade, making it perfect for shade-loving plants. Three Delaware white azaleas (*Rhododendron 'Delaware Valley White'*) bloom profusely in the springtime. In the center of the bed, growing on a wrought-iron trellis, is a Henryi clematis. Between the azaleas is a collection of specimen wildflowers including Jack-in-the-Pulpit (*Arisaema triphyllum*), trillium (*Trillium grandiflorum*), and Solomon's Seal (*Polygonatum biflorum*). With the addition of a few more plants, this bed will become a moonlight garden.

Across the path is a small arbor where two people may sit and have a private conversation. Growing up on either side of this small arbor is a tangerine crossvine (*Bignonia capreolata*). The bright orange blooms in the early spring attracts many pollinators and the first hummingbirds. There are hostas planted in containers on each side of this smaller arbor. Facing the left side, there is a large tree. This is the tree that we call the tree of life.

As we walk to the back of the barn, we see a potting bench made from an old door and treated lumber. Above the bench are two shelves featuring handmade pottery, most of which was crafted by our daughter-in-law, June. Because this bench gets almost no sun, these pots are planted with a variety of shade-happy plants.

On either side of the potting bench are two specimen plants. To the right is a purple rhododendron (*rhododendron elegans*). It is the only variety of rhododendron that I have found to be successful in our garden. To the left of the potting bench is an Annabelle hydrangea (*Hydrangea arborescens*). This flower is a cultivar of wild hydrangea native to our area.

Positioned between the rear of the barn and the border fence is a play area first enjoyed by our children and now our grandchildren. A sturdy swing set built out of treated lumber features five swings. I placed the swing set so that Clare could watch the children from her kitchen window. What a delight it is to see our grandchildren and their friends enjoying the freedom of the swings.

Further along, there is a large double deck structure, also constructed from treated lumber, built specifically for children. This play structure has been a pirate ship, a doll house, a flower shop, and a jungle treehouse. Its function is limited only by the imagination of the children who use it. From the top floor, there is access to a zip line, a fire pole, and a sturdy ladder. On the opposite side of this play structure, there is a sliding board.

The front of the play structure has three shelves where potted plants bloom throughout the summer. Annual flowers in these pots include begonias, petunias, pansies (*Viola tricolor var. hortensis*), and coleus (*Coleus scutellarioides*). An old wooden ladder serves as a trellis up one side of the play structure where I plant a Mandevilla vine (*Mandevilla splendens*) every summer which travels up this ladder and travels across the face of this play structure. The chain link fence behind the play structure features a sweet autumn clematis (*Clematis terniflora*) which usually climbs to the top of a pole for outdoor lighting.

In a small nook next to the fence is a wild flame azalea (*Rhododendron calendulaceum*). I first saw this plant on a canoe trip on the north fork of the New River in North Carolina. Ours was purchased at the Asheville Farmer's Market.

If we continue around the barn to the east-facing side, there is a display of old garden tools covering the entire side of Pappy's barn. These tools consist mostly of handcrafted wood implements. One wrought iron trellis supports a clematis vine (*Clematis occidentalis*). A bed made from railroad ties and good soil is home to a collection of Asiatic lilies (*Lilium auratum*) and a few dinner plate dahlias (*Dahlia pinnata*).

Anchoring the far-left corner of this side of the barn is a Miss Kim lilac (*Syringa pubescens*). This Korean flower is the only lilac I have been able to grow with our soil. The fragrant pink blossoms perfume the night air when this lilac is in bloom. On the barn's right side is an 'Incredi-Belle' hydrangea (*Hydrangea arborescens*) which features hardy blooms.

If we continue our walk to the back of our home, shelves and flower boxes feature many different kinds of annuals and some perennials. A bed along the back of the house is home to an array of black-eyed Susan (*Rudbeckia hirta*), purple cone flowers (*Echinacea purpurea*), and midnight nay salvia (*Salvia sylvestris*). On the right-hand corner of this expanse is a purple Butterfly Bush (*Buddleja davidii*). On the far left-hand corner is a rich blue rose of Sharon bush, which is not a rose, but a hibiscus flower (*Hibiscus syriacus*).

Our backyard is a large grassy area. The lawn is a mixture of bent Bermuda grass (*Cynodon dactylon*) and Kentucky 31 bluegrass (*Poa pratensis*). I do not use herbicides on my lawn, my basic motto is "if it is green and growing, leave it alone." For that reason, our yard is host to several large patches of clover (*Trifolium repens*). Though it gets cut frequently, the clover blooms continuously, attracting many pollinators, including honeybees.

Along the edge of the yard are several specimen trees including many varieties of Japanese maples (*Acer palmatum*). Recent additions to our garden include vegetable beds on the east side of our yard. Our son-in-law, Jay, takes care of these vegetable beds. While I have grown vegetables in the past, Jay's efforts reliably put food on the table.

The back of our yard features a shack constructed with treated lumber and a tin roof. This roof is best to sit under during summer rain. One can enjoy a soft symphony, the music of rain falling on the metal.

The front of the shack is completely covered in a Lady Bank rose (*Rosa banksiae*). This climbing rose is covered with many yellow flowers. While it blooms only once a year, this rose puts on quite a display. If you are going to see the rose in full bloom, you need to come within a narrow 3-week period in the early spring. On the left side of the shack is a sweet autumn clematis that blooms profusely in August and September. On the right side of the shack is a vigorous star jasmine. Between the shack and the play structure is a double wide swing that will accommodate two large people or three small ones. Climbing up the right-side support is a Zéphirine Drouhin rose. The left side provides a trellis for an orange trumpet vine.

At the very back of our yard is an English style litch-gate which can accommodate seating for six people. Also built with treated lumber, this structure features a canopy of yellow trumpet vine. Hummingbirds enjoy sipping nectar from these blossoms throughout the summer until the first frost. Beyond the litch-gate, we have a small greenhouse and a canister compost bin.

The gate is centered on a circular bed made from railroad ties and spans the length of the shack. This bed is planted with a variety of flowering shrubs including David Austin roses, knockout roses, ornamental grasses, calla lilies, sedum, and other low-growing plants.

In front of this large bed, our daughter, Betsy, and her husband, Jay, have created a beautiful sitting area. It features a paved area with garden tiles and decorative gravel. Nearby is a Pawleys' Island hammock, a sturdy picnic table, and a trampoline for the kids. This area also features a firepit, suitable for roasting hot dogs and marshmallows. We enjoy having a small fire and good friends on pleasant evenings.

In this area, there is a raised circular flowerbed constructed from the same stone used for the firepit. This bed features three blooming day lilies and a fairy garden for the children.

My garden is a low-maintenance garden with continuous blooms and fragrances. However, this description is a composite of how you may see it at any one time. You can see the attached map at the beginning of this chapter which I hope will make it a little easier to visualize the stops we have made along this garden walk.

So, there's a quick tour of our garden. I must tell you, if you came and walked through our garden, you wouldn't see the flowers all blooming at once.

As we walked around my garden together, did you notice the dead tree which needs to be removed? Did you see the broken limbs in need of trimming? Were you aware of the greenbrier (*Smilax rotundifolia*) that is climbing one of my prized delaware azaleas (*Rhododendron 'Delaware Valley White'*)? Did you get any mosquito bites? I certainly did.

Also, did I mention to beware the large copperhead that resides in the English ivy (*Hedera helix*) near the tree of life? Yes, like Adam and Eve, there is a snake in my garden too. In fact, there are many snakes in my garden, most of them non-venomous, but there is this copperhead.

Having a garden is never a destination, it is always a journey. We plant annuals and perennials and they bloom for a season or two, then they disappear. Even my perennial tulips give up after about three years. While I have made several attempts to grow peonies, they just don't do well in my garden. The same is true of one of my favorite flowers, the foxglove (*Digitalis purpurea*). While the plants are really biennials, there is a perennial variety that in my experience lasts only four seasons.

Please let me add one more thing. As I have taken you on this virtual walk around our garden, I hope in your mind's eye, you see a place of beauty. You may even think to yourself, "Why doesn't my garden look like that?" Please remember: my garden doesn't look like that either. Even as our children use their imagination, I also imagine our garden as better than it really is.

Every plant I've mentioned in this description has found a home in our garden. A garden is always a work in progress. For example, one year I planted six different varieties of peonies spaced in even intervals in the circular bed at the back of our yard. Only one remains, the Sarah Bernhardt peony (*Paeonia lactiflora*). Even that peony doesn't flourish well in our garden. I've had the same experience with delphinium and other beautiful perennials. We have to learn what works and what doesn't.

One of the interesting things about gardening is that it is never complete. It is a lifelong work of love and labor. If we take the time to think deeply, it is a partnership with the Divine Creator, who created the perfect garden and folks, just like us, messed it up. As far as I'm concerned, the challenges we face in gardening only enhance the joy. Even God has to take what is broken and repair it. Redemption doesn't happen just once; it is an ongoing process. Beautiful gardens, like the people who tend them, are always being redeemed, remade, and restored.

God's Sanctuary

"The Lord is in his holy temple;"
-Habakkuk 2:20a, NIV

A garden is a holy place. The prophet Habakkuk speaks of all creation as God's temple. "The earth is the Lord's and the fullness thereof; the world and they that dwell therein" (Psalm 24:1, NIV). The Psalmist reminds us that all of creation is God's domain.

That certainly must include my one acre of red clay here in the upstate of South Carolina.

A garden is a sacred place where we may encounter the living God. An old hymn by c. Austin Miles called "I Come To the Garden Alone" puts this in anthropomorphic terms:

> I come to the garden alone
> while the dew is still on the roses,
>
> And the voice I hear falling on my ear,
> The Son of God discloses
> And He walks with me and He talks with me,
> And He tells me I am his own;
> And the joy we share as we tarry there,
> None other has ever known.
>
> He speaks, and the sound of his voice \
>
> Is so sweet the birds hush their singing,
> And the melody that He gave to me
> Within my heart is ringing.
> And He walks with me and He talks with me,
> And He tells me I am his own;
> And the joy we share as we tarry there,
> None other has ever known
>
> I'd stay in the garden with Him,
> Though the night around me be
> falling.
>
> But He bids me go; through the voice of woe
> His voice to me is calling.
> And He walks with me and He talks with me,
> And He tells me I am His own;
> And the joy we share as we tarry there,
> None other has ever known.

Every garden needs a gate. The entry does not need to be elaborate, but it does need to be inviting. The entry to my garden is a double arch with benches on each side so that two people can sit under the archway and have a conversation and maybe a cup of coffee.

When we walk into the garden, we do so with a humble spirit and a sense of reverence. This place belongs to God. We are here as guests, worshippers, and servants. In my garden, I have plenty of places to sit down. These include two Charleston benches next to a small pond at the bottom of the waterfall. Adults and children alike enjoy stopping to watch the falling water.

Nestled beneath a mountain hemlock tree (*Tsuga mertensiana*) is a stone bench erected with great effort from a large slab of granite found in the middle of the highway after a rock slide. Not only do people enjoy this stone bench, but squirrels often hang out to munch on acorns or pecans gleaned from the yard. Near the playground, we have two old-fashioned steel gliders. Clare remembered that her grandparents had this kind of outdoor seating in their side yard. I found these two in a reclaimed furniture sale. They make the perfect place for young parents to sit and swing their infants while their preschoolers enjoy the playground. Under our arbor, we have black wrought iron furniture, and in the shack, we have white wrought iron furniture. All these pieces were hand-me-downs from our parents.

The seating areas, in whatever form, become like pews in a sanctuary where people sit down to meditate, read scripture, or pray.

Along one side of our yard, we have an impressive grove of oak trees. Our arborist friend suggested that we prune some of the lower branches off of these trees to create a sense of open space beneath the canopy above. The trees themselves are like temple columns. They not only serve to provide shade in warm weather, but in the springtime, they provide a nesting place for many songbirds.

Sometimes, I sit outside and just listen. In the early morning or after dark, I can enjoy a symphony in my own yard. I have to consciously screen out the noise from the highway in front of our house and from the railway behind our house. More difficult is screening out the noise of my own heart. Once I get quiet and listen, I can hear the music. Tree frogs, cicadas, and crickets provide the rhythm; bullfrogs in the pond add the bass, and the melody comes from songbirds. In the early morning, I often hear a Carolina wren or a wood thrush singing their clear-throated songs. At night, the song of a whippoorwill or the medley of a lonely mockingbird seeking a mate fills the air. The music is sacred.

The garden that I tend has been in the making for 83 years. The pecan trees (*Carya illinoinensis*) were planted by my grandfather. A crepe myrtle tree (*Lagerstroemia indica*) was planted by my grandmother. We have a few Virginia bluebells (*Mertensia virginica*) that were transplanted from Clare's grandparents' farm in Saluda, South Carolina. Throughout our garden, we have many pass-along plants. Each one of these plants is a reminder of the special people who contributed to this garden. The plants themselves become a living prayer book. The diminutive, but fragrant, lily of the valley (*Convallaria majalis*) came from my mother's yard. Clare's mother, Miz Lib, allowed me to take cuttings from her beautiful azaleas. Transplanted from sandy soil in her garden to the red clay of our garden, these cuttings have transformed beautifully.

Clare especially remembers her mother when the azaleas bloom. One year for my birthday, I received an 'August Moon' hosta. It was given to me by a lady in the church who died later that same summer.

Twenty years ago, a man called me and asked if I could use some tall-bearded iris (*Iris germanica*). His wife had recently died, and he wanted her beloved iris to have a home where they could bloom beautifully. I accepted the gift, and every year since, the irises have put on a springtime show. These are just a few of the pass-along plants that are reminders to pray for other people.

In the garden, the basic elements of earth, wind, water, and light all add to the sacramental nature of space. The earth is a reminder that God created all things *ex nihilo*, out of nothing. But the scriptures also tell us that God created humankind from the dust of the earth. "From dust you are, and to dust you will return" (Genesis 3:19, NIV). Water is a reminder of our baptism. The wind is sacred music and a reminder of the presence of the Holy Spirit. "The Spirit is like the wind..." (John 3:8, NIV).

One of the things I enjoy about my garden is the play of light filtering through the trees. In the ancient temple in Jerusalem, there was always an eternal flame, a symbol of the presence of God. When an acolyte moves forward at the beginning of a worship service to light the candles, it is a reminder to those who worship that God is with us. The filtered light in a garden is a further reminder that this is God's place, and God is here.

The Tranquil Garden

"They went to a place called Gethsemane, and Jesus said to His disciples, 'Sit here while I pray.'" -Mark 14:32, NIV

O n a recent trip to the North Carolina Arboretum, I noticed several cozy nooks carved out of that beautiful garden space. These are places to stop and rest, have a quiet conversation, or spend time alone in blessed solitude. These quiet areas, usually in the shade, invite those who stop and take a break to breathe more deeply, meditate, or pray. I noticed this pattern of quiet places in many of the large, formal gardens. This encouraged me to include tranquil places in our own garden.

In Saluda, North Carolina, along Old US 176, I came upon a large flat rock that had dislodged from the mountainside and tumbled into the roadway. I was in my pick-up truck, so I drove around the obstacle, parked in front of it, turned on my hazard lights, and undertook the back-breaking task of loading this granite slab into the bed of the truck. It took me nearly 15 minutes, but by lifting one end of the stone and then the other, I was able to muscle it into the truck. I had done a service to my fellow travelers, though that old stretch of road is not often used. Better still, I had found the natural bench for a secluded pew. Thanks to the help of two other people, that stone bench now resides under eastern hemlock near our waterfall.

Some years ago, at a yard sale in Prosperity, I found five Charleston benches. The slats were rotted and broken, but the wrought iron supports, though quite rusted, were still strong and sturdy. I bought all five for thirty dollars. I had the wrought iron pieces sandblasted to remove the rust and replaced all the slats with treated lumber. I painted the benches with flat black enamel paint, they now serve as places to stop and take a break in our garden.

Clare remembered that her grandparents had two old-fashioned gliders in the shade of a large sycamore tree in their yard. She asked me if I could find some of those old gliders. I searched high and low and found a few, but they were all in terrible condition. Finally, I looked online and found a place that sold them. I gave Clare two for her birthday.

We have worked to create a tranquil garden. I have some ideas that might help you create such spaces in your backyard. Find a place in the shade, preferably one that offers a cool breeze. Incorporate some hardscape near these quiet nooks. It may be a simple bird bath or a gazing ball.

One of the things I hope to include in my garden in the future is a Zen garden near the gazebo. I already have a Japanese Maple planted there. The beauty of a Zen garden is its simplicity. Try not to crowd your spaces. You don't need gardening tools in these quiet spots.

If you can arrange for some flowing water, it adds to the sense of serenity. It can be as simple as a bird bath bubbler. As odd as it may seem, you don't need to spend much time toiling at creating tranquility, rock slabs in the middle of the road notwithstanding. One of the things I enjoy in our garden is a Pawleys Island rope hammock. It is located beneath the tin roof of the shack; what a place to take a nap on a rainy afternoon! Finishing touches might include a strand of Christmas lights, a fire pit, or a chiminea.

A poem by John Greenleaf Whittier was made into a hymn. It is a prayer for tranquility through our connection with God.

> Dear Lord and Father of mankind,
> Forgive our foolish ways;
> Reclothe us in our rightful mind,
> In purer lives Thy service find,
> In deeper rev'rence, praise.
>
> Drop Thy still dews of quietness,
> Till all our strivings cease;
> Take from our souls the strain and stress,
> And let our ordered lives confess
> The beauty of Thy peace.
>
> Breathe through the heats of our desire
> Thy coolness and Thy balm;
> Let sense be dumb, let flesh retire;
> Speak through the earthquake, wind, and fire,
> O still, small Voice of calm.

The Elemental Garden

The spiritual garden begins with a basic plan and a defined structure. While it is certainly true that some things just happen and seem right, most of the work in gardening requires forethought. Consider how you use or will use these basic elements.

If you read the Creation account in Genesis 1 you will see that this was the second step in the way God made everything else. He started with nothing – *creatio ex nihilo*. Fortunately, we don't have to begin there. He has provided these basic elements for us to use.

EARTH:

"But the seed falling on good soil refers to someone who hears the Word and understands it." -Mark 13:20, NIV

While hydroponic gardening has come into its own, most of us who garden depend on the good earth as the foundation of our efforts. Soil comes in many varieties. It is important to have an analysis done on our soil type and composition from time to time. Avid gardeners do this every year. The process is simple and inexpensive, but it does take a little time. Every state has a college or university with an agricultural department to test soil.

In my state of South Carolina, Clemson University has an extension service with an office in many towns across the state. The extension office and the people who work there are among our most valuable resources in cultivating a garden. Soil sample kits are available with careful instructions about how to obtain a good sample. Once mailed to the address on the box, an analysis will be done that will advise on amending the soil in your particular garden. This will include how to change the acidity of the soil, improve the nutrients in the soil, and modify the consistency of the soil.

In my garden, with its red clay base, I have to add composted material and lime every year and with every planting. Red clay does not drain well, if at all. So good compost is a necessity. I have a compost tumbler at the back of the garden, which I used for years. More recently, we have used a compost service. These good folks come by once a week and collect from our porch two buckets full of table scraps and other compostable material. From time to time, we receive a bucket of rich compost to use in the garden.

When you develop good soil, you ensure that plants will be happy. Mulching is one of the ways to take care of plants. Too much mulch is counterproductive. We want to use enough mulch to keep the soil moist and aerated. On this acre of red clay, double-ground bark mulch is my favorite. It protects well in the winter, keeps the root system of the plants cool and moist in the summer, and it is an attractive way to landscape.

Hardscape, while not soil, is a first cousin to the good earth. Garden paths are an attractive addition to any garden. In my garden, I use small, smooth gravel on most paths. In some places, I use stepping stones. Hardscape also includes well-placed railroad ties around raised beds. I like to use large rocks, usually field stones, as points of interest, or even as a place to sit in the garden.

It is well worth the effort to take care of the soil. The Psalmist is right: "The earth is the Lord's and the fullness thereof" (Psalm 24:1, NIV). Stewardship of the earth means taking care of the soil.

WIND:

"The wind blows wherever it pleases. You hear its sound, but you cannot tell where it comes from or where it is going. So it is with everyone born of the Spirit."
-John 3:8, NIV

The poet Christina Rossetti wrote, "Who has seen the wind? Neither you nor I." That is exactly right, but we certainly see the effects of the wind in the garden. Some years ago, I decided to plant several varieties of ornamental grass. I did it because I enjoyed watching these grasses move with the wind.

During a thunderstorm, I enjoy watching the trees sway together like a giant chorus line. Their movements seem synchronized. The storms may be thought of as an exercise session for the trees. The movement keeps them healthy, but thunderstorms also serve the purpose of pruning the trees. After a storm, I'll walk through the garden and collect fallen branches to use as firewood in my chiminea.

While we cannot see the wind, the wind provides music in the garden. The weeping branches of a willow tree (*Salix babylonica*) or a cherry tree (*Prunus avium*) make a distinctive swoosh in the wind. In my garden, I have windcatchers, wind screws, and a windmill strategically placed to catch the currents of the wind. I also use windscreens to protect some tender plantings from wind damage.

Among our favorite garden accessories are wind chimes. My father-in-law, Mr. Jack, made wind chimes from an aluminum electric conduit. With a hacksaw, he cut the sections to precise lengths so the windchimes would ring in harmony. Some of them did. Even the ones that clanged were pleasant to the ear. After a while, wind chimes break. Every summer, I take a day or two to repair broken wind chimes. I have a small tool bag with all the supplies I need for my wind chime clinic. I invite my brothers and sisters to give me their broken wind chimes. In fact, I enjoy wind chimes so much that sometimes I arrange an oscillating fan to stir the air just so I can hear the music.

WATER:

"The water I give them will become in them a spring of water welling up to eternal life."-John 4:14, NIV

When God created the first garden, he included water. Water, of course, is necessary for all of life. For plants to thrive they must have sufficient water. From the grass in our lawns to shrubs and trees, plants require water.

I overheard a conversation in a garden shop. A woman customer said, "I want a shrub for the corner of my garden. It needs to be something that doesn't require any water. In that corner, the plant won't even get rain, and I am certainly not going to water it. What do you suggest?"

The owner of the garden shop looked at me and said, "This man is a master gardener, why don't you ask him what to plant there?"

I responded, "If the plant is not going to get any water either from rain or from you, you only have three choices. The first one is, to plant something already dead. The second is an artificial Christmas tree. It'll stay nice and green all year without water. Your third choice is a big rock."

The woman decided to find a big rock.

When I took the master gardening course, my two teachers were Winston Hardigree and Joe Maple. They both agreed that every garden needed some form of irrigation. Winston's preference was an above-ground sprinkler system. Joe recommended a drip irrigation system. Either will work. If your garden is going to thrive, you have to have a way to provide water, especially to plants that are not well-established.

Water features are an attractive way to enhance the garden. Here, on our one-acre plot, I have a natural hill that slopes down to our side yard. It was the perfect place to construct a waterfall with a small pond. I spent months collecting rocks for this project. I dug the pond with a shovel. It was back-breaking work. I had a professional install the recirculating pump, the filters, and the plastic liner for the waterfall and the pond. The entire project was labor-intensive and expensive. Clare and the children, and now the grandchildren, all believe the effort and the cost are worth it. I too enjoy the waterfall and the pond. I sometimes wonder if I wouldn't have been better off trying to find a place in the mountains with a natural water feature constructed by the Master Gardener.

There are many other ways to add a water feature to your garden. A simple birdbath is a delightful feature. The water can be changed regularly with a garden hose and birds of every feather will come to drink.

Perhaps the best water feature I have is the metal roof I put on our shack. Rain, especially the gentle type, is a welcome feature. To sit in the shack during summer rainfall is a natural tranquilizer with no harmful side effects. The sound of rain on a metal roof is music to the soul.

LIGHT:

"And God said, 'Let there be light,' and there was light." -Genesis 1:3, NIV

When creation began, one of the first orders of business was to divide the light from the dark. Both are equally important in the garden. Respiration plants require sunlight for photosynthesis to work. During the daylight, plants are breathing carbon dioxide and exhaling oxygen. At night, the cycle is reversed. In a recent discussion on global warming and solutions to climate change, a panelist offered this advice, "People ask me what one person can do to help with this overwhelming problem. My best answer is to plant a tree, grow a garden, enlist the aid of plants to help clean the air."

There are many ways to bring light into the garden. We have a small, plastic gazing ball in a dark corner. The reflected light brightens that corner. I have seen heavier, and perhaps more durable, gazing balls made from old bowling balls. The bowling ball was affixed atop a tripod of sturdy sticks, fitted into the finger holes in the bowling ball. The ball itself was spray-painted with reflective aluminum paint.

In our garden, we use Christmas lights throughout the year. Strands of white lights bring a soft glow to the gazebo, the arbor, and the shack after dark. I also use sun catchers to refract the light. We have several of these inside our home placed to catch the sunshine and create fanciful tiny rainbows. Any kind of prism will work. In the garden itself, I have three large windows that were removed from a church in eastern North Carolina. The heavy windows are concrete with irregularly shaped pieces of stained glass. These heavy windows are wired to the chain-link fence on the side of our garden. When the sun shines through the pieces of stained glass it creates a splash of color in the garden.

A comforting fire can be a pleasant addition to the garden on a cold day or at night. I enjoy sitting outside by my chiminea. It's a safe place to build a small fire. Other people prefer a fire pit or an outdoor fireplace. The most important thing is to be careful, especially if you have small children or grandchildren. To sit by a fire and swap stories is a delightful pastime. To sit by a fire in complete silence is bliss.

The most common trait of all primitive peoples is a reverence for the life-giving earth, and the Native American shared this elemental ethic: The land was alive to his loving touch, and he, its son, was brother to all creatures.

Stewart Udall

Behold, my friends, the spring is come; the earth has gladly received the embraces of the sun, and we shall soon see the results of their love!

Chief Sitting Bull

The Sensual Garden

"Taste and see that the Lord is good;"
-Psalm 34:8, NIV

Some people will have difficulty thinking of the garden as spiritual. To add sensuality to the mix may be confusing to them. However, God has in divine grace given us five senses.

In the gospel of Mark, in chapter 6, we have the account of Jesus feeding the five thousand. There are many things we could say about the remarkable miracle. However, the notable thing is that this event is recorded in all four gospels, showing how great of an impact it made on all the disciples.

Later, in chapter 7, Jesus heals a deaf and mute man. He looks up to heaven with a deep sigh and says *"Ephphatha!"* which means "to be opened." In chapter 8, Jesus again feeds a multitude. This time it was four thousand people. So, in a short time, the disciples have witnessed the feeding of over nine thousand people.

Following that miracle, they got in a boat and forgot food, except for one loaf. The disciples begin worrying about their low supplies, despite the miracles they had just witnessed. Jesus comments, "Do you have eyes but fail to see, and ears but fail to hear?" (Mark 8:18, NIV). Ho goes on to remind them of the miracles He just performed with the food. He tries to show them how He provides despite and apart from doubt. The chapter continues with them arriving in Bethsaida and Jesus healing another blind man.

The story of deaf and blind men brackets the comment on hearing and seeing. Jesus says don't be distracted, but pay attention. This is how we should also approach the garden. As we go into the garden, we must say the same thing --- be open to all senses, not merely sight and sound. If people somehow lose one of their senses, the others may compensate to some extent. These are the ways that we experience the garden.

The perfect clinical example of this truth is a case study of Helen Keller. She was born in Tuscumbia, Alabama. At a young age, she lost her sight and hearing from an unknown illness, now thought to possibly be scarlet fever. Her father – a local newspaper editor – brought her a companion, Anne Sullivan, who taught Keller language through reading and writing. Helen Keller became the first deafblind person to attend Radcliffe College at Harvard University where she earned a Bachelor of Arts degree.

For Helen, the sense that took over for the absence of sight and hearing was the sense of touch. Her first word was the word water. Her senses learned to adapt to continually take in the world. It was Helen Keller who said, "The only thing worse than being blind is having sight but no vision." Her words echo Jesus's words in this passage about comprehension and listening over simply hearing.

Our plantings can include planning for areas and progressions that delight all five of these avenues into the human spirit. As we enter the garden, and throughout the day, we might all pray that we may "*Ephphatha!*" That we may be open and receptive.

a. Seeing

Gardening requires paying attention. Often, we will be surprised. For most of us, our initial enjoyment of the garden probably comes through our vision. Only the seasoned gardener can enjoy walking through the garden in wintertime. As one person recently said to me, "If I'm going to put in the time, effort, and money to grow plants, I want to see flowers all the time. Otherwise, the plants are not earning their keep." When we understand the life cycle of plants, we know that even the best perennials do not bloom all the time.

As I mentioned earlier in this book, Clare and I have dubbed the red geranium our signature plant. I have the bright red and green plants on our front porch from spring through fall. For several years, I keep the plants on the porch all winter long. I would cover them with fleece blankets when the temperature went below 35 degrees F. Usually, the geraniums bloomed beautifully through Christmas here in the upstate of South Carolina. Some years, the red geraniums did well for two full blooming seasons. After a time, the plants become leggy and the blossoms are smaller. This is a sure sign that the geraniums need to be replaced.

A while ago, the geranium plants on the front porch suffered from the intense heat of our summer and early fall. I decided to discard the spent plants and replace them with a mixture of pansies and violas. Then, in mid-February of the following year, our front porch had never looked so beautiful. We received many comments from those who visited our home. Most importantly, Clare was delighted with the new flowers.

Every gardener knows that each season and each location in the garden requires discovering and rediscovering what works best. I have tried to plant so that we can enjoy a progression of blooms. Soon after Christmas, as early as January 1st, the Lenten roses show their first blooms. Pansies, violas, and snapdragons are usually prancing at the same time. Spring bulbs take center stage in February. Early crocus and narcissus will bloom even in the snow. These are followed by their showier cousins, daffodils, hyacinths (*Hyacinthus orientalis*), Dutch iris (Iris hollandica), and scilla. Finally, tulips and tall bearded iris complete the progression of spring bulbs.

After the final frost, perennials and annuals join the parade. Many gardeners focus only on the early summer flowers. Take the time to look through garden catalogs to see what plants will thrive in your garden during the summer and fall. Some of the more reliable are daylilies (*Hemerocallis fulva*), as well as 'Oriental' lilies (*Lilium orientalis*) and Asiatic lilies (*Lilium auratum*). Many gardeners enjoy multiple plantings of gladiolus (*Gladiolus communis*). Peonies (*Paeonia lactiflora*) are a favorite old-fashioned plant. While I have a few, they are not very satisfactory in this red clay.

For the fall, chrysanthemums (*Chrysanthemum indicum*) and asters (*Symphyotrichum patens*) will always be reliable, but there are other perennials that you may want to try. Consult your full-service garden shop and look at the catalogues that come in the mail.

You may also want to do a designated planting that will attract flying flowers. Butterflies and moths, hummingbirds, and dragonflies are attracted to many of the same plants. Zinnias (*Zinnia elegans*), salvia (*Salvia officinalis*), and coneflowers (*Echinacea purpurea*) are easy to grow and are a good place to start.

In addition to annuals and perennials, consider flowering shrubs and vines. Yellow jasmine (*Gelsemium sempervirens*) is the state flower of South Carolina. The one covering my arbor blooms profusely in the early spring. Later, the star jasmine (*Trachelospermum jasminoides*) does the same. Through the years, I have enjoyed a selection of roses, especially climbing varieties, David Austin roses, and more recently, knock-out roses. Some of the rose aficionados in my circle of friends consider these fake roses, but these low-maintenance varieties work for me.

My favorite flowering trees are dogwoods, redbuds, and sassafras. Yoshino cherry trees (*Prunus yedoensis*) and sergeant crabapple trees (*Malus sargentii*) grow beautifully in our area. Avoid Bradford pear trees (*Pyrus calleryana*) at all cost. In South Carolina, they naturalize and become an invasive species, not to mention their blooms smell like old fish.

As you can see, it is not difficult to create a progression of blooms, especially here in the southern United States. It does require some planning, but even that is a part of the joy of gardening.

Seasoned gardeners know that a winter garden has its charm. Evergreens have their day in the sun after deciduous trees have lost their leaves. Trees with exfoliating bark, such as sycamores (*Platanus occidentalis*) and river birch (*Betula nigra*) add interest to the winter landscape. Even the spent seed heads of *rudbeckia* are attractive to people and birds.

Gardeners tend to look down, after all, that is where the plants are. However, there is much to see overhead. Lean back in a hammock and look up. You will see things you might have missed. It's enough to see the green foliage against the blue sky. It's also interesting to identify shapes in the clouds. When we look up, we may even catch a glimpse of a pileated woodpecker hammering away on a tall snag. You may see, as I did one year, a newly born albino squirrel.

We have heard the expression, "The eyes are the window of the soul." If that is true, and I believe it is, when we open our eyes in the garden, our soul will surely find delight.

Selah.

b. Hearing

Sometimes, when you're in your garden, close your eyes and listen. When I do this in my garden, I'm likely to hear a dog barking, 18-wheel trucks driving by my house, one of the many trains traveling on the tracks behind our house, or a cacophony of these sounds mixed with others. At first, all of this noise may seem distracting; however, if we listen carefully, we will hear beyond the noise. As I indicated earlier, sometimes the noise that interferes most is my own restless heart. In moments like these, I call to mind one verse from the Psalms. "Be still and know that I am God" (Psalm 46:10, NIV).

These words become a mantra that serves as a call to worship, that calms my spirit, quiets my soul, and makes me more attentive to the world around me. The words of a hymn come to mind:

> This is my Father's World
> And to my listening ears
> All nature sings and round me rings
> The music of the spheres.

Our sense of hearing enables us to experience the garden beyond what we can see. Once, I listened to the clear-throated song of a Carolina wren. The small brown bird with a perky tail is fun to watch, especially when she is building her nest. Whether we can see her or not, her song is a garden favorite. She sings to stake out her territory, to guard her nest, or to warn her neighbors of an intruder, such as a cat, a snake, or a hawk. Her music may also serve to attract her mate

One of the joys of gardening for me is learning to identify birds by their call. Some are unmistakable, like a catbird, a crow, a mourning dove, a blue jay, or a mockingbird. Others require a trained ear. One night, I was sitting in my garden listening to a mockingbird sing incessantly from the top of a weeping willow tree. Occasionally, the lonely mockingbird would pause. In that space, I could hear a pair of bullfrogs adding bass notes to the concert. High in the trees, cicadas and tree frogs chimed in. Fortunately, I do not have tinnitus, but Clare does. She hears tree frogs even in the dead of winter.

One of the things I've learned is to allow distracting sounds to serve a higher purpose. A shrill siren may become a call to prayer. Whenever I hear a siren, I know someone is in trouble. I try to pause and breathe a prayer for the person in trouble and for the first responders rushing to help. Inevitably, closing my eyes and paying attention to my sense of hearing leads me to moments of worship.

Selah.

c. Smelling

In gardening, the sense of smell is one of our greatest assets. The seasoned gardener knows when the soil has soured. A gardener can also appreciate the aroma of freshly tilled earth. In the process of composting, which is important for every garden, the odor of a compost pile can inform the gardener about the readiness of the compost to be used. Any gardener who incorporates manure into a soil amendment program knows the difference between green manure and clean manure simply by the smell.

In my garden, I have a variety of extraneous smells. Some are pleasant; some are not. The aroma of wood smoke at a distance is pleasant. Up close, the same smoke can be an irritant. I do not like the smell of petroleum products, especially in the garden. I do enjoy the fragrance of many of the trees, shrubs, and plants in my garden.

In the same way that I have tried to create a progression of color in the garden, I have also tried to plan for a succession of fragrances. In my yard, winter daphne has a difficult time. It is a delightful plant that does not like wet feet. I have had some success planting a winter daphne in a large container. On our front porch in the wintertime, a daphne provides an early fragrance. I also plant pansies and violas in boxes and hanging baskets on our front porch. The pansies have little or no fragrance. The violas make up for it. To come home at the end of the day and catch the sweet aroma of violas on the evening breeze is a delight.

Carolina jasmine (*Gelsemium sempervirens*) grows profusely on an arbor in our backyard. It provides an early spring display of bright yellow blooms accompanied by a pleasing fragrance. Miss Kim lilac (*Syringa pubescens subsp. patula*) is the one variety of lilac I have been able to grow in my garden. It is smaller than most lilacs but blooms profusely, yielding a familiar lilac aroma. Star jasmine vines twine around the post on our shack. Tiny white flowers have a surprising and pleasant scent in mid-spring. I allow wild honeysuckle to grow on a chain-link fence. I try to keep it contained by cutting it back after it blooms. It continues to sally forth and fill the night air with a distinctive sweet aroma.

Roses are known for their fragrance. While I am far from a rose expert, I do enjoy several low-maintenance varieties. Among my favorites is the Zéphirine Drouhin. It is a vigorous climber; an almost thornless pink rose with a strong bourbon scent. The Zéphirine Drouhin works well in my garden because it can tolerate some shade. I have them planted on either side of our entrance and either side of a double swing.

When I walk through the garden, I enjoy plucking a few needles from hemlock trees and red cedar trees. I crush them in my fingers and enjoy the aroma. Aromatic herbs also make a strong contribution to the fragrant garden. Among my favorites are rosemary, lavenders, basils, mint, pennyroyal, and fennel.

Selah.

> One of the plants you might want to try is a daphne plant with variegated leaves (*Daphne aureomarginata alba*). It is quite aromatic and can perfume an entire garden by itself. It remains attractive all year long with its dark green leaves and attractive gold edges. However, it is a plant that is very picky. It demands soil that is consistently moist, but not wet. I have found it does best in a pot with good soil and good drainage. It is one of the first plants to bloom in early January. We enjoy having one by our front door. The scent mixes with the violas in our baskets and creates a pleasing aroma for all those who enter our front door.

d. Tasting

Those of us who have had a basic anatomy class know that smelling and tasting are close cousins. Keep that in mind the next time you visit a dairy barn or a pig sty. In the garden, tasting was the way that Adam and Eve got into trouble - by eating the forbidden fruit. You will notice that the scripture never identifies the fruit. It almost certainly was not an apple.

The scripture gives an invitation to "Taste and see that the Lord is good" (Psalm 34:8, NIV). Walking through the garden allows picking a ripe strawberry, a fresh muscadine, a bright red cherry tomato, or a sugar pea. Rinsed under a garden hose, these mini harvests remind us of the scripture.

My dad loved to garden. It was a necessity for our family of ten people. All of us worked in the garden.

I'll never forget my dad thinning radishes. His favorite variety was the scarlet globe. Dad would pull a handful from the ground, wash them off with the garden hose, pull a packet of salt out of his pocket, and pass around the fresh red vegetables. Seasoned with a little salt, this became a special garden treat.

Every year, I try to plant a variety of basil (*Ocimum basilicum*), and several *nasturtiums*. Basil plants are good companions to tomato plants. Basil leaves are the perfect complement to fresh sliced tomatoes and mozzarella cheese. This combination makes a good Caprese salad with a vinaigrette dressing.

In World War II, people were encouraged to plant victory gardensSome gardens are mostly for show but some are mainly for food. That brings up the question, "Why should we even consider planting a garden when so much fresh produce is available at our local market?"

When I was growing up, my family had a big vegetable garden. At least once a week, my whole family worked the plot together, but my dad, my brothers, and I worked in the red soil almost every day. A garden provides for a family in many ways. It can save on grocery bills, but it can also contribute to the healthy growth of family relationships.

Food marketed as organic is increasingly popular. However, being able to grow food without pesticides and eating it straight from the garden is superior in every way. When you walk in your garden, you can pick a vegetable, wash it off the garden hose, and eat it right there. That's the beauty of growing it yourself.

As we garden, we are also contributing to the health of our planet. We enrich the soil and do a small part to confront climate change.

Gardens can also be a community activity. Clare's brother, Ben, has volunteered to help plant gardens in Cincinnati, Ohio. These block gardens provide fresh vegetables throughout the summer months. Those who help work the garden also help share the produce. In my hometown, the master gardeners tended a large vegetable garden. Each participating member took care of one row. When the harvest came in, the produce was taken to shelters for those in need and the local soup kitchen.

Clare's father, Mr. Jack, planted a large garden after his retirement. He tended nearly a half-acre of a beautiful black soil garden on the sand ridge of South Carolina. Mr. Jack was an exacting executive before his retirement. When it came to his beautiful vegetable garden, he was just as thorough in his garden practices. He had grown up on a red dirt farm in Saluda County.Living in Lexington County gave him the opportunity to reclaim and hone his old skills. I remember watching him put mineral oil on the silks on the developing ears of corn in his garden. He had three or four long rows. This mineral oil kept away corn earworms.

There was no way Mr. Jack and Miz Lib could consume all the produce from their garden. Family, friends, and neighbors were the beneficiaries of this overabundance. Of course, with their depression mentality, they canned and froze much of the bounty to use throughout the winter months. There was never a meal on Miz Lib's table that did not have at least two nutritious, homegrown vegetables.

One of the joys of gardening is sharing with others. Gardening is good for the human soul. Many people describe gardening as therapeutic. Therapy comes from the Greek word for healing. Gardening contributes to good physical and mental health. Fresh air, exercise, a break from our daily work, a space for creativity, the list of benefits is endless. One woman who had been gardening for years said, "Gardening is my way to create a work of art in my backyard. Not only that, it keeps me from spontaneously screaming at irritating people."

I often consult our South Carolina extension service for my garden. Their website provides multitudes of helpful information on all aspects of gardening. Consult your own local extension agency for a plethora of valuable information about gardening. If you're just beginning to grow a vegetable garden, start small, then expand as space and time allow. Remember the basics: good soil, adequate water, full sunlight, and a vigilant eye.

All vegetables taste better when they are grown in your own garden. I want to suggest six that you can consider including in your garden. In early spring, usually around Valentine's Day where I live, plant red potatoes and sugar snap peas. When the soil becomes warmer, plant radishes in the same row as carrots. The radishes will germinate and mature quickly while the carrots take a long time. Plant some spinach, maybe some kale, and Bibb lettuce. On Good Friday, plant everything but the hottest weather crops, like lima beans and okra. I would suggest one yellow crookneck squash hill and one zucchini hill. If you have room, you can add one patty-pan squash hill. I would start with one hill of each because I started with three hills of zucchini and it took over my garden. My garden overflowed with an abundance of zucchini, some as large as baseball bats. I was quickly overwhelmed with this intense flood of food.

Plant three varieties of tomatoes. One of them should be a cherry tomato. If space allows, plant two rows of sweet corn on the north side of the garden. As the plant matures, the leaves should grow to touch each other, setting them up for good cross pollination. My favorite varieties for corn are the 'Silver Queen' and the 'Golden Queen.'

As your garden grows and expands, you can always add and experiment. Fresh cucumbers are always a part of my garden, but only a vine or two. I've also had great success with cantaloupe. The problem with cantaloupe is that all of the fruit tends to become ripe at the exact same time. I had one cantaloupe vine a long time ago that grew beautifully. However, I then had twenty-one fresh cantaloupe all harvested on the same day. While I gave many away, Clare and I thoroughly enjoyed our bounty of this sweet fruit.

Selah.

e. Touching

Textures in nature are another way that we enjoy the garden. To run my hand over the bark of a tree planted by my grandfather is a reminder of how much Pappy enjoyed the feel of lumber. To sink my hands into freshly tilled soil makes me grateful for the experience of growing plants from seed. To handle a smooth rock, polished by a mountain stream, helps me feel at one with the earth.

The sense of touch can best be experienced when we pull off our garden gloves. I use gloves much of the time when I am gardening, but I take them off when I want to feel the reward of my labor. I enjoy showing my children the soft, fuzzy leaves of lamb's ear, a plant whose name is well taken. On a hike with scouts, I often stop at a wild mullein plant and explain how indigenous peoples of North America often used the soft leaves as insoles in their moccasins. I also take the time to point out the leaves of poison oak (*Toxicodendron pubescens*) and poison ivy (*Toxicodendron radicans*), plants that should not be touched or burned.

Sometimes, when I sit in my garden, I just want to think. I take out my pocket knife and whittle on a piece of red cedar. The fragrance is enjoyable but the wood itself has a feel of something substantial. A while ago, I was doing just that, whittling on a piece of red cedar. For a bit of context, my grandchildren call me PK, short for Papa Kirk.

My grandson asked, "PK, what are you doin'?"

"I'm piddlin' and whittlin'," I said.

"Will you teach me how?" he asked.

Some things can only be taught at the slow pace a garden provides. Learning at a slower pace is necessary for grandfathers and grandchildren alike.

"As iron sharpens iron, so one person sharpens another." -Proverbs 27:1, NIV

Selah.

Forget not that the earth delights to feel your bare feet and the winds long to play with your hair.
Khalil Gibran

Common Sense is that which judges the things given to it by other senses.
Leonardo da Vinci

I have the habit of (paying) attention to such excess, that my senses get no rest - but suffer from a constant strain.
Henry David Thoreau

The Garden of Love

"Blessed are the pure in heart, for they will see God." Matthew 5:8, NIV

Companions at the Gate

"The Lord God said, 'It is not good for the man to be alone. I will make a helper suitable for him.'" -Genesis 2:18, NIV

Clematis 'Henryi'

Companion planting is a way of combining plants in the garden. When two plants are grown together, it may be of benefit to both. Some varieties of herbs and flowers have natural substances that can repel or attract certain insects. Marigolds (*Tagetes erecta*), when planted near cabbage, are said to discourage nematodes. Bee balm (*Monarda didyma*) attracts pollinators and so is a suitable companion to eggplant. Other plants seem to promote growth among their neighbors. Basil, for example, is said to promote healthy growth and improved flavor for tomatoes. Fresh basil and homegrown tomatoes layered with mozzarella cheese and drizzled with a vinaigrette make a tasty summer salad.

In our garden, I plant some things together simply to enhance their beauty. Zéphirine Drouhin is an antique climbing rose. It has been cherished for generations for its rich perfumed scent and its large deep pink blossoms. Zéphirine Drouhin is one of the few roses that can tolerate poor soil and air pollution. Even in partial shade, it blooms beautifully.

Henryi clematis is a variety of clematis that thrives well in the Piedmont. Also a vigorous climber, this plant features large pure white blossoms. It is a favorite mailbox decorative vine because if the roots are protected, it tolerates our southern heat. Henryi is one of the most reliable of all clematis plant varieties.

On either side of our gate, we have a Zéphirine Drouhin rose and a Henryi clematis planted next to each other. They climb to a height of nearly twelve feet, intertwining with each other and thriving together. Most of the time they alternate in their blooming, but there are occasions when they bloom simultaneously. It is a sight to behold, a striking display of pink and white, accented by green and darker green leaves. It took more than three years for the two plants to become established, but it was well worth the wait.

Because both the Zéphirine Drouhin rose and the Henryi clematis are climbers, they must have support. The rose and the clematis offer each other some support. But when a clinging vine clings to a clinging vine, the result can be disastrous. The vines fall to the ground and are trampled underfoot. If they bloom at all, they bloom poorly. Sooner or later, one or both will die.

As I've said before, every garden needs a gate. It is a sign of hospitality. The gate in the white picket fence that opens into our garden doubles as a sturdy trellis. It was built from treated lumber and red cedar lattice with the help of one of my good friends, Wid Jenkins. The entire structure is painted with durable oil-based white paint that penetrates and protects the wood. The trellis provides the support needed for both the Zéphirine Drouhin rose and the Henryi clematis.

The gate into our garden is a picture of marriage. From the very beginning, God saw the beauty of marriage. When two people are rooted and grounded together in faith, when they are nurtured together through the seasons of life, and when they grow together holding fast to each other, there is the potential for this rare beauty. They must, however, have a support stronger than either of them individually, stronger than the two of them together. I believe that support comes from God, the Creator of life.

In the Greek language, the word *eros* describes the love that we most often associate with romance. It is the passionate, spine-tingling love that first brings two people together in courtship. *Eros,* alone, cannot endure. The Greeks had another word for love, *agape,* best described in the love chapter in the Bible: Love "bears all things, believes all things, hopes all things, endures all things. Love never fails" (1 Corinthians 13:7-8, NIV).

Agape is the love that gives strength and stability to marriage. It is not a feeling but a decision, not an emotion but an act of the will. It is like a trellis to flowering vines. It is committed love that becomes the sturdy support for marriage. Agape love allows partners to become lifelong companions, to grow strong together, and to bloom most beautifully.

Grow old along with me!
The best is yet to be,
the last of life, for which the first was made.
                                    Robert Browning.

I think of marriage as a garden. You have to tend to it. Respect it, take care of it, feed it. Make sure everyone is getting the right amount of sunlight.
                                    Mark Ruffalo

Cardinals

Cardinalis cardinalis

Perched in the bough of a mountain hemlock on a snowy day, tending a nest among the flowers of a dogwood, chirping a clear "No trespassing" while guarding a berry-laden pyracantha bush (*Pyracantha coccinea*), or darting and dipping in low flight, the bright red cardinal is always an honored guest in our yard. The redbirds were named cardinals by colonists for the male's red body and crest, reminiscent of a Roman Catholic cardinal's attire. It is the state bird of seven states, more than any other bird: North Carolina, West Virginia, Ohio, Illinois, Indiana, Kentucky, and Virginia.

My mother loved "red birds" as she called them. Though they can be found all across the South, the correct name is the Northern Cardinal (*Cardinalis cardinalis*). It is one of the birds most easily recognized by novice birdwatchers. However, it still brings a thrill to the hearts of seasoned ornithologists. A cardinal's spiritual meaning is really in the eye of the beholder. Some people believe that if a cardinal flies across your path, it means that a romantic relationship is nearby. For a single person, that might mean that a new significant other will soon come into their life. For a person who is married, it may be taken as a sign of fidelity to the one to whom they are betrothed.

People who are grieving often find the cardinal to be a source of comfort and joy. Recently, I conducted a funeral where a bright red male cardinal flew into the tent and perched on a flower arrangement next to the casket. The family interpreted this as a quiet visitation from the Spirit of God, bringing them comfort in one of their darkest hours.

An old legend from colonial times says that "cardinals appear when angels are near." Many cardinals have been associated with dearly departed loved ones. When my mother saw a red bird, she would often say "I feel like Granny is nearby to tell me that everything is going to be all right." Cardinals will always bring joy to my soul.

Here is an ode to the Northern Cardinal:

> Wearing the vestments of a Roman cleric
> Winging in undulating flight
> Perching in a flowering dogwood
> Chirping over black oil sunflower seeds
> Chanting sweet liturgy
> Invoking the presence of the Spirit
> Bidding my soul
> "Be still and know that I am God."

Attracting cardinals to the garden is reason enough to have seed feeders within sight. Filling the feeders around our yard is a never-ending task, but it can also become an act of devotion.

I call to mind the words of Jesus found in Matthew 6:25-27: "Therefore I tell you, do not worry about your life, what you will eat or drink; or about your body, what you will wear. Is not life more than food and the body more than clothes? Look at the birds of the air; they do not sow or reap or store away in barns, and yet your heavenly Father feeds them. Are you not much more valuable than they? Can any one of you by worrying add a single hour to your life?" (NIV).

Dirty Hands

"Clean hands and a pure heart" -Psalms 24:4, NIV

A chicken and a pig lived together on a farm. They became friends and often took walks together. One Saturday morning, they were strolling together down a country road when they passed a church. The sign out front read:

FREE BREAKFAST TODAY
ALL DONATIONS APPRECIATED

The chicken said to the pig, "We could each make a donation. I could give a couple of eggs, and you could offer ham, bacon, and sausage."

After a long pause, the chicken said, "Come on. It would be a kind thing to do. What do you think?"

The pig replied, "What you suggest is easy for you. You can give a couple of eggs and go back to the farm. For me, it would require total commitment!"

Gardening is more than a pastime. For those of us who enjoy being outside and sinking our hands in the good earth, gardening is total involvement. Committing to tilling, cultivating, watering, fertilizing, and weeding is a down-and-dirty endeavor. I often wear a pair of garden gloves. But I enjoy peeling the gloves off to feel the texture of loamy soil and to enjoy the aroma of rich earth.

It was a typical South Carolina summer day, hot and humid. I was cleaning a flower bed along our picket fence in the front yard. I started with garden gloves but pulled weeds with my bare hands. I used a garden mattock to loosen the soil, digging deep to get the intruding roots.

After working a couple of hours, I stood up, brushed the dirt from my knees, wiped my brow with a bandana, and then my hands. I was covered with red clay, sweaty and filthy.

An automobile slowed and pulled into our driveway. There were two women in the late model Lexus. The one on the passenger's side powered down her window and asked, "Do you do this kind of work often?"

"Yes," I said. "Especially here, in this yard."

"May I ask what you get paid?"

I thought for a moment and then quipped, "Well, the lady that lives here lets me sleep with her."

End of conversation.

The Lexus zoomed out of the driveway into the four-lane, tires squealing, never to return.

I honestly don't know any way to tend a garden without getting down on your knees and getting your hands dirty. It's part of the joy of gardening. And as you can see, it has its advantages.

Our yard has an outdoor sink fully equipped with Lava soap. The strong hand soap contains pumice that removes much of the dirt from my hands. Our basement has a utility sink in the laundry room with liquid detergent soap and a fingernail brush. We also have a shower with Dial soap.

When I have been working in the garden, I often have to make a stop at all three washing stations, putting my garden clothes in the washing machine along the way.

Octagon soap used to be indispensable in Southern households. From scrubbing dirty work clothes to lathering hands that had come in contact with poison ivy, the yellow lye soap with eight sides scented with lemongrass had multiple uses.

My mother, who had a strong aversion to dirt, always kept a bar of Octagon soap close at hand. Mama expected us to wash our hands up to our elbows before meals, whether they needed it or not. We were allowed to go barefooted after the first day of May, but that required additional foot washing. If we made an ugly comment about another person or uttered a bad word, she washed our mouths out with the same yellow soap.

When I went fishing with my grandfather, I usually picked up a few choice phrases to add to my lumberyard vocabulary. Mama employed my own toothbrush and yellow Octagon soap to scrub Pappy's colorful language from my mouth.

"I want you to enjoy being with your grandfather," she said. "But I don't want you to talk like him."

She almost cleansed me from all of Pappy's profanity, but not quite.

I have found that whenever I wash my hands in a public restroom, trying to dry them with an automatic dryer is annoying. Those machines never get my hands completely dry. Have you ever exited a restroom after using one of those machines, drying your hands, rubbing them on your clothing, only to meet someone who wanted to shake hands? Meeting the public with water on your hands is embarrassing.

Meeting the public with blood on your hands is incriminating. Pilate, the Governor of Judea, washed and dried his hands in public, attempting to rid himself of any responsibility for the death of Jesus.

Scripture records, "Pilate … took water and washed his hands before the crowd saying, 'I am innocent of this man's blood...'" (Matthew 27:24, NIV). Nice try, Governor.

Even Octagon soap would not have washed away his guilt. No amount of washing could wipe his hands clean of the death soon to occur on Golgotha, the place of the skull.

Simon Peter made a bold vow on the night of Passover, "Lord, I am ready to go with you to prison and to death" (Luke 22:33, NIV). By dawn the next morning, when the rooster crowed in downtown Jerusalem, Peter had asserted three times that he didn't even know Jesus. Scripture says that he punctuated his denials with cursing.

Mama would have certainly washed out his mouth with soap.

Before the Last Supper, on the night he was betrayed, the Gospel says that Jesus "poured water in a basin and began to wash his disciples' feet..." (John 13:5, NIV). All twelve disciples were there for the foot-washing – Peter, Judas, all of them. The scrubbing was not enough to clean up the act of Peter, Judas, or the rest. Maybe the Lord should have used Octagon soap.

For many Christians, some days are set aside for reflection and self-examination, acknowledging our sins, and seeking forgiveness. There is a time to come clean with God.

Have you tried to wash your hands of responsibility like Pilate? Have you denied Jesus like Simon Peter? Have you betrayed the Lord like Judas? The cleansing we need concerns not only hands, mouths, and feet. The purging we need is the deep, inner cleansing of our hearts.

David phrased it well, "Create within me a clean heart, O God" (Psalm 51:10, NIV). Christians affirm that the one who died for our sins offers forgiveness and pardon. If we confess and receive, by faith, His mercy and His grace, our hearts will be clean. It is cleansing that goes far beyond the reach of Octagon soap.

Roses

"A rose by any other name would smell as sweet." -William Shakespeare

Rosa 'Queen Elizabeth'

My grandmother loved roses. She had a small rose garden in the backyard of this house. Hers were not the hybrid varieties but what some called "old-fashioned roses." Along the back fence of the property, near the railroad track, she planted a climbing rose known as 'Seven Sisters.' It was a vigorous grower that bloomed only once a year, but when it did, it offered a magnificent display and a sweet fragrance.

The rose is a symbol of love; I used to send them to Clare when we were dating. Once we moved to this home, she asked me not to send cut roses anymore. Instead, she wanted me to plant the kind that blooms year after year.

Clare and I enjoy roses. I prefer the low-maintenance varieties. We have several David Austin roses; one, known as 'Falstaff,' is deep ruby red. A large yellow variety is called 'Teasing Georgia.' I have a friend, an expert in English gardens, who calls the popular knockout roses "fake roses." We enjoy them anyway.

Among the climbing roses in our garden are a white Cherokee rose, which blooms just about Mother's Day, and a spectacular Queen Anne rose that blooms profusely in the late spring with small yellow blossoms draping like a flowering curtain across our shack. We enjoy an early blooming pink Zéphirine Drouhin, which is nearly thornless and does well in semi-shade. We have a wild Irish rose that I did not plant. I suspect it was planted by the birds who delight in eating the tiny rose hips.

Years ago, when our oldest son was in high school, he played the part of Sir Lionel in the musical *Camelot*. That spring, I found a Camelot rose at a discount store and planted it near the climbing Cherokee rose. It did beautifully for several years… as long as I kept the aphids off it.

In our garden, we have a climbing rose, a rescue plant from a local garden shop. I spoke to the owner and asked for a special price. I knew that even when it was just about dead, I could bring it back to life.

He said, "If you'll take it home and plant it, I'll give it to you."

I took my new scraggly rose back to my shack and planted it. During the first year, the rose came to life and climbed a few feet. By the second year, it had climbed to the roof. Now it covers all sides of the shack.

It has no thorns and puts out many small yellow flowers which provide cover for many birds. This rose puts on a gorgeous display one time every spring for three weeks.

If you are looking for a specimen that is easy and low maintenance, look no farther than the yellow Lady Bank rose (*Rosa banksiae*).

Thyme

"Just as bees make honey from thyme, the strongest and driest of herbs, so do the wise profit from the most difficult experiences." -Plato

Thyme is a member of the mint family. There are more than 350 species of thyme. For my garden in South Carolina, the two most important varieties are *thymus vulgarius* and *thymus serpyllum*. *Thymus vulgaris* is native to the Mediterranean and is a relative of oregano used for cooking. *Thymus serpyllum* is native to northern Europe and often called creeping thyme, as it grows low to the ground, while the Mediterranean variety grows into a bush. The flowers of thyme are attractive to pollinators, especially bees. It has long been associated with the fairy world. In Shakespeare's *A Midsummer Night's Dream*, thyme is associated with the fairy queen, Titania.

In ancient Greece, Theophrastus, a third-century BCE Greek philosopher and naturalist, gave thyme its name. The herb was used to restore vigor and mental acuity. It was burned as a religious incense to give Greek soldiers courage. It was burned in ritual altar fires to purify the sacrifice to the gods. It was burned at funerals and placed in coffins because it was believed that the soul of the deceased could be assured of safe passage to the afterlife.

How did this plant become associated with courage? In Greek, "thymus" sounds like "thymos," the Greek word for courage. It was tucked into the armor of Greek soldiers. Greek athletes applied crushed thyme or thyme oil to enhance their courage. The creeping thyme of northern Europe was not known to the Greeks;

however, ancient Greeks and Romans called several species *thymus serpyllum*. Oddly that name was later given by Linnaeus to ordinary creeping thyme.

The reason the name was used was that, in both cultures, folklore held that thyme repelled snakes. Aemilius Macer wrote in the 11th century, "The smoke of thyme drives away all serpents and all other venomous beasts. Therefore, it is the custom for reapers to mix thyme with their food, so that such venomous beasts would flee from them and do no harm if they fell asleep in the field."

One ancient Christian belief was that the hay in the manger bed of the infant Jesus was mixed with thyme, protecting the child. In northern European mythology, creeping thyme attracted fairies who would gather to dance wherever the herb grew.

In medicinal practice, thyme has been used for respiratory congestion, to rid the body of parasites, and for headaches.

Today, it is used in mouthwash, skin lotions, chewing gum, and candy. Thyme oil is frequently used in aroma therapy. The liquor Benedictine contains thyme. In my garden, I prefer creeping thyme of several varieties. I plant it in a path between stepping stones where it can be crushed underfoot, releasing its fragrance. It may keep snakes away from the path, but not out of the garden.

One particular variety of thyme is my favorite. It's a small creeping variety called pennyroyal *(Hedeoma pulegioides)*. Pennyroyal is a strong insect repellant. I remember a time when I was fishing on the outer banks of North Carolina. I went into a bait shop and asked for insect repellant. The mosquitoes on the outer banks are notorious if the wind is blowing from the Pamlico Sound toward the ocean. The lady who checked me out told me I needed to get myself some of the "Skin-So-Soft" from Avon. She said all the local fishermen used it, that it was better than Off! or any other intentional repellant. I said, "Well, what is it that makes it that way?" She said the primary ingredient was pennyroyal.

My brother-in-law, Dr. Jule Hedden, is a family physician, a gentleman doctor, and a fellow gardener. Conservative by nature, Jule often prescribes for his patients a "tincture of time." He doesn't mean "thyme." In his wisdom, he knows that some things just take time, so my recommendation to you is to plant some time. Everybody needs a little more thyme.

Bees

"Out of the eater, something to eat; out of the strong, something sweet."
-Judges 14:14, NIV

Anyone who has gone barefooted in a patch of clover has, sooner or later, stepped on a honey bee. Bee stings are to be avoided. But, bees are essential insects.

Writing for the *Southeast Farm Press*, Roy Roberson reports that beekeepers in the United States generate approximately $200 million annually in honey production. As pollinators, honey bees are valued at more than $34 billion. This figure is calculated by multiplying the total value of crops and the percent of each crop requiring honey bees for pollination. This includes field crops, fruit crops, vegetables, and nut crops.

Nationwide, the honey bee industry directly impacts approximately one-third of all agricultural food products. Three-fourths of all flowering plants rely on pollinators for fertilization. These include most food crops and some that provide fiber, drugs, and fuel. In South Carolina, crops that are primarily dependent upon honey bees for pollination include cucumbers, peaches, apples, blueberries, strawberries, melons, and squash.

In 1622, early European colonists brought the first honey bees to the Americas. Many of the crops that depend on honey bees for pollination have also been imported since colonial times. Swarms that escaped, known as wild bees, spread rapidly as far as the Great Plains, usually preceding the colonists.

My grandmother, who suffered from asthma, believed that a spoonful of local honey taken every day helped control her allergies. A jar of honey was the best gift we could give to her.

Last Christmas, I received a quart jar of local honey from a friend. The sweet elixir came with a block of honeycomb. My friend expressed a concern. "I'm worried about my bees," he said. "Something is hurting them." His concern reflects a nationwide problem. Honey bees are disappearing.

A mysterious illness is killing tens of thousands of honey bee colonies across the country, threatening honey production, the livelihood of beekeepers, and crops that need bees for pollination. The ailment is called Colony Collapse Disorder. Commercial beekeepers, some that keep thousands of colonies, have reported losing more than 50 percent of their bees.

One Pennsylvania beekeeper, traveling with two truckloads of bees to California to help pollinate almond trees, found nearly all of his cargo dead on arrival. An analysis of dissected bees revealed a high number of foreign fungi, bacteria, and other organisms and weakened immune systems. Dubbed the "Honey Bee Flu" by some beekeepers, the destructive aliment attacking bee colonies is a significant threat to United States agriculture.

The country's bee population had already been shocked in recent years by a tiny, parasitic mite, which has destroyed more than half of some beekeepers' hives and devastated most wild honey bee populations. The mite is so small it lives within the breathing trachea of the honey bee. This is the mite that is considered to be the cause of the loss of almost all of the honey bees in Great Britain during World War II.

A series of hurricanes in 2004, followed by Katrina in 2005, destroyed thousands of honey bee colonies, decimating the vital Gulf Coast bee industry. Many of the pollinators for other parts of the country came from Gulf beekeepers. The ultimate economic impact of these storms, especially Katrina, is yet to be determined.

Researchers are also looking into the effect pesticides might be having on bees. There is a possibility that newer insecticides are being applied to crops and then being transferred into the pollen that bees are gathering. When they bring it back to the hive, it affects the entire colony.

The two European countries with the largest honey bee populations are France and Italy. These two countries banned certain pesticides in recent years because beekeepers there became convinced that systemic pesticides were killing honey bees. So far, neither France nor Italy has reported the collapse of honey bee colonies.

Some have said that honey bees are a canary for the human race. In times past, a canary was sent into the coal mines to see whether there was oxygen enough for the miners to do their work. If the canary died, it was time to get out of the mine.

Penn State University researchers have concluded that the mysterious ailment affecting honey bees is causing a breakdown of the immune system in the insects. They raise an important question:

"If the immune system is compromised in honey bees, will this also affect humans?"

Already the mysterious disappearance of honey bees is making an impact in at least twenty-two states. The busy insects pollinate about one-third of the food supply around the world. In the United States, an absence of bees could mean the country that once fed the world will be required to import food to make up for our lack of production.

Albert Einstein once said, "If the honey bee becomes extinct, mankind will follow within four years." Though agriculturists aren't predicting such dire consequences for humankind, all agree the impact has already been significant.

That's the latest buzz on honey bees.

What can we do? Here are four suggestions:

- 1. Be careful using pesticides. Overkill destroys helpful insects as well as pests.
- 2. Buy local honey when it is available. Beekeepers need our support.
- 3. Plant a garden with flowers and vegetables. They feed the bees.
- 4. Some of our greatest blessings come in small packages. Be thankful for honey bees, even if one happens to sting you.

If the bee disappeared off the surface of the globe, then humanity would have only four years of life left. No more bees, no more pollination, no more plants, no more animals, no more humans.

Albert Einstein

When I heard that the bees were in trouble, the fact that they're disappearing and not coming back to the hive, is a big issue, since a third of the food we eat comes from plants.

Louie Schwartzberg

Poet's Corner

"Write, therefore, what you have seen..." -Revelations 1:19, NIV

When Clare and I moved into this house, there was a structure in the backyard made of concrete block on three sides and open on one side where a previous tenant had kept sand. The sand was used to make concrete tiles. At first, I thought this would be a good sandbox for our children, so I put a piece of 2 x 10 treated lumber across the front and bought a new truckload of sand. The children loved it and played there but, before long, every cat in the neighborhood discovered it and, oh my goodness, used it as a litterbox. Clare and I decided we'd have to find a new purpose for it.

I began to envision a structure built on the foundation of those concrete blocks. I knew a young man that did excellent carpentry work, who had a young family, so I asked him to talk with me about what kind of structure might be built. He suggested an open shelter with a tin roof. He gave me a reasonable price and we built what became known as "The Shack."

The Shack has room for a hammock as well as some hand-me-down yard furniture. It also houses three kayaks. Every spring, I cover the floor with a fresh supply of cedar shavings. Early in my gardening adventure, I realized the value of vining plants. Anyone who has ever walked through a tangle of blackberry vines or had the misfortune of wading through poison ivy may have a low opinion of vining plants. Any gardener who has tried to dig up greenbriers or waged war against kudzu knows that some vines are incredibly maddening.

However, vines that bear flowers, or those that bear fruit, are always welcome in the garden. In my garden, I have even found wild honeysuckle (*Lonicera periclymenum*) creeping along the chain link fence. The vine covers the fence and offers a sweet fragrance to the rest of the garden, especially at night. Further down, along the same fence, we have a wild Irish rose (*Iris germanica*). While the rose only blooms for a few weeks every spring, it is a good occupant of the space. Flowering vines are among my favorite plants in the garden, I especially like the older varieties which are known for their resilience and covered with blooms.

Some farmers in our area grow scuppernong (*Vitis rotundifolia*) and muscadines (*Muscadinia rotundifolia*). These wild grapes are native to the South, can be easily grown, and have a unique flavor. My Uncle Wesley often enjoyed eating bronze-colored muscadines. They ripen from late summer until early fall. The muscadine grapes have tough skin and are full of seeds. The trick to enjoy eating them is to spit out the skin and the seeds rather than trying to digest the skin. My favorite verse is from the gospel of John, chapter 15, verse 5 where Jesus says, "I am the vine; you are the branches. If a man remains in me and I in him, he will bear much fruit; apart from me you can do nothing" (NIV).

The Shack is a perfect place for vigorous flowering vines. On one end of the structure, I have a large star jasmine which blooms profusely in mid-spring. On the other end, I have a sweet autumn clematis. Delicate white flowers cover the plant and the end of The Shack in early autumn. In the middle of The Shack, I have a Queen Anne rose which I found in a broken pot at one of my favorite nurseries. When I asked the price of the plant, the owner said "if you take it and plant it, you can have it for free" so I did just as they requested. The plant has thrived and become a curtain across the front of The Shack. In mid to late spring, it is absolutely covered with delicate, bright red flowers.

These plantings of sweet autumn clematis, star jasmine, and a Queen Anne rose, weave together and drape the structure, making a shady place to sit on a hot summer day. There is even an electrical outlet where a fan can be plugged in, or a radio, or a computer. One end is designated the Poet's Corner.

The Poet's Corner is a great place to write, even in a summer shower. The tin roof provides adequate cover and a rhythmic sound. Though I am certainly not an accomplished poet, some of my children are. I have included, on the next page, a couple of verses that I have written in this secluded spot.

Luna Moth
With fluttering flight
Through the dark night
Traveling from afar
Drawn to the light
Shining so bright
Of our Moravian star

Under full moon's glow
As soft breezes blow
She came on gossamer wing
How did she know
With dew grass below
She could rest on our porch swing?

Homegrown Tomatoes

"By their fruits you will know them."
- Matthew 7:20, NKJV

A while ago, a visitor wearing a medical mask came to our door.

She brought us a grocery bag full of vine ripe tomatoes grown by her husband. The man has a debilitating muscular disease that requires the use of a motorized scooter. He grew the plants in raised boxes on his deck. The tomatoes were just right, the best I had that summer. Clare and I enjoyed tasty tomato sandwiches all week. In ordinary times, I would have purchased tomatoes from Bellew's Market on Garner Road in Spartanburg.

Cherokee purple is my favorite heirloom variety. But when good friends show up at our front door with homegrown tomatoes, we are thankful. Mid-summer is the time of year when tomatoes are at their peak in color and in flavor in the Upstate.

Before I retired, I was often asked, "Preacher, do you have a vegetable garden?"
"No, I don't," I explained. "I have more fresh vegetables without agarden than I ever had when I planted a garden of my own."

Church members kindly shared the bounty of their gardens with our household. Sometimes we would know who to thank. At other times, these gifts were left, anonymously, on our doorstep.

Dave Sikma is an Illinois farmer who plants two dozen or more tomato plants in his garden. Dave is our daughter Betsy's father-in-law. He told me that the first time Betsy visited their farm. She plucked several bright green tomatoes from his plants and prepared fried green tomatoes for the family. Following a family recipe, Betsy makes delicious fried green tomatoes. But Dave was not so impressed with this Southern delicacy. His opinion was that the fruit is best when left on the vine to ripen as the good Lord intended.

When Clare and I traveled to our family vacation at Pawleys Island, we often stopped for lunch at Thomas Café, one of our favorite eateries in the Lowcountry of South Carolina. Clare usually ordered shrimp and grits while I selected flounder. Both plates were served with a side of fried green tomatoes.

A lifelong devotee of this distinctly Southern fare, I would search high and low for unripe tomatoes during our week at Pawleys. At roadside stands in the summertime green tomatoes are as scarce as hen's teeth. In hot weather, even tomatoes that are picked green in the early morning soon start turning pink. Good fried tomatoes require the use of bright green fruit that is as firm as a potato. Absolutely no pink!

Here is my recipe for fried green tomatoes. Caution: these have a kick, and the
preparation is messy. The flavor is worth it!

Kirk's Spicy Fried Green Tomatoes
Ingredients

- 4 large green tomatoes, (all green, no pink, hard as a rock)
- 2 eggs
- 1 cup buttermilk
- 1 cup all-purpose flour
- 1 cup cornmeal
- Crushed red pepper flakes
- Garlic powder
- Coarsely ground salt
- Freshly ground black pepper
- Red pepper hummus
- Jalapeño pimento cheese
- Sour cream or goat cheese
- Vegetable oil for frying

Dredging

- Slice tomatoes 1/2 inch thick. Discard the ends. You need to use four bowls.
- Into the first bowl pour only half of the buttermilk and dip tomato slices.
- Into the second bowl, put the flour only. Lightly dip tomato slices coating both sides.
- Into the third bowl whisk eggs and the rest of the buttermilk together, and
  dip tomato slices coating both sides.

- In the fourth bowl mix cornmeal with red pepper flakes, garlic powder, coarsely ground salt, and freshly ground pepper, and thoroughly cover tomato slices on both sides.

Cooking
- In a large skillet, pour vegetable oil (enough so that there is 1/2 inch of oil in the pan) and bring to medium heat.
- Place tomato slices, coated in batter, into the frying pan in small batches, depending on the size of your skillet. Fry a few at a time.
- Do not crowd the tomatoes. Give them plenty of room! They should not touch each other.
- When the tomatoes are lightly brown, flip and fry them on the other side.
- Drain them on paper towels.

Serving
- On individual plates, spoon a heaping tablespoon of roasted red pepper hummus.
- Place the first fried green tomato in the hummus.
- Stack the fried green tomatoes three or four high with a spoonful of jalapeño pimento cheese between slices.
- Top with a dollop of sour cream. Goat cheese is also good on top.

We always enjoy delicious red tomatoes served in various ways. Some folks swear by tomato pie. Others prefer the summer delight in salads of many varieties. My specialty is "Neely Soggy Tomato Sandwiches." In years past, this was my sandwich of choice at the annual Neely Family Fourth of July Picnic. In our home, we enjoy this favorite kitchen sink sandwich as long as tomatoes are in season.

You can find our favorite tomato sandwich recipe below.

Neely Soggy Tomato Sandwich
Ingredients
- 2 vine-ripe tomatoes
- Duke's Real Mayonnaise
- 6 slices of white bread
- Salt
- Freshly ground pepper

Instructions

- Take six slices of white bread. Don't use anything that is good for you - just plain ole white sandwich bread.
- Slather Duke's Real Mayonnaise heavily on all six slices. Only use Duke's. Use about twice as much mayonnaise as you ordinarily would.
- Grind fresh black pepper on all six pieces of bread.
- Stack thinly-sliced, vine-ripe tomatoes three layers deep on three pieces of the bread.
- Salt the tomato slices.
- Mash – not lightly press – the remaining three pieces of bread, mayonnaise side down, on top of the tomatoes.
- Turn the sandwiches over and mash again.
- Cut the three sandwiches in half. Let them come to room temperature.
- Stand over the kitchen sink to catch the drips as you enjoy these juicy sandwiches.

Until colonial times, some people thought the tasty red treat was poisonous. Long
before it was considered fit to eat, it was grown exclusively as an ornamental garden
plant.

The mistaken idea that tomatoes were poisonous probably arose because they
belong to an unusual plant family. A nightshade plant, from the Latin word *solanum*, it
includes the *matura*, *mandrake*, and *belladonna*, all considered poisonous. Take it from me. Tomatoes are not poisonous!

Close relatives are paprika, chili pepper, potato, tobacco, and petunia. The unpleasant odor of tomato leaves and stems contributed to the idea that the fruits were unfit for human consumption. Tomatoes originated as wild plants in the tropical foothills of the Andes Mountains of Peru. Gradually, they were carried north into Central America. Because of the highly perishable nature of the fruit, the tomato was slow to be adopted as a cultivated plant by indigenous peoples of that region. Mayans used the fruit in their cooking. Tomatoes were grown in Mexico by the sixteenth century. The Pueblo people believed that those who ate tomato seeds were blessed with powers of divination.

Spanish explorers in the sixteenth century introduced the tomato to Europe. Italians were the first Europeans to grow and eat tomatoes. Later the tomato was grown in English and Spanish gardens, not as food, but as a curiosity. The French gave it the name *pomme d'amour*, translated as love apple in English.

The earliest reference to tomatoes being grown in North America is from 1710, when herbalist William Salmon reported seeing them in South Carolina. They may have been introduced to our area from the Caribbean. By the mid-eighteenth century, tomatoes were grown on numerous Carolina plantations. Even then, they may have only been of ornamental interest.

Thomas Jefferson learned of the vegetable in France. The Virginia farmer grew them at Monticello as early as 1781. Tomatoes were grown as food in New Orleans as early as 1812, no doubt because of French influence.

Tomatoes are now the most common garden vegetable in our country. Along with zucchini squash, the plants have a reputation for out-producing the needs of the grower, thereby encouraging the sharing of garden bounty.

A friend who tends her garden with care recently reported a serious problem with her tomatoes. "I found healthy plants at my local garden shop. I put them in good soil with fertilizer and adequate water. The plants produced lovely big tomatoes, but they would not turn red. I waited and waited until they finally started changing color. Lo and behold! I had mistakenly purchased a golden yellow variety. They were never going to turn red! Still, they are delicious."

Tomatoes are regarded as one of the healthiest foods in our diet. Rich in vitamins A and C, tomatoes contain lycopene, a chemical that gives them, as well as watermelons and red grapefruit, their color. Lycopene, an antioxidant, helps reduce the risk of heart disease and cancer.

Although the tomato is technically a fruit, a member of the berry group, it is also considered a vegetable. In fact, it is the state vegetable of New Jersey and Arkansas. Health experts claim that we need five to ten servings of vegetables and fruits every day. When they are in season, we should all take advantage of local homegrown tomatoes to meet our daily quota.

Tomatoes are my special favorite. Several years ago, I wrote these lines as an expression of my gratitude.

God is great. God is good.
Let us thank Him for our food.
By His hand we all are fed.
Give us, Lord, our daily bread.

Wholegrain bread, rye, or lite,
A sourdough loaf, or just plain white.
And please, dear Lord, some Duke's mayonnaise,
And homegrown tomatoes for these summer days.

Add lettuce, and bacon, or maybe cheese,
But especially, Lord, I ask You please,
For vine-ripe tomatoes, sliced thick and round,
To make the best sandwich I've ever found.

On days that grow weary with muggy heat,
A soggy tomato sandwich just can't be beat.
With a tall glass of something cold to drink,
I'll eat my lunch over the kitchen sink.

I'm grateful for corn, that good Silver Queen,
For cantaloupe, peaches, and fresh green beans,
For squash, and okra, and small red potatoes,
But nothing is better than homegrown tomatoes.

God is great, and God is good.
Let us thank Him for our food.
I know His kindness never ends
When given tomatoes by special friends.

The Garden Of Hope

"Blessed are the meek, for they will inherit the earth."
Matthew 5:5, NIV

Saving Seed

"…Have faith as small as a mustard seed…"
-Matthew 17:20, NIV

You may have heard the expression, "Big oaks, from little acorns, grow." In the natural order of things, the life cycle of plants is a continuous drama of growth, flowering, fruit-bearing, and reseeding. Horticultural developments have circumvented this process with hybrid varieties of many plants that do not reseed. Seedless grapes and seedless watermelons are the last of their breed.

But from the beginning, it was not so.

People who garden take delight in cultivating the soil, planting seeds, and experiencing the joy of growth. When we garden with children, we learn to plant radishes, squash, lettuce, and other plants that germinate quickly and yield something good to eat within a month or so after planting. Other vegetables, like carrots, corn, and tomatoes, take much longer.

I tried to imagine what it must have been like for John Chapman, who is said to have planted apple seeds wherever he went--thus the name "Johnny Appleseed." Can you imagine how long it takes for an apple seed to grow into a tree and bloom and bear apples? Johnny Appleseed must have been a patient man. We often use the Johnny Appleseed blessing as table grace at our house with our grandchildren:

> Oh, the Lord's been good to me.
> And so, I thank the Lord
> For giving me the things I need:
> The sun
> And the rain
> And the apple seed.
> The Lord's been good to me.
> Amen.

The practice of saving seeds is well-established among seasoned gardeners. I save empty prescription bottles for this purpose. I have successfully saved seeds from hollyhocks (*Alcea rosea*), foxgloves, zinnias, moonflowers (*Ipomoea alba*), Missouri primrose (*Oenothera macrocarpa*), sunflowers (*Helianthus annuus*), and black-eyed Susan, just to name a few.

Sometimes I till a small patch of ground and sow these seeds to make a butterfly garden that is attractive to a variety of pollinators and is beautiful to the human eye. The practice of saving seeds is one of the reasons we have heirloom plants. Years ago, I was visiting my father-in-law in Leesville, South Carolina. In his tool shed, he had a Mason jar filled with bent and rusted nails.

"Mr. Jack," I asked, "why are you saving those old nails?"

"It's something I learned from my own father," he said. "I'm saving 'em for seed, I guess."

The vegetable life does not content itself with casting from the flower or the tree a single seed, but it fills the air and earth with a prodigality of seeds, that, if thousands perish, thousands may plant themselves, that hundreds may come up, that tens may live to maturity; that, at least one may replace the parent.
Ralph Waldo Emerson

Iris

"As a flower of the field, so he flourishes."
-Psalm 103:15, NKJV

Iris x hollandica

Spring in our garden has always been spectacular! The irises put on an outstanding show. Dwarf irises (*Iris pumila*) are among the first flowers to bloom. These small sturdy plants are cousins to the wild blue iris (*Iris missouriensis*) found in pine forests throughout the Southeast. Dwarf irises display their array of colors as the opening act to their taller family members.

On either side of our garden gate is a welcoming committee of pure white intermediate irises (*Iris germanica*). They make delightful companions to dancing yellow daffodils. They conclude their blooming just as the tall bearded irises come into flower. From late April into May these stately debutantes make their début.

In our garden many of the tall irises are pass-along plants from the gardens of mothers and grandmothers on both sides of our family. Our son and daughter-in-law shared solid purple, gold, and pink bloomers from their first home. Some were given by a grieving husband. He wanted his wife's irises to have a good home.

In mid-April I was pleasantly surprised by a stunning sight. A bed of reblooming irises planted in the fall was in full display. They have names like Immortality and Resurrection. They came from my friend and pastoral colleague, Everette Lineburger.

Everette is known among his fellow Master Gardeners as the 'Iris King.' Early in his ministry, when he was called as Pastor of Grace Lutheran Church in Rock Hill, the parsonage had a cottage garden planted by the previous pastor. Everette learned about the flowers he had inherited.

In 1955, he bought nine iris plants. Since that time, he estimates that he has nurtured more than 1500 varieties. His irises have won awards from Charleston to Spartanburg. He has developed, named, and introduced thirteen new varieties. One is named for his wife, Ann; another, Deb's Sunshine, is named for their daughter. He became such an authority on the lovely flowers that he served seven years on the Board of the American Iris Society.

When Everette retired from St. John's Lutheran Church in Spartanburg, he started his backyard iris business at Quail Hill Gardens in Inman. At one time he had 750 varieties.

Irises are hardy, easy to grow, and have spectacular showy flowers. There are many varieties to try, Dutch, Japanese, Siberian, dwarf, and the all-bearded iris. Several years ago, I created a special iris bed to show off the beauty of these flowers. It is a circular structure with a brick wall. I filled it with good soil, a bag of gypsum, and a bag of 10-10-10. The bed is planted with reblooming irises only. Some of the names of these iris are Immortality, Resurrection, and Splendor. Every garden, no matter the size, can benefit from irises. Irises that rebloom put on an awe-inspiring show in the spring and again in the fall.

The colorful flowers were named for the goddess of the rainbow, Iris. The Greeks believed that Iris took messages from heaven to earth via the arc of the rainbow. Greek men planted an iris on the graves of their wives to insure that their souls would arrive in the Elysian Fields.

The iris is the national flower of France. Legend holds that upon his conversion to Christianity Clovis, king of the Franks, was presented a golden iris by an angel. Joan of Arc carried a white flag bearing the fleur-de-lis, a stylized iris, when she led French troops to victory over the English.

The fleur-de-lis was used by the monarchs of France as a royal decoration. King Louis VI became the first French monarch to use the emblem on his shield. Everette Lineberger is not French royalty. But he is the Iris King!

When you take a flower in your hand and really look at it, it's your world for the moment. I want to give that world to someone else. Most people in the city rush around so, they have no time to look at a flower. I want them to see it whether they want to or not.
Georgia O'Keeffe

Pass-Along Plants

"Share and share alike."
-Daniel Defoe

The pink crepe myrtle tree in our side yard is blooming just as it has done for almost eighty years. A great aunt who lived in the Lowcountry of South Carolina gave the shrub to my grandmother about the time I was born. Mammy planted it next to a small goldfish pond that my grandfather had built. At some point they decided that, as interesting as the goldfish pond was, it was unsafe for their thirty-six grandchildren. So, the pond was filled with soil and transformed into a flowerbed nestled beneath the crepe myrtle tree.

The home that we live in was built in 1937 by my grandfather following the Great Depression. Old photographs of the house under construction show a landscape completely devoid of trees. My Uncle Asbury, a builder, filled the deep clay pit next to the new structure with construction rubble — brick bats, broken slabs of concrete, and fragments of cinder blocks. The resulting hill was graded with packed red clay and covered with a layer of topsoil. Little would grow on the slope except grass.

At the bottom of the hill on the north side of the property, my grandfather transplanted two water oak saplings from his native Tennessee. On the opposite side of the spacious yard, he planted three small pecan trees dug from the sandy soil of the Lowcountry plantation where my grandmother lived as a child. These trees, now more than seventy years old, tower above our two-story home. They anchor our landscape. I think of them as the pillars of our outdoor sanctuary.

Many other heirloom plants in our garden are smaller shrubs and perennials with interesting histories. Clare's father, Mr. Jack, was raised on a red dirt farm in Saluda County, South Carolina. The spring after a fire destroyed the heart pine farmhouse, Mr. Jack discovered his mother's Virginia bluebells in full bloom. He transplanted several of those flowers to his yard in Macon, Georgia. When Clare and I lived in Louisville, Kentucky, Mr. Jack presented some of the bluebells to us. As we moved, first to Winston-Salem, North Carolina, and later to Spartanburg, some of the plants made the moves with us.

Our garden includes azaleas, camellias, and Hosta given to us by my mother and Clare's mother. My mother also donated blue periwinkle and lily of the valley. Clare's mother added yellow jasmine and daylilies to our collection. One of our most cherished heirlooms, a Don Juan rose, came from Clare's grandmother in Leesville, South Carolina.

Sometimes people ask us why we live where we do. After all, our home place is located between a busy four-lane highway and the main Norfolk Southern railroad between Spartanburg and Columbia. We live here because it is part of our heritage. A part of the mystique of the place is our heirloom plants. They remind us of the loved ones who nurtured us.

But there is more. When we moved to Spartanburg I brought with us several small trees — a dogwood, a redbud, and three hemlocks. All have thrived in their new home.

Some of our most treasured florae are pass along plants. Southern lore holds that saying thank you for a transplant from another garden will mean certain death for that plant. The proper response is to make a gift in kind. Many of the beautiful flowers, trees, and shrubs in our yard have come to us from friends. Among our favorites are a weeping cherry (*Prunus pendula*) and a Cherokee dogwood (*Cornus florida*).

I often refer to our yard as a prayer garden. Not only does the foliage help make it a sacred space, but it also serves as a reminder to pray for the people who favored us with a gift.

God has given us two hands - one to receive with and the other to give with. We are not cisterns made for hoarding; we are channels made for sharing.
Billy Graham

Life is all about sharing. If we are good at something, pass it on.

Mary Berry

Rosemary

"I let rosemary grow all over my garden, not only because my bees love it, but because it is the herb sacred to remembrance and to friendship."
-Saint Thomas More

Rosmarinus officinalis

An evergreen perennial shrub native to the Mediterranean region, *Rosmarinus officinalis* is quite common in the Holy Land. The leaves are similar to evergreen conifers but with a silver tint. The leaves contain essential aromatic oils that have a camphor-like taste and smell. This plant can grow to six feet tall but is better pruned into a shrub shape.

Ancient Greeks and Romans knew this shrub well. In their world, it enjoyed a reputation for improving memory and rejuvenating the spirit. Greek scholars wore garlands of rosemary in order to improve their memory and concentration. Rosemary also symbolizes loyalty and friendship. In ancient Greece, brides wore it in their hair as a wreath symbolizing their fidelity.

Traditionally, rosemary was used internally as a tonic and as a stimulant. It also treated dyspepsia, and mild stomach upsets. Rosemary baths were used to stimulate circulation and calm the nerves. These baths were used to treat colds, headaches, and nervous tension. Rosemary was burned and the smoke was inhaled to ward off sickness.

The herb is used in cooking meat and game dishes. It is a favorite with roast lamb. It is also used in sausages, soups, sauces, stews, soups, and salads. Rosemary is used to flavor wines, vinegar, oil, and butter. Sprigs of rosemary tossed into barbecue grill will impart flavor to meat. Rosemary branches make perfect skewers for grilling shrimp and scallops.

The origin of this herb's name is woven into folklore. It is associated with Mary, who is thought to have draped her cloak over a rosemary bush on the Holy Family's flight to Egypt. This is why rosemary blossoms are blue. Thereafter the plant was called Rose of Mary.

Christians called rosemary the holy herb. Traditionally it was associated with baptisms, weddings, and funerals. It is drought tolerant.

One of the most unusual women I've ever known was named Rosemary. She suffered terribly with rheumatoid arthritis. Rarely did I hear her complaint. Instead, she was always concerned about other people. If Rosemary is the herbal symbol for faithfulness, this woman could not have been more aptly named. She was faithful to her husband, to her children and grandchildren; she was faithful to her church and to her Lord. When she died, I conducted her funeral. I went to the large rosemary bush in my backyard and cut sprigs to give to each member of her family after her funeral. I told them, "You might consider planting one of these bushes in your yard. It has tiny, blue beautiful flowers and a fragrant aroma. It will be a pleasant reminder of this dear woman.

Hope is always difficult to define in words. It is best expressed in symbols. To me, rosemary is one of the best.

Blue Jays

"Look at the birds of the air."
-Matthew 6:26, NIV

Cyanocitta cristata

S ally Middleton is a North Carolina artist who specializes in wildlife paintings. When I first became familiar with her work, I noticed in almost all of her paintings a single blue jay feather. I knew that there must be a story behind this pattern in her work. Blue jays do not enjoy the best reputation in the world of ornithology. Legend says that on Fridays, this raucous bird carries sticks to the Devil to keep the fires of Hell stoked. Why, I wondered, was Sally Middleton so consistent in including a blue jay feather in her paintings?

I later learned the story. One gray day, burdened with family problems and financial concerns, Sally Middleton took a walk in the woods near Ashville, North Carolina. As she walked, a blue jay feather floated down in front of her. She caught it in her hand and took it as a gift of grace. From that day on, the blue jay feather was her personal symbol of hope.

I have told the story many times. I mailed to Sally Middleton a copy of a sermon in which I used her story as an illustration. Her kind response was that the blue jay feather had become a source of hope for many others who treasure her paintings.

Several years ago, I was asked to participate in a funeral service for a young man who died in a drowning accident during the first month of his senior year in high school. His death, of course, was very difficult for his family, especially for his parents. The funeral service was at a Methodist church filled to overflowing with teenagers, parents, and teachers, as well as family friends. The body was cremated for the committal at a camp where this young man had spent several happy summers.

The committal service was for family and a few close friends only. I was invited to travel to the camp to lead the service at a beautiful spot beside the lake. I had been trying to think of a symbol of hope for the parents and siblings of the young man. As I walked along a path through the woods, I found one blue jay feather and then another. Picking up both feathers, I put them in my Bible. When we arrived at the burial site, a shovel with a stirrup handle had been pushed into the ground behind the simple wood and brass urn containing the ashes. The shovel stood like a marker above the place of interment.

At the gravesite, I read scripture and shared the story of Sally Middleton. I gave both the father and the mother one of the blue jay feathers, suggesting that they might become for them signs of hope. We had a closing prayer including the words of committal. Just as I concluded the prayer, a blue jay squawked, flew through the circle of those gathered, and perched on the handle of the shovel just above the urn. The audible gasp in unison of the assembled mourners gave way to a holy silence. No one made a sound, not even the blue jay. It was a singular moment of quiet reverence.

Later in the week, the young man's mother returned to the camp to place flowers on her son's grave. As she stood weeping with a friend, she was astonished when a blue jay landed on her shoulder. The bird flew away after a moment or two.

The Camp Ranger gave a logical explanation for the blue jay's behavior. During the summer, the camp staff had fed peanuts to the blue jay training him to perch on their shoulders. When the camping season ended, the blue jay, unafraid of humans, continued to beg for peanuts whenever they visited his domain. For those parents, the reasonable explanation did nothing to diminish the blue jay and his feathers as symbols of hope.

Emily Dickinson wrote:

> "Hope is the thing with feathers –
> That perches in the soul."
> So, it is.

Butterflies

"Agent of God's grand design"
-For the Beauty of the Earth

Papilio glaucus

In my backyard, I have a volunteer sunflower, now taller than I. It sprang up when a sunflower seed escaped a birdfeeder and landed in a flowerbed. Out of curiosity, I decided to let it grow. Recently, I have noticed that several of the leaves have been chewed to a pulp. I have yet to see the caterpillar that is doing the damage. I imagine his eating binge occurs after dark.

Caterpillars have been rightly called eating machines. They can devour the foliage of plants seemingly overnight. Some cause great destruction and do millions of dollars in damage to agricultural crops each year. There are literally millions of species in the biological order *Lepidoptera*. Every one of them has a larval stage we know best as caterpillars. There are both Jekyll and Hyde varieties. The boll weevil has wreaked havoc in cotton crops across the South. Armyworms attack cotton and soybean crops. Every vegetable gardener knows to be on the lookout for cabbage worms and tomato horn worms. Earlier this summer I noticed a webbed tent, the characteristic abode of tent caterpillars, on the branch of a pecan tree.

Some caterpillars are desirable. Every fisherman knows that the delicate purple blossoms of the catalpa tree attract moths that lay eggs. When the eggs hatch, catalpa worms start eating the large green leaves of their host plant. Bream fishermen treasure these tiny worms because bluegills consider them to be such a delicacy.

Other caterpillars are raised because of their economic importance. The silk worm is perhaps the best example. The minute threads secreted by the silk worm are used to make valuable cloth to be fashioned into fine garments.

By late summer, my garden is aflutter with flying flowers, butterflies of all varieties. Once they take wing, they are drawn to flowering plants that provide a feast of nectar. Creating a butterfly garden requires a little planning and some maintenance. It is well worth the effort. Among some of the butterfly's favorite plants are ageratum, aster, butterfly bush, bee balm, black-eyed Susan, catmint, coneflower, coreopsis, cosmos, goldenrods, honeysuckle, hyssop, lantana, marigold, phlox, salvia, sedum, verbena, yarrow, and zinnia.

Butterflies are difficult to count because they are constantly on the move. One sunny afternoon last month, I drove into our driveway and paused to look at the lantana. There were no fewer than thirty on, above, and around the lantana. There were several varieties including majestic monarchs, deep orange fritillaries, and an American painted lady. The lantana, attended by a bevy of flittering guests, created quite a display.

In my garden, I have planted bronze fennel (*Foeniculum vulgare*). The dark green plants make a nice backdrop with their lacy leaves. Its fragrance reminds me of licorice. I have fennel in my garden because it is a favorite host plant for a particular kind of caterpillar, the larvae of swallowtail butterflies.

Near the back of my property grows a patch of wild flowers. There is some tall goldenrod (*Solidago altissima*), but more importantly, there is plenty of milkweed (*Asclepias tuberosa*). The orange blossoms of the milkweed plant attract monarch butterflies and they then lay their eggs on the leaves.

All butterflies begin life as caterpillars. After a time of chewing on leaves, they hang upside down and enfold themselves in the silken case they spin. In this chrysalis stage, they resemble a dead leaf until the moment comes when they emerge from their cocoon. Spreading their newly formed wings they fly away, gloriously transformed.

This metamorphosis has made butterflies a symbol for new life. Sometimes butterflies are released at weddings, just as the bride and groom are pronounced husband and wife, to mark the beginning of their new life together. Early Christians saw in the butterfly an apt symbol for the resurrection.

I shall never forget the funeral service for a woman who loved butterflies. She had decorated her home with a butterfly theme. She tended a special garden in her backyard designed to attract her flying flowers.

After her death, following an extended illness, it was only natural at her memorial service to emphasize her enjoyment of butterflies. Flower arrangements sent by friends and family members included silk butterflies.

At the cemetery on a mountainside, the crowning touch to her service came as a complete surprise. As I finished reading the scripture, a monarch butterfly fluttered into the funeral tent and descended upon the Bible I held in my hands. The tiny orange and black creature perched like a bookmark between the opened pages. For a few silent seconds we marveled in amazement. The choreography in that service was beyond anything I could have scripted.

Monarchs are among the most amazing and regal of all butterflies. These orange and black beauties are migratory. The majestic insects fly three thousand miles each fall to winter in the high mountains of central Mexico. Those who intentionally set out to attract butterflies usually find special satisfaction when they are graced with a visit from a monarch.

I once sat with a man who was dying of lung cancer. We were in his backyard next to his butterfly garden which included several varieties of *buddleia*, the butterfly bush. The afternoon was pleasant; the air was still. The garden was alive with flying flowers. Spicebush, swallowtails, monarchs, buckeyes, and mourning cloaks all sipped nectar from the array of blooms.

We sat in silence for a time before he spoke.

"They're beautiful, aren't they?" he asked.

"Yes," I agreed. "You know the butterfly is a symbol of resurrection."

After a long pause, he said, "No wonder I enjoy them so much."

Rainbows

"I have set my rainbow in the clouds…"
-Genesis 9:13, NIV

The sorrow of grief is depicted as colorless. A photographer whose wife died with a brain tumor said, "I am living in a black and white world. There is no color, only shades of gray."

From 1901-1904, the artist Pablo Picasso painted all of his pictures in shades of blue. His subjects during this Blue Period were the lonely, suffering, poverty-stricken outcasts from society. At the time, Picasso was despondent, nearly penniless, and perhaps unable to afford a variety of colors. Certainly the Blue Period in his work corresponds to a blue period in his life. When people are despairing, they are often described as feeling blue. An entire genre of music, the Blues, puts the sorrow of life into song.

Try to imagine Noah standing on the deck of the ark. The rains have ended, but the sky is heavy and overcast as it has been for the five months since it stopped raining. The noise and the stench within the ark are almost unbearable. The waterlogged world before him is desolate. Thoughts of unspeakable death flood Noah's mind. He is looking for some sign of hope.

As he searches the barren horizon, Noah spies a small bird flying toward him: the same dove he had released earlier, which is returning as it had seven days before. On that occasion, the dove had returned with no sign of hope. Now, as the dove wings its way closer, Noah can see that the bird carries something in its beak. He reaches out his hand to receive the bird and sees the fresh green tip of an olive branch. Not much of a gift, to be sure, but it is a sprig of hope, just enough green in a gray world to make the eyes of a six-hundred-year-old man brim with tears.

When the ark finally finds a resting place and the animals return to nature, Noah worships God. As he does, the gray skies break with a shaft of sunlight. For the first time, Noah witnesses the colors of hope: the multitudinous colors of the rainbow.

The story of Noah's rainbow has three distinct meanings.

1. Through the flood the world was purified. The cloud is connected to the Jewish observance of Yom Kippur. This type of cloud, which is for the purpose of revelation, also teaches about the concept of repentance. It is similar to the cloud of the smoke of the

incense of Yom Kippur that comes through the repentance of Yom Kippur. Through the service of repentance that is a level of "returning light," a spiritual rainbow is created that has within it three primary colors which correspond to God's "primary" attributes of Kindness, Judgment, and Mercy. "I erased like a thick cloud..." (Isaiah 44:22). Thus, the impure powers are completely erased, in a way of purity.

2. Covenant. "This is the sign of the covenant ... My bow I have set in the cloud." This comes in the way of a covenant that "All the days of the Earth, planting and reaping, cold and heat, winter and summer will not cease." (Gen. 8:22).

3. God's glory. The glory of God is revealed in the spectrum of light that we experience as rainbows. I have seen rainbows many times. Five of those times have been especially memorable for me. I stood above the Zambezi River gazing at Victoria Falls. In the mist of the falls, there was a rainbow. I'm told it is almost constant. The thundering water fell more than four hundred feet into the gorge below, creating a constant cloud of water droplets. When sun shines through that cloud, there is a magnificent rainbow. This is also one of the only places visitors can see a moon bow.

I have stood at Mt. Carmel, where Elijah contested the prophets of Baal with a cloud shaped like a hand. Suddenly, the drought was over. As I stood there reflecting on this story, a rainbow stretched from the top of the mountain down to the Mediterranean Sea below, beyond the city of Haifa.

On another occasion, I stood on the Golan Heights near a kibbutz. There they grew and sold perennial bulbs from around the world. I had a perfect view of the Sea of Galilee, also known as Lake Gennesaret. This word also means harp. From that vantage point, I could clearly see how the sea was shaped like a shepherd's harp. On that day, I saw a rainbow stretch from the heights all the way down to the sea.

When my friend Ron Wells died, I had a part in the funeral. He was the Minister of Music at First Baptist Church. As we walked out of the church, Dr. Alastair Walker pointed to the sky where a full rainbow stretched over us, a sign of hope. Several hours later, when we came out of the mausoleum after the commital, a beautiful rainbow still stretched across the sky, a sign of God's grace and provision.

When Adam in *Paradise Lost* asks Michael the meaning of the "color'd streaks in Heaven," his angelic teacher instructs him that they have been placed there to remind the sons of Adam that

Such grace shall one just Man find in his sight,
Over the earth a cloud, with therein set
His triple-color'd bow, whereon to look
And can to mind his Covenant.
The rainbow bending in the sky,
Bedecked with sundry hues,
Is like the seat of God on high,
And seems to ten this new:
That as thereby He promised
To drown the world no more,
So, by the blood which Christ hath shed,
He will our health restore [Book XI, 11. 890-71].

On more than one occasion, I have stood with a family at a graveside under a gray sky. As if choreographed by the Divine Director, sunlight breaks through the clouds, creating a multicolored rainbow. In another setting, these rainbows would be of momentary interest, briefly enjoyed and then forgotten. For a bereaved family, the rainbow becomes an enduring, colorful symbol of hope.

The way I see it, if you want the rainbow, you gotta put up with the rain.   **Dolly Parton**

I've always taken "The Wizard of Oz" very seriously, you know. I believe in the idea of the rainbow. And I've spent my entire life trying to get over it.
                                        Judy Garland

The Strawberry Patch

"It was as sweet as honey in my mouth."
- Revelation 10:10, NKJV

A while ago, I visited a South Carolina Certified Roadside Market. The tables and bins were loaded with fresh produce, most of it from Upstate farms. I purchased tomatoes, squash, Vidalia onions, and a few plums. However, the main attraction was fresh strawberries. I bought a gallon bucket of the delicious red fruit. We were at the peak of the strawberry season in the Upstate.

The Beatles' song, "Strawberry Fields Forever," was released on a 45-rpm vinyl record back in the old days. It was on the other side of "Penny Lane." What is the meaning of the seemingly senseless lyrics? An answer can be found at www.Songfacts.com.

Strawberry Fields was a Salvation Army orphanage in Liverpool, England. Having lost his father and his mother, John Lennon felt a kinship to the homeless boys. He had fond memories of the place, especially the garden that inspired this song. In an interview, Lennon explained:

> "Strawberry Fields is a real place. After I stopped living at Penny Lane, I moved in with my auntie, into a nice place with a small garden. Paul, George, and Ringo lived in government-subsidized housing. Near our home was Strawberry Fields, a boys' reformatory where I used to go to garden parties with my friends. I used it as an image, Strawberry Fields forever."

John donated money to the orphanage before his death. One of its buildings is named Lennon Hall. The title of the Beatles' song reminds me of Strawberry Hill on Highway 11 in northern Spartanburg County. The strawberry fields near Cooley Springs are abuzz with activity in the summer.

A few summers ago, I made a telephone call to the folks at Strawberry Hill. James Cooley reported that favorable temperatures, rainfall, and sunshine earlier that year give promise for a plentiful crop of delicious berries. Strawberry season was in full swing!

For an all too brief time every year, locally grown strawberries take the produce spotlight. Imported berries from

California or Florida get us through the colder months, but we look forward to the unsurpassed flavor of the Spartanburg County beauties. From Cross Anchor to Landrum, from Cowpens to Lyman, the succulent red strawberries, grown on the rolling hills of our county, are the fruit of choice from mid-April through late June. On an early Saturday morning in April several years ago, I brought home a gallon bucket of Spartanburg County's finest. When I walked in the front door of our home, Clare exclaimed, "Oh, boy! Strawberries!" Three of our adult children and their families had come for Saturday morning brunch. Those strawberries never made it past the kitchen sink. Clare rinsed them, and the family clustered around to eat their fill. The berries evaporated. Later that day, Clare sent me out to fetch another bucket of the tasty treat.

My mother was a master chef. Strawberry shortcake was among the many rich dessert offerings at Mama's table. She constructed her masterpiece with either angel food cake or old-fashioned homemade pound cake. The freshly baked delicacy was sliced into thin layers. Each section was saturated in turn with sweetened puréed strawberries and topped with a thick coating of whipped cream. There was nothing short about Mama's reassembled cake! The towering structure was crowned with more whipped cream and decorated with fresh sliced strawberries. Just writing about Mama's strawberry shortcake makes my mouth water and raises my cholesterol level.

I preached a series of sermons at a revival for a country church in the Lowcountry several years ago. On the final night, we enjoyed a church picnic. At the outdoor supper, an alarmingly large man sat beside me. His dinner-sized paper plate sagged under a heaping portion of strawberry shortcake. I thought for a moment that the folding chair beneath him would buckle under his weight. The large serving might have been the proverbial straw that broke the camel's back. The chair held secure. When the last morsel of the dessert was consumed, and the platter was licked clean, the man turned to me and said, "Now, preacher, that's the way we're gonna' eat in heaven." I thought to myself, "Probably sooner than later."

In my childhood, my dad was, to me, the master strawberry grower. Dad planted his own strawberry field, a long narrow bed of Ozark Beauties next to a stand of tall yellow pine trees. The pine needles provided the mulch to protect the plants in the winter. In the early spring, the pine needles were removed to allow the plant crowns to bud. Delicate white blossoms gave a pleasing portent of the harvest to come. When the strawberries were ripe, we took turns picking. The family rule was, "Put ten in the bucket for every one you eat."

Thank goodness! Otherwise, the bucket would never have been filled. When I was a boy, fresh berries were on our table three times a day throughout the spring. Now, as then, for eight to ten weeks each spring, strawberries are a daily treat in our home.

Strawberries brighten the flavor and the appearance of a bowl of cold cereal. The red berries sparkle in a salad of fresh fruit. Strawberries over vanilla ice cream are an outstanding finale to a summer supper. By the way, did I mention Mama's strawberry shortcake? That must be an all-time favorite for our family and for many other folks as well. Come to think of it, strawberry shortcake really might be served in heaven!

When Clare and I lived in Louisville, Kentucky, I wanted to plant my own strawberry field, a small patch in our backyard. In the fall, I tilled several bags of composted cow manure into the garden plot to enrich the clay soil. In the early spring, I set out twenty-five strawberry plants and side dressed them with more composted cow manure. My mom and dad came for a visit at precisely the time the strawberries were ripe. Though few in number, the berries were plump and delicious. I proudly put a bowl of strawberries in front of my dad, the master at growing strawberries.

He admired the bowl of fresh, red berries, "Tell me what you put on your strawberries."

"Composted cow manure," I said.

He looked at me with a twinkle in his eye and a playful smile on his face.

Then, he quipped, "Have you tried cream and sugar?"

To each their own, I guess.

The Garden of Joy

"Blessed are the poor in spirit, for theirs is the kingdom of heaven."
Matthew 5:3, NIV

Hummingbirds

"Hope is the thing with feathers"
-Emily Dickinson

Archilochus colubris

The first week of September brought blessed relief from the oppressive heat and humidity of our dog day afternoons. One Monday, I enjoyed a delicious summer lunch with a gathering of friends on a screened-in back porch overlooking a well-tended flower garden. Hummingbirds provided the entertainment for our midday meal. The tiny, feathered creatures put on quite an aerial display as they competed for the sweet nectar of the flowers and the sugar water in a feeder.

At the end of the day, as the sun was setting, Clare and I sat on our own back porch. We were treated to an amazing air show. As we enjoyed our supper, we witnessed an incredible display of aerobatics. Agile flying machines were buzzing our yard, staging mid-air combat maneuvers that would impress even Air Force top guns. September is the prime season for hummingbirds.

Hummingbirds are always interesting to watch. Their activity increases as the summer days grow shorter. From late August through much of September, the tiny hummers become frantic in their feeding habits and combative toward all competitors. They put on quite a performance as they prepare for their long migration to Central and South America.

Their excited pace and almost perpetual motion are at once fascinating and wearying to the observer. Earlier in the spring and summer, two or three hummingbirds might share the same feeder, but in early autumn they become territorial and will attack any intruder, even fellow hummers. Like feisty siblings quarreling over dessert, the petite birds quarrel with each other over which one will have the next turn at their sugar water treat.

A hummingbird in flight can be easily mistaken for a large stinging insect. The hummingbird's tiny wings move so rapidly they make a buzzing sound. This flight pattern, filmed in slow motion, reveals their remarkable ability to speed forward, to pause, and to reverse directions. Hovering, darting, and diving in their heightened frenzy, the aerial gymnastics performed by the humming creatures with tiny wings provide a constant show. It can also be disarming.

A friend who welcomes hummingbirds to her garden with feeders and flowers wanted to put fresh flowers in an arrangement for a dinner party at her home. She cut several late blooming red gladioli from her cottage garden. As she did, what she thought was a large buzzing insect began to bother her. The pest attacked from the rear, moving up her neck underneath the tresses of her new hairdo. The well-mannered lady ran, clutching gladioli tightly in one hand, swatting wildly with the other.

She stopped when the buzzing nuisance confronted her at eye level. It was a hummingbird, clearly annoyed that the lady had cut the flowers from which it had been feeding. The woman held the red gladioli at arm's length, as if making a peace offering. The hummer moved from one blossom to the next in the handheld bouquet, drinking its fill, before flying off without further conflict.

Hummingbirds are attracted to a variety of blooms. Fiery red salvias (*Salvia splendens*), cup-shaped hibiscus (*Hibiscus rosa-sinensis*), and even the common trumpet vine (*Campsis radicans*) provide nourishment to these tiny creatures that are constantly in search of a meal. Their frenetic activity demands a continual supply of sugary food. They sip nectar and can be enticed into view with feeders filled with fresh sugar water. A mixture of one part sugar and four parts of water meets the dietary requirements of these small birds. It is best for the health of hummers if we do not add red food coloring.

Accounts of close encounters between human and hummers abound. The tiny birds are frequently trapped in garages and on screened porches, usually drawn into these unfriendly confines by something bright red in color. A red toolbox or a red fire extinguisher can lure a hummingbird into an open garage. One was even seen attempting to extract nectar from a red plastic bicycle horn.

Several years ago, a ruby-throated hummingbird, attracted by an artificial flower arrangement, entered a large sunroom in a nursing facility. The patients all suffered from dementia or Alzheimer's disease. Most of the patients were in the final stage of the illness, sometimes known as the living death. The nursing staff was unaware of the hummingbird's presence until they noticed something they rarely saw. Several of the patients were smiling, some for the first time in months. With the aid of a towel, a nurse was able to capture the tiny bird and release it outdoors. The bird flew away, but not before bestowing a gentle blessing on a room full of people who needed a touch of tender mercy.

Hope is the thing with feathers that perches in the soul - and sings the tunes without the words - and never stops at all.

Emily Dickinson

Sunshine And Moonlight

"God called the light 'day,' and the darkness he called 'night.' And there was evening, and there was morning—the first day."
- Genesis 1:5, NIV

I was on the fourth day of creation that God made the lights to separate day from night. The greater light was the sun (Genesis 1:14-16, NIV). People who were members of the Flat Earth Society thought that the sun came up out of the ocean in the early morning and went down into the ocean in the evening. During the night, it got back into position to do its work the next day. In other words, they believed the sun was rotating around the earth.

The scientist Galileo was excommunicated from the church because he dared to suggest that, in fact, the Earth was rotating around the sun. This notion was considered heresy in Galileo's day. In a way, it is understandable. All of us like to believe that we are the center of the universe. A part of growing up and growing wiser is learning that things do not rotate around us. Our lives, instead, have to revolve around something else. We need a center.

The sun is our nearest star. Scientists tell us that it is ninety-three million miles from Earth. But who's counting, right? The thing that matters is when God placed the Earth in orbit around the sun, He determined the correct distance and the tilt of the earth that would give us here in red clay country the seasons we all enjoy.

We often think of spring and summer as growing seasons and fall and winter as dormant seasons but, in our neck of the woods, plants are always flourishing. Bulbs that are buried six inches in the ground and covered with mulch are growing the root system needed to produce the beautiful blooms we anticipate every spring.

Trees, too, are constantly growing. Evergreens, like pines, cedars, and hemlock, drop a few needles as new ones take their place. Broadleaf evergreens, like magnolias, rhododendron, and camelias, bring a splash of green to even the coldest days of winter. This green color that we see comes from chlorophyll, manufactured within the leaves. This process of photosynthesis, another part of God's creation, allows the garden to flourish. As John Denver says, "Sunshine on my shoulders makes me happy." Just as we thrive on sunshine, so do the plants.

The foliage of daffodils, tulips, crocus, and other spring bulbs, begins to shrivel and fade after the blooms are spent. The reason we remove those withered blooms is so the sun can produce new nutrients for the bulbs. This prepares the plants for a new growing season.

Some plants thrive in the hot summer sun. Cotton and okra are first cousins and require a long, hot growing season in full sun. Some plants prefer dappled light, more shade than direct sunshine. Among my favorite shade-loving plants are hostas, in all their many varieties. Coleuses, impatiens, and astilbe all do well in the shade, but they are also dependent on filtered sunlight.

However, on the fourth day of creation, God made the moon and the stars. You can read more about stargazing in Chapter 47 of this book. The moon rotates around the Earth as the Earth rotates around the sun.

When I was a student at Furman University, a physics professor pointed out that the moon is roughly the same size as the Pacific Ocean when measured by volume. This led to speculation that the moon may have been created from a piece of the Earth. It seemed to me like a plausible concept and acts as a simple reminder that, from the beginning, God was working in mysterious ways with wonders to perform.

The moon is no less important to the Earth than the sun. Scientists have long known that the moon controls the tides. Fishers know that the moon has an effect on the animals that occupy the sea and the fish that live in the rivers and streams. People who fish also know that night fishing is best on a full moon. For example, avid bream wranglers know that the full moon in May is the best time to get Shellcrackers and Blue Gills.

The moon also strongly affects the garden. Several years ago, I attempted to create a night garden and had moderate success. A night garden is sometimes referred to as a moon garden. It is a treat for the eyes and for the nose. White blooms reflect the light of the moon better than cut flowers and several of those night blooms are more fragrant in the dark rather than the light of day. Not only that, but nighttime pollinators will also enjoy your moon garden.

I have had success with Angel's trumpet (*Brugmansia*), Cape gardenia (*Gardenia jasminoides*), white lily (*Lilium 'casa blanca'*), evening primrose (*Oenothera biennis*), flowering tobacco (*Nicotiana alata*), four o'clocks, also known as Marvel-of-Peru (*Mirabilis jalapa*), night phlox

(*Zaluzianskya ovata*), and, last but not least, vining moonflower (*Ipomoea alba*). These are just a few suggestions from me, but if you search the internet, you will find plenty of other suggestions for your moon garden. If you have a small space near a patio or a deck, you may want to try a night garden of your own.

There are many reasons to enjoy sitting in the garden at night, especially when the days are long and hot. Time in the garden can be refreshing, even if you need to wear a copious layer of mosquito repellant. The sounds of the garden are entertaining. whippoorwills, owls, and even watching bats fly around in the low light is fascinating. Most of all, resting in the garden at night in a comfortable chair or hammock yields time to pray with our eyes wide open.

"When I consider your heavens, the work of your fingers, the moon and the stars, which you have set in place, what is mankind that you are mindful of them, human beings that you care for them?"
- Psalms 8:3-4, NIV

Lady Bugs

"Even the tiniest things can be miracles."
-Anonymous

Coccinella septempunctata.

One year, our daughter, Betsy, presented me with a necktie for Father's Day. Bright yellow, the tie was adorned with a colorful assortment of ladybugs.

"Wear it with a light blue shirt," Betsy advised. "The ladybugs are cute!"

Even beyond the world of men's apparel, the bright red beetles with black spots make a fashion statement. Ladybugs stand out in the *Coleoptera* family whose members are usually black and brown.

The proper name for these fascinating insects is the ladybird beetle. Over time the name was shortened to lady beetles. In the United States they became known as ladybugs.

During the Middle Ages, hordes of voracious insects descended upon the fields and orchards of central Europe. Fearful that all their food crops would be destroyed, the people prayed to the Virgin Mary for help.

According to legend, red and black beetles appeared, making a feast of the invading insects. The crops were saved. People called their winged rescuers the beetles of Our Lady. Their red wings were said to represent the Virgin's cloak. The black spots were symbolic of both her joys and her sorrows.

Lady beetles are among the most helpful garden predators. The brightly colored insects picnic on aphids and mealy bugs. One tiny ladybug can polish off a hundred aphids in a day!

More than four thousand species of ladybugs are found worldwide. In the United States the hard shell is usually red with black spots. During flight, the shell opens, allowing the wings to beat up to eighty-five times a second.

Ladybugs hibernate during the autumn and winter in logs or piles of leaves. Sometimes they find shelter beneath the siding of a home. As the spring sun warms them, they may emerge inside the dwelling, causing considerable consternation among residents. A vacuum cleaner removes them best. They can then be released outside where they belong.

Many folks in various cultures consider the presence of a ladybug to herald good luck. Killing one is said to bring sadness and misfortune.

The French believe that if a ladybug lands on you, any ailment you have will fly away with the insect. People in Belgium believe that if a ladybug crawls across a young girl's hand she will be married within a year. The black spots on the back of the insect indicate the number of children the couple will have.

Many Bretons believe that the arrival of ladybugs will bring fair weather. When Swiss children ask where babies come from, parents tell them that ladybugs deliver newborn infants. In Norway romance will surely blossom for a man and a woman who spy a ladybug at the same time.

People living in Victorian England believed that a ladybug alighting on your hand predicted that you would receive a new pair of gloves. If one landed on your head, a new hat would soon be yours.

In some cultures, ladybugs were thought to have divine powers. According to a Norse legend, Thor sent the ladybug, riding on a bolt of lightning, as a gift to earth. Some Asian cultures believe that ladybugs understand human language and function as interpreters for the gods.

Many legends in this country harken back at least as far as the pioneer days. Finding a ladybug in a family's log cabin during the winter was considered a good omen. Ladybugs even played a part in pioneer medicine. In the 1800s, some doctors treated measles with the foul-smelling fluid that ladybugs secrete to make themselves distasteful to birds! Physicians also believed that putting a mashed ladybug onto an abscessed tooth would stop the throbbing pain.

Farmers say that seeing numerous ladybugs flying around during the spring months is a harbinger of bountiful crops. Folklore suggests that the number of spots on a ladybug found in your home reveals how many dollars you will soon find. Making a wish, while holding a ladybug in your hand, brings good luck. Watching the direction it flies off your hand can indicate the source of this luck.

Legends notwithstanding, the ladybird beetle is a beneficial insect. In the 1880s, a destructive scale insect was killing large groves of lemon and orange trees. The California Citrus Growers released thousands of ladybugs into the orchards. Within two years the infestation ended, and the trees began to bear fruit again. The ladybugs had singlehandedly saved the entire citrus industry. Since then, ladybugs have been employed around the world to help control outbreaks of pests.

On one of the first warm days of spring, I was walking in my garden examining various plants that were off to a fresh start. I paid particular attention to the climbers – scarlet honeysuckle, several varieties of clematis, and the rambling roses. Ordinarily, I will find a few aphids on some of the tender shoots of these vines. But one clematis was heavily infested with these tiny sucking invaders.

Later that day I purchased a bottle of insecticidal soap. When I returned to the affected clematis, I discovered the plant was covered in ladybugs. The small beetles were feasting on the aphids. I put the spray bottle away allowing the ladybugs to dine to their hearts' content.

Master gardener Joe Maple taught me that if you kill a beneficial insect, you inherit his job. When it comes to ladybugs, my motto is borrowed from highway construction crews.

"Let 'em work. Let 'em live."

The Garden Cat

"One cat just leads to another."
–Ernest Hemingway

I have learned that when Clare senses something is amiss, I need to pay attention to her. While house hunting in Winston-Salem, we visited one picturesque abode. We got no further than the front door when Clare said, "Yuck! The previous family had cats! Many cats!" After that, we turned around and left straight away, unwilling to consider it for a home.

Several years ago, we were sitting quietly in our den when Clare smelled something burning. I sniffed and detected nothing. Clare insisted that I look around the house with her. Reluctantly, I left my chair to join the search. I could not smell smoke.

But there was! And it was my fault! I had come home from work, pulled off my necktie, and flung it toward a chair in our bedroom. One end of the silk tie had flipped over a lampshade, and was touching the hot lightbulb. The end of the tie was smoldering, just before bursting into flames. Clare's keen olfactory awareness saved us from a more serious problem.

Clare often wears two pairs of glasses. Her prescription lenses are perched on her nose and a pair of reading glasses is at the ready on top of her head. But her unaided eyesight is amazing. She can spot a dead bug on our basement floor at thirty paces. She can see a stain on my shirt and identify the source before I am even aware of the problem. She carries a laundry stick in her purse, just to keep me presentable.

My wife's hearing is equally as sensitive. Last spring during a booming thunderstorm, Clare thought she heard a baby crying. I, of course, heard nothing. But I have learned to pay attention when Clare senses something strange. As I listened, I heard only rumbling thunder, whistling wind, and pounding rain.

"I hear something that sounds like a baby crying," Clare insisted. I listened more closely, and I heard what she had heard.

I went out into the storm to investigate. Sure enough, Clare was right! It was a baby crying – a baby kitten.

I reported my find. "Don't bring that cat into this house!" she instructed.

I heeded her warning. I have never regarded myself as a cat person. Dogs are more to my liking. At the same time, I felt compelled to provide some comfort for the black and white foundling. The little kitten had obviously become separated from her mother during the storm. I could not be sure how old the kitten was. She was so small I could hold her in the palm of one hand.

Placing an old towel in a garden basket, I made a bed for the tiny trembling stray. Cold, wet, hungry, and frightened, she continued to cry. She even tried to nurse my little finger. That didn't work.

I called a good friend, a retired veterinarian, who gave me sound guidance. At a local pet store, I purchased a formula substitute for mother's milk. The little orphan lapped it up and promptly fell asleep in the crook of my arm. I am not really a cat person, but I had become the unexpected caretaker of a kitten.

Our daughter named the cat. "She was delivered to your porch by a thunderstorm. You have to name her Stormy." So, Stormy she is.

My veterinarian friend advised me on immunizations and on the proper time to have her spayed. Those health issues were taken care of by the good folks at our local animal shelter.

My responsibilities are relatively few. I make sure Stormy has her regular ration of food, that her water bowl is freshly filled each day, and that she has a routine tick and flea treatment. I also take a little time to scratch her ears. When I sit down on a favorite bench in the yard near the tree of life, Stormy still enjoys climbing into my lap for a snooze. I, who am not really a cat person, enjoy that, too.

Stormy has made herself at home in our garden. She quickly found the patch of catnip and enjoys a daily tumble in the fragrant foliage. She has her favorite lookout posts and napping places. She has climbed most of the trees in our garden and knows how to descend as well as ascend each one.

Early in our relationship, Stormy and I reached an agreement. She is free to stalk and capture any varmint that crosses the estate. However, she is under strict orders to leave the birds alone. So far, Stormy has done pretty well with that contract. We have been gifted with a variety of artifacts at our front door. These have included an assortment of deceased moles, voles, mice, and chipmunks, and at least three gray squirrel tails. I don't know what she did with the other end of the squirrels. Perhaps there are three tailless squirrels bounding through our tree branches.

Late one night, I heard the sounds of a major catfight. Actually, Stormy had cornered a possum. She wasn't quite sure what to do with the critter, so I ran it off with a shovel.

As far as I can tell the bird casualties have been limited to one starling. I reminded Stormy of our bargain, but, honestly, I wasn't a bit upset by the demise of the pesky starling. She is a discerning cat.

In one corner of our garden, I have a cast iron chiminea that I bought from a fellow in Commerce, Georgia. Sometimes on cool nights I build a small fire in the rusty stove. Stormy ventures over to check me out. Then, just like she did when she was a little kitten, she will hop on my lap. I am not really a cat person, but I scratch her ears. Stormy purrs, and we enjoy the dying embers together.

Perhaps one reason we are fascinated by cats is because such a small animal can contain so much independence, dignity, and freedom of spirit.
Lloyd Alexander

The Artist's Corner

"So, God created humankind in his own image."
-Genesis 1:27, NIV

What does it mean to be created in the image of God? This theological concept of *imago Dei*, in the image of God in Latin, is a puzzle. My own take on it is that the image of God means that we are created with an ability to think and to reason. We have an ability to distinguish right from wrong. We have an enormous capacity to love and care about other people. When God created us, He bestowed on us a childlike sense of wonder, a kind of curiosity. To say that the Divine Creator made us in His image is to say that a gracious God created us to be creative.

Our home is decorated with art, most done by our family. Our children brought many pieces of art home from school. As adults, they have continued to express their creativity in multiple ways, including visual arts.

On Father's Day 2010, they encouraged me to try my hand at painting.

I have done a lot of painting in my time, most of it on furniture and walls. I had never before tried to be an artist.

When our children suggested it, I protested. "I can't do that. I'm colorblind."

They, of course, know that. Through the years they have noticed my mismatched socks. Our son Erik once quipped that my choices in neckties harkened back to a time before the invention of color.

"Dad, you ought to try painting," they still encouraged.

My first tentative attempt was on canvas. Our son Kris, Chair of the Art Department at Spartanburg Methodist College, viewed my efforts.

Ever the teacher, he asked, "Are you happy with it?"

"No!" I answered. "It doesn't look a thing like the picture I had in my mind."

Kris said, "Let's talk about it. Dad, you might try painting on wood. It's a lot more forgiving."

Forgiveness is not a word I had thought of using in connection with art. But, looking at my first canvas, the idea of forgiveness seems appropriate. I must confess I felt like a school child presenting a piece of art, hoping it would be displayed on the refrigerator door.

I've done a lot of painting on wood. I spent most of one summer trying to paint a fence for my Uncle Wesley. The rough pine boards drank gallon after gallon of white paint. By the end of the summer, it looked like a bad whitewash job.

Having grown up on a lumberyard, I know a little bit about wood. I gathered two pieces of Oriented Strand Board I had in my barn. The Strand Board is called by contractors OSB. I am hesitant to use the initials OSB for fear I might get them mixed up and say something I do not intend. To be safe, I just call it strand board.

I assembled a few paints, dragged out an easel our children used when they were preschoolers, scrounged together some old paint brushes and a forgotten shaving brush, and dared to try.

For a time, our son, Kris, owned and operated Wet Paint Syndrome, a local art studio at the Hillcrest Shopping Center in Spartanburg, SC. Once a month, he created a unique opportunity for local artists at his gallery. On special pop-up nights, he allowed any artist the privilege of displaying two works of art for three hours for a small fee. Amateurs, as well as experienced artists, accepted this unusual invitation. I decided to show my first two pieces at the pop-up night. The two paintings I entered were still wet, appropriate for his enterprise. A group of seventeen young artists gathered around my paintings. Most of them offered kind comments. All of them were encouraging, making helpful suggestions.

They, like my children, said, "You need to keep at this."

My first two paintings were of crosses. In itself, the cross is an odd symbol when you think about it. Most of the world's great religions use an object of beauty to identify their faith: the Star of David, the crescent moon, the lotus flower. Christians have chosen the cross, a cruel instrument of execution. It might just as well be a guillotine or an electric chair! Through death by crucifixion the Romans devised a way to inflict severe pain and suffering.

For me, there is a compelling beauty in the cross. It is a reminder of divine love.

So, I paint crosses.

Now that I have embarked on this new venture, I see crosses everywhere—in the shape of a tree, the form of a dragonfly, a constellation in the night sky, and the markings on a hawk. Some crosses are literally in your face. Others are far more subtle.

I am a novice artist, and I am colorblind. My mother, Mama, was the first to discover my color impairment. She could tell from the drawings I brought home from school. I couldn't distinguish red roses on a green bush.

As a teenager I drove through a town in Georgia one dark night. A police car tailed me straight down main street. Just beyond the city limits, the officer pulled me over.

"Son, are you colorblind?" he asked.

"Yes, sir, I am."

"Colorblind folks have trouble here. When they installed our stop lights, they hung 'em upside down. I followed you all the way through town. You stopped at every green light and went through every red light! I'll warn you this time, but don't let it happen again."

In the 1960s, when I was at Furman, Army ROTC was a required class for freshmen and sophomore men. The US Army was preparing all male students to be officers in Vietnam. We were given a routine colorblind test. The Colonel called me aside.

He barked, "Neely, this army needs you in reconnaissance!"

Turns out, colorblind people are not easily fooled by camouflage. The life expectancy for a reconnaissance officer in Vietnam was something like two days. I respectfully declined and went to seminary instead.

My children comment on my paintings, "Dad, you have such an unusual use of color, and the colors are so vivid."

I cannot see the colors, but I can read the labels on the tubes of paint. Like a young kindergartner, I am an old man having fun.

This world is but a canvas for our imagination.
                              Henry David Thoreau

The true work of art is but a shadow of the divine perfection.
                              Michelangelo
Gardening is another form of creating and playing with colors.

                              Oscar de la Renta

Lilies

"Consider the lilies…"
-Luke 12:27, NKJV

I am allergic to the pollen of lilies. My sinuses stop up, my eyes itch, and I am constantly clearing my throat. Decongestants and antihistamines have helped some. The problem would be completely avoidable except for the fact that I am a pastor. The church I serve has a long tradition of decorating the sanctuary at Easter with beautiful white lilies.

The folks on our flower committee have gone the extra mile in trying to help me. For the past several years, they have removed the stamens from the blooms. Since these pollen-producers are considered the male parts of the flower, I suppose the resulting blossoms are somewhat like steers and geldings in the animal world. Thank you, flower committee, for emasculating the lilies.

Florists and garden shops are well supplied with Easter lilies. These fragrant white flowers will be given as gifts to hospital patients and nursing home residents. Cemetery plots will be adorned with lilies. By Easter Sunday morning, the traditional white flowers will be in full display.

According to Roman mythology, the white lily is associated with Juno, the queen of the gods. It is said that when Queen Juno was feeding her baby son Hercules, some of her milk fell from the sky. The part that remained above the earth formed the Milky Way. Where drops of milk fell to earth, pure white lilies bloomed.

In Greek mythology, the lily was dedicated to the goddess Hera, the wife of Zeus.

The lily was a popular flower in ancient Jewish civilization. The flower is mentioned several times in Hebrew scripture.

In Christian art, the angel Gabriel is pictured giving the Virgin Mary a bouquet of pure white lilies when he announces that she is to be the mother of the Christ child. In other paintings, early saints are depicted bringing vases filled with white lilies to Mary and the infant Jesus.

The Easter lily (*Lilium longiflorum*) is a symbol of purity and hope. They were said to be growing in the Garden of Gethsemane where Jesus prayed prior to His arrest. A legend says that when the women visited the tomb of Jesus following the resurrection, they found the grave empty and a bouquet of white lilies where the body of Jesus had previously been placed.

If you enter a church Sanctuary on Sunday, you may see lilies at the foot of the cross, around the altar or the communion table, or in the church foyer. These white trumpet-shaped flowers signal the resurrection.

The Easter lily is native to the southern islands of Japan. In the 1880's, lilies were cultivated in Bermuda, and bulbs were shipped to the United States. Around the turn of the century, the Japanese took over the growing of Easter lilies. Prior to 1941, the majority of the Easter lily bulbs were exported to the United States from Japan. World War II eliminated the dependence on Japanese-produced bulbs and commercial bulb production shifted to the United States.

The Easter lily industry is an American success story. It all began with a World War I veteran, Louis Houghton. He brought a suitcase full of hybrid lily bulbs to the south coast of Oregon in 1919. Houghton freely distributed bulbs to his friends and neighbors.

After the Japanese attacked Pearl Harbor in 1941, the source of bulbs was abruptly cut off. The value of lily bulbs skyrocketed. Many who were growing lilies as a hobby went into business. The Easter lily bulbs were called White Gold. By 1945, there were about 1,200 growers producing bulbs up and down the Pacific coast.

Producing quality lily bulbs proved to be an exact and demanding science with specific climatic requirements. Over the years, the total number of bulb producers dwindled to just ten farms. All are located in a small, isolated coastal region straddling the Oregon-California border. This region, called the Easter Lily Capital of the World, produces nearly all of the bulbs for the Easter lily market.

Bulbs are harvested in the fall, packed, and shipped to commercial greenhouses. They are planted in pots and, under controlled conditions, are forced into bloom for the Easter holiday. 'Nellie White' is the bulb most commonly used for potted Easter lilies. James White developed the hybrid and named it after his wife. 'Nellie White' has large, white, trumpet shaped flowers with a soft yellow throat.

Lilies are among the most dramatic and easy to grow flowers in the home garden. Good drainage is the key for success with lilies. Raised garden beds amended with good soil are best in our red clay Piedmont. Form, color, and fragrance contribute to the charm of garden lilies. Tall stately *Asiatic lilies* and fragrant *Oriental lilies* are the two favorite varieties for the Upstate. The corms, also called bulbs, may be planted in the fall or the spring. *Asiatic lilies* and *Oriental lilies* grow best in full sunlight.

'Nellie White' Easter lilies also do quite well in our area. They can be transplanted immediately after the blooms have died.

In the Sermon on the Mount, Jesus said, "Consider the lilies ... "

Our flower committee has done just that. They have figured out how to decorate the Sanctuary with Easter lilies without inflicting pollen on the pastor. The church will be adorned as usual for Holy Week this year.

However, this Easter, all of the lilies will be silk.

Flowers always make people better, happier, and more helpful; they are sunshine, food and medicine for the soul.

Luther Burbank

Bluebirds

"He made their glowing colors"
-All Things Bright and Beautiful

Sialia sialis

S everal years ago, as I left my driveway, a bright bluebird flew directly in front of me. When I arrived at the church, a pair of bluebirds was perched on top of one of the nesting boxes placed along the road leading to the parking lot. The day began with blessing of bluebirds.

One of the perennial joys of spring and summer is the visitation of bluebirds. The sight of these beauties lifts my spirits.

Bluebirds are associated with happiness. In the movie *The Wizard of Oz*, Judy Garland's Dorothy sang of bluebirds that fly over the rainbow. The lyrics to a song from the World War II era proclaimed, "There'll be bluebirds over the white cliffs of Dover" as a harbinger of peace.

Songs about bluebirds abound, but there was a time when the bluebird was an endangered species. Bluebirds are found in South Carolina year round. When insect populations decrease with frost and cold weather, the bluebirds expand their menu to include berries, mistletoe, Virginia creeper, red cedar, hollies, and dogwoods. In a single season, a nesting pair will rear two broods of four or five fledglings each. Though the birds will nest in any cavity, bluebird boxes, mounted four or five feet above the ground, facing south over an open area, are almost sure to attract a mated pair.

The Cherokee call the bluebird the "bird that carries the sky on its back." The bright blue feathers, accented with chestnut throat and white belly, make this winged visitor a welcome addition to any backyard.

Once, as I was working in my garden, I saw a pair of bluebirds making their second nest of the season in one of the several nesting boxes I provide. Since the fall of 2000, bluebirds have become, for us, a sign of grace.

November in South Carolina is usually a mild month. Not until after Thanksgiving does the weather begin to feel like winter. On November 19, 2000, we had an accumulation of snow in the Upstate. It was the day of our 27-year-old son's funeral.

Erik died on November 15, 2000, at his home in Charleston. Temperatures in the Lowcountry were normal. The day we returned from Charleston to our home in Spartanburg, the sky was bright and sunny. Sunday morning, the day of the funeral, dawned grey, cold, and damp. Temperatures continued to fall through the day. By the time we arrived at the church for the funeral, light snow was falling. When we went to the cemetery for the committal service, the ground was covered with snow.

Some of our friends expressed regret that the weather was inclement on the day of our son's service. In our imagination, we thought that Erik had put in a request to the Almighty. Something like, "Lord, you know this will be a hard day for my family. Could you do something to surprise them?"

In my first sermon after Erik's death, I interpreted the snow as a gentle touch from God, a gift of grace in our grief, and a symbol of hope. Many of the Christmas cards and Christmas presents we received that year included a snow theme. As Christmas approached, we decided to decorate our Christmas tree only with snowflakes and snowmen ornaments. Hand-cut snowflakes adorned our windows.

As spring approached, Clare and I knew we needed a symbol of hope for the warmer months. In late February, I conducted a funeral for a church member at Greenlawn Memorial Gardens, the same cemetery where Erik's grave is located.

At the conclusion of the service, I stopped the car near our son's newly-placed tombstone. I could see an eastern bluebird perched atop Erik's marker. I called Clare on the cell phone just as the bird flew away.

"I think I have found a new symbol for spring and summer," I said when she answered. "It's a bluebird that has just flown away."

"Just wait a minute or two. Maybe he will come back," Clare said.

Sure enough, the bluebird returned. He perched on Erik's gravestone and was joined by his mate, giving us our new symbol of hope.

Nesting boxes in our yard invite bluebirds to make their home near ours. Every spring since Erik's death we have enjoyed two or three winged families as visitors in our yard. They are, indeed, a symbol of hope, a tender mercy, and a touch of grace.

Sialia sialis, the Eastern Bluebird, primarily feeds on insects. Crickets, grasshoppers, caterpillars, and Japanese beetles are all a part of a bluebird's diet. Because they are insect eaters, the native population of bluebirds was reduced to critically low numbers by the overuse of pesticides. Through conservation efforts, the species has made a remarkable recovery. You can invite bluebirds to your garden with bluebird boxes.

You can find patterns online. Be aware that these boxes require a specific size hole, no perch, and that they must be well positioned six feet above ground, facing south. I have several boxes in my garden. I clean them out every January just in time for the bluebirds to arrive about Valentine's Day.

Lavender

"Lavender is grown for its purple flowers and fragrant scent. It promotes calmness, wellness, and relaxation."
-Anonymous

Lavandula angustifolia

C lare's grandmother, Dena Leone Rheney Mitchell, whom Clare called "Mother Dee," used Yardley lavender soap. She bathed with it and used it as a fragrance for her lingerie and her towels and her other items of clothing. My grandmother, Mamie Lawton Neely, whom I called "Mammy," used lavender water as a perfume. The fragrant herb lavender has enjoyed a long and well-deserved reputation as an antiseptic, a protective, a fragrance, and a love-inducing perfume.

Ancient Egyptians used lavender in their process for mummifying the dead. Even before her death, Cleopatra was reputed to have used lavender as one of her secrets for seducing both Julius Caesar and Mark Antony. When the tomb of King Tutankhamen was opened, archaeologists discovered that it had been filled with lavender. Some of the ancient flowers still had a slight fragrance when the tomb was opened.

The Greeks and Romans prized lavender for its medicinal and magical properties as well as for its scent. The Arabs were the first to cultivate lavender. They used the herb to reduce stress, calm the nervous system, and encourage a good night's sleep. Arab physicians used lavender to cleanse wounds and promote healing. Ancient Arabia first developed the distillation process for making essential oil from lavender. The technology is still used today.

In time, lavender made its way along the ancient spice trail from Arabia and through Europe to the British Isles. King Charles VI of France demanded that his pillow always contain lavender so he could get a good night's sleep. Queen Elizabeth I of England requested fresh lavender in the vases of her parlor every day of the year. Lavender was used among the wealthy and the poor to scent bed linens and clothing. It was hung above entrance doors to protect against evil spirits and added to bath water to comfort tired bodies. Lavender oil is still used in homeopathic medicine to treat migraines and insomnia. Medieval churches in Europe included lavender in their gardens. The flowers were strewn in the aisles on holy days of obligation. Physicians and midwives recommended lavender as an aid to childbirth.

During the Black Death, or the Bubonic Plague, Four Thieves Vinegar was used as a protective and antiseptic agent, combining the herbs of thyme, sage, lavender, rosemary, mint, and garlic. Four Thieves was a concoction of vinegar infused with those six herbs. The story behind the name is that, during the Plague in the town of Marseilles, four thieves had been caught robbing the sick and the dead. The punishment for their crimes was to bury the dead. They survived their sentence through the power of this concoction. This potion is still available, sometimes still under the name of Four Thieves Essential Oil.

For all of its medicinal uses, lavender as the herb of love is the subject of folklore in many cultures. Even in India, ancient Hindu practitioners associated lavender with the heart chakra A study done by the Chicago Research Foundation revealed that the scent of lavender was one of the most arousing to male subjects. Long before the Chicago research, young ladies tucked small lavender bags in their cleavage to lure suitors.

In my garden, I have tried several varieties of lavender, especially French and English. I have had most success with common English lavender. These perennials can be short-lived, so periodic replanting is helpful to keep a good supply. There is much to love about this plant. It is easy to grow; it is heat loving and drought tolerant. It is deer and rabbit resistant. Healthy plants return bigger and better every year. If you have a hot dry spot in a flower bed where nothing else will grow well, try lavender.

The Garden of Mercy

"Blessed are the merciful, for they will be shown mercy."
Matthew 5:7, NIV

Greenbriers

"...greenbriers and thorns will grow there."
-Isaiah 5:6, NIV

Who knew that the Bible would mention greenbriers? Leave it to the prophet Isaiah, one of my favorite books in the Old Testament, to reference these prickly vines.

In the city of Jerusalem, there is a church named Saint Anne's. Near the church are twin pools identified as the pools of Bethesda. According to the fifth chapter of John's gospel, this was a place where people sought healing. Here the sick and the lame, the blind and the paralyzed gathered in the shade of colonnades by therapeutic waters. In Aramaic, the word Bethesda means "house of mercy." There a person, paralyzed for thirty-eight years, received the miracle of restored health from Jesus.

The garden can also be a place of mercy and healing. In my garden, a small waterfall sings gently in the shade. It is a wonderful place to rest and experience the tender care of God. In this shaded place among hostas and ferns, delicate shade-loving plants thrive. Forget-me-nots (*Myosotis sylvatica*) offer their calming display of tiny blue flowers, reminding me of people now gone on to heaven. Here, too, is an old-fashioned favorite which bears dangling, rosy heart-shaped flowers, true to its name, bleeding heart (*Dicentra spectabilis*). The names of these flowers suggest that this shady Garden of Mercy is an inviting place to release sorrow, a place where broken hearts can mend, where loved ones will not be forgotten, where the soul can be restored.

In our garden, there is a peaceful spot, a shady corner with a Charleston bench. A place where the sound of wind chimes and flowing water soothe the spirit, there is an invader even here. Even in the heat of summer, it offers quiet solitude. Among the hostas, the ferns, and the bleeding hearts, greenbriers also spring up. When I kneel with garden gloves and trowel, I work to dig out the brier root. It is deeply buried, with ugly yellow sections between hard knotty nodes. Even the roots have thorns.

As I mentioned earlier, the Cherokee people have knack for finding good uses for plants in the wrong place. Greenbriers have a wax coating all along the stem. When a greenbrier stem is cut into foot-long pieces, the bundle can be used as a fire starter. At a Boy

Scout camp one fall, we experienced rain for three straight days. The rain started as a two hour long torrential downpour. After a soggy night, most of our clothing and all of our sleeping bags were soaking wet. Nearby was a pavilion with a fireplace where we had planned to boil our morning eggs. We tried to build a fire with the small stack of oak logs, but the rain had thoroughly drenched everything, making the task feel impossible.

A Cherokee man, who was part of our group, said, "Give me a few minutes. We'll have a fire to boil those eggs, make some coffee, and maybe even have some toast."

"One more thing," he said before he left, "hang those sleeping bags from the rafters and as much of the wet clothing as you can." He then added, "If you find an old bird's nest, put it on the stack of oak logs next to the fireplace."

The man then left the pavilion carrying a hand ax and a sheath knife. Meanwhile, we hung up all the sleeping bags and wet clothing and managed to find two old, vacated bird's nests. One was a robin's nest, which was large, soft, and dry. It was made from pine needles, straw, a few stray feathers, and a piece of string. The other was a wren's nest made from tiny sticks.

No sooner had we hung our wet laundry from the rafters than the Cherokee man reappeared from the woods with an armload of wet white pine sticks (*Pinus strobus*) and a bundle of greenbrier twigs.

He explained, "If you go under the canopy of a white pine tree, you can always find a few dead limbs. No matter how wet the weather, those limbs are drier than anything on the ground."

With his large sheath knife, he peeled the bark off of the white pine limbs, revealing dry wood filled with pine sap. At the fireplace, he stacked four oak logs in a log cabin-style. Next, he put down three pine sticks and the robin's old nest. He then added four more oak logs, three more pine sticks, and the wren's nest. After that, he added another four logs, three more pine sticks, and the bundle of greenbrier. With one log remaining, he placed it on top with the two more pine sticks.

Taking a piece of flint from his pocket, he chipped sparks off the rock using the back of his sheath knife. After hitting the rock two or three times, the robin's nest caught on fire. It blazed up through the sap-filled pine sticks, to the twigs of the wren's nest, and onto the greenbrier which popped and cracked, igniting the topmost layer of pine. Before long, the center of the fire structure collapsed and the man rearranged the oak logs. In short order, we had boiled eggs, hot coffee, and lightly toasted bread.

As I work in the shade beneath a winged elm tree at the top of the waterfall, I rejoice in the beauty of wood squill and lily of the valley. But even here, there is greenbrier, an unwelcome intruder. I am reminded of the wisdom of the writer of Hebrews: "Let no 'root of bitterness' spring up and cause trouble" (12:15, NIV).

The shaded soil in which Virginia bluebells and forget-me-nots thrive is also a place where thorny briers prosper. So, too, when the human heart is bleeding and sorrowful, longing for peaceful healing, the root of bitterness can take hold. The difficulties of life can lead us to blame others for our pain. Our hearts can be invaded by jealously and envy, by hate and anger. The mercy of God is the forgiveness of God. It is the willingness of Christ, with hands pierced by nails and with thorns on his brow, to probe deeply into our hearts with gentle, yet powerful, forgiveness. His mercy can rid us of bitterness and bring healing to our spirit.

Sometimes after being on my knees struggling with thorny roots and thorny thoughts, I rest. I listen to the sounds of water and wind. I watch dappled sunlight on delicate blooms. I brush the dirt from my knees, and I pray the words of the old hymn by Robert Grant:

> Frail children of dust, and feeble as frail,
> In Thee do we trust, nor find Thee to fail:
> Thy mercies how tender, how firm to the end,
> Our Maker, Defender, Redeemer, and Friend.

It is a moment of mercy, and I am renewed. It is a time when, by the tenderness of God, thorns can be removed from our soul, making room for new growth, new life, and new beauty.

Fireflies

"...you will shine among them like stars in the sky."
-Philippians 2:15b, NIV

I called my grandmother Granny. She lived on South Converse Street in Spartanburg. From the time I was ten years old, I cut her grass with an old-fashioned push reel lawn mower. Granny's yard was so small that I could mow her grass in about a half an hour.

In the summertime, I went to Granny's house after supper, cut her grass, drank a glass of lemonade, and sat on the porch until dark watching the fireflies come out.

One of my favorite summertime memories is running barefooted through Granny's grass catching lightning bugs, also known as fireflies.

When is the last time you saw a lightning bug?

Some folks have seen increasing numbers of these night visitors. Other people believe the twinkling flying lights are vanishing. One time, I posed the question to the breakfast crowd at Dolline's Restaurant in Clifton with mixed results.

"Growing up I saw fireflies all the time, now I don't see them anymore," answered one fellow.

"I've got plenty of them at my place down near the river," responded another.

Firefly Watch, based at the Museum of Science in Boston, has researched the question. They provide good information and possible solutions.

Lightning bugs are actually beetles. Fireflies are winged, distinguishing them from other luminescent insects commonly known as glowworms. They are surprisingly long-lived, but they spend most of their lifespan, two years or more, as grubs underground. The nighttime lights that we see represent only about the last two weeks of their lives.

That magical display is all about producing more fireflies. They use those tiny lights to attract a mate. The males are the ones flying around flashing. Females are perched in tall grass blinking subtly, waiting for a rendezvous with one of the show-offs.

This is where the plot thickens. There are more than two hundred species, each with a distinctive blinking pattern. Females hiding in the grass use these flash patterns, not only to attract a mate, but also to fool others. Some mimic the patterns of another species and then eat the hopeful mate. Call them femmes fatales.

Where firefly populations have dwindled researchers offer several remedies.

- Remember that lightning bugs are not flies; they are beetles. So, if you want these flying nightlights to grace your garden avoid using pesticides that target beetles.
- Since, these delightful guests spend most of their lives underground, anything that disturbs the soil or kills grubs will diminish the firefly population.
- Mature fireflies prefer tall grass and moist soil. Frequent mowing grass too short contributes to drier, packed soil and negatively affects grub habitat.
- Outside artificial lighting affects the ability of lightning bugs to find mates.

When Clare's mother died, we were cleaning out her home. Under her kitchen sink she had a stash of Duke's mayonnaise jars.

"Why did she save all those jars?" I asked.

"So, we could catch lightning bugs!" chorused our children.

It is one of the simple pleasures of summertime.

Like stars that hover close to ground.
Surrounded by rivals all around.
With taillight blinking pursuing his fate,
The firefly beetle finds his mate.
__Kirk H. Neely__

Balm

"Is there no balm in Gilead?"
-Jeremiah 8:22a, NIV

Melissa officinalis

The Balm of Gilead

Balm is an herb with many cousins. The varieties range from low-growing ground covers to tall plants with fragrant blossoms. After his brothers threw Joseph into the pit, they sold him to an Ishmaelite caravan on their way to Egypt. According to the scriptures (Genesis 37:25), they were on their way from Gilead to Egypt with their camels bearing spice, balm, and myrrh.

During the final years of the kingdom of Judah, Jeremiah raises the question, "Is there no balm in Gilead?" (Jeremiah 8:22) From the prophet Ezekiel, we learn that Hebrew merchants carried balm to the market of Tyre (Ezekiel 27:17). According to 1 Kings 10:10, balm was among the many precious gifts the queen of Sheba gave to King Solomon. So, the herb balm has its roots in the Bible. In Greco-Roman times, the ancient city of Jericho was believed to be the only place where true balm grew. There, it was confined to two gardens.

Biblical balm, also called the balsam tree, was indigenous to Palestine, the Transjordan, and Arabia. It was greatly valued by the Romans. Pompei exhibited branches of the tree as treasured spoils of the newly conquered Palestine. The fragrant herb graced the triumphal parade of other Roman conquerors. It is mentioned in the writings of Josephus. Pliny mentions three different species of the plant.

In the Talmud, balsam is an ointment of great value. There was a product of Jericho; the main use was medicinal, rather than cosmetic. The early rabbis composed a special blessing for the herb. After King Josiah, balsam oil was used to anoint new kings. In the Christian era, balm was mixed with olive oil to make the chrism used in the anointing of newly confirmed Christians.

One tradition says that the plants were brought to Egypt by Cleopatra and were planted in the town of Ayn Shams near a freshwater spring. Both Muslims and Christians stopped at the spring for refreshment in their travels. It was at this same spring that Mary, the mother of Jesus, was said to have washed the swaddling clothes on her way back to Galilee after her sojourn in Egypt. The clothes were scented with balm from the nearby trees. Now, the tree, *Commiphora Gileadensis*, grows wild in the Valley of Mecca.

Lemon Balm

Melissa officinalis is a member of the mint family. It is native to southern Europe, the Mediterranean, Iran, and central Asia. It has been naturalized in the Americas. The leaves have a mild lemon scent. During the summer, they produce small white flowers full of nectar. It attracts honeybees, therefore the name, "Melissa," which means "honeybee" in Greek. Something I didn't know. The leaves are used to make herbal tea. The essential oil extract is used for aroma therapy. Called "The Elixir of Life" in medieval Europe, lemon balm came to North America during the American colonial period. It was among the herbs cultivated in Thomas Jefferson's garden at Monticello. Additionally, lemon balm tea and lemon balm extract improve the quality of sleep. The herb is also used to alleviate anxiety and depression. It increases calmness and improves mood and cognitive performance.

Bee Balm (*Monardia*)

Every garden can benefit from a patch of bee balm, a native of North America. Common names for bee balm are "horse mint," "Oswego," and "bergamot." The plant was named for the Spanish botanist Nicolas Monardes. This perennial will grow to a height of three feet. The flowers are usually single, but some cultivated forms have double flowers. Colors vary from red to pink to light purple.

Seeds collected from these plants do not yield plants identical to the parent.

The plant was used by many indigenous people of the Great Plains as a medicine. They recognized the strong antiseptic actions of the plants and used them in poultice for skin infections and minor wounds. It's also used to alleviate stomach and respiratory ailments. Indigenous people also use the herb to season wild game. The plants are widespread across North America and can be found in meadows and on hillsides up to 5,000 feet in elevation. The plants attract pollinators such as hummingbirds and honeybees.

Apart from its many uses, balm deserves a place in the garden. Here are the first lines of a hymn about balm:

> There is a balm in Gilead
> to make the wounded whole.
> There is a balm in Gilead
> to heal the sin-sick soul.
>
> Sometimes I feel discouraged,
> and think my work's in vain,
> but then the Holy Spirit
> revives my soul again.

Calloused Knees

"God opposes the proud but shows favor to the humble."
-1 Peter 5:5, NIV

Which resident of the Lowcountry is tall, bald, and has knobby knees?

When I first heard the riddle, my Aunt Gladys Hutson Sowers came to mind. She lived with her husband and eight children in a cabin on the edge of the Okefenokee Swamp. Her hair loss probably came from raising those children. Maybe it was the frequent visits by alligators that crawled out of the swamp into her backyard, enticed by her chickens.

You can probably think of several acquaintances that fit the riddle's description. But the correct answer is not a person at all. It is one of Aunt Gladys's close neighbors, the bald cypress tree.

I have three cypress "knees" in my backyard garden in the Upstate of South Carolina. I suppose that having the unusual root formation in a piedmont garden is odd. We might say these are dislocated knees, a painful thought for anyone with aching joints. For me these three cypress knees have devotional significance.

First, there is a Biblical connection. The Good Book says that on the third day of creation, the Almighty created all the plants and trees, everything that bears fruit with seeds. Among these was a Lowcountry native with knobby knees, the bald cypress tree.

The South Georgia swamp behind Aunt Gladys's cabin is Okefenokee National Wildlife Refuge. Before that conservation effort in 1937, extensive logging operations had seriously depleted the boggy forest of cypress trees.

The coastal plain of the southeast is heavily populated with cypress trees. The bald cypress is closely related to the sequoias of California. The tree is called bald because, though a conifer, its leaves are shed in the fall. This interesting evergreen grows best in the rich, wet soil along riverbanks, on the margin of wetlands, or in the middle of swamps. It can grow to a great age and large size, sometimes 150 feet high and seventeen feet in diameter. Its durable wood is often called the wood eternal.

Cypress lumber resists insects and chemical corrosion as well as decay. It has a fragrance resembling that of cedar. It is a close-grained yellow or reddish wood, so resinous that it resists rotting even after prolonged submersion in water. Cypress products include coffins, acid tanks, docks, pilings, poles, and railroad ties. There is a Biblical connection that usually goes unnoticed. The King James Translation reports that God told Noah to build the ark of gopher wood. The New International Version translates the text, "Make an ark of cypress wood" (Genesis 6:14).

The massive trunk of the stately tree tapers upward from its wide, flaring base, where roots entangle to form supporting buttresses. The roots of cypress trees form knees that protrude above the surface of the water. Scientists believe that these knobs provide aeration for the roots that are otherwise completely submerged in water. They also give balance to the tall trees that might topple over under their own weight in the soggy soil.

Though the trees grow throughout the deep South, the largest remaining old-growth stand of bald cypress is at Corkscrew Swamp Sanctuary, near Naples, Florida. Some of those trees are around five hundred years of age.

In the second place, there is a family connection.

My grandmothers were reared on Lowcountry plantations. Aunt Gladys' home in the Okefenokee put her in a familiar environment. Though the Upstate has long been my home, the cypress knees bespeak a connection that stretches below the fall line.

For years, my family and I were privileged to spend a week at Pawley's Island each summer. One hot Saturday while on vacation there, I met Thomas, a big man, standing tall and stately like a cypress tree. He had large hands, callused from years of hard work. His skin, the color of ebony, glistened in the heat and humidity of the Lowcountry like wood with a coat of high gloss varnish. His voice was quiet and gentle, and he spoke in reverent tones.

Thomas began his life on a farm. Even as an elderly man, he continued to work the land. "But," he said, "years ago the Lord called me into the swamp and showed me the beauty of cypress knees."

Between McClellanville and Georgetown, along Highway 17, Thomas was known as the Cypress Knee Man. Several days a week, Thomas put on a pair of high-water boots and wades into the swamp, chainsaw in hand, to harvest these unusual root formations. "I cut them above the water line," he said. "That way the trees won't die. They just make more knees."

I met Thomas along the highway at Pawleys Island. His vintage Ford pickup was parked next to a hardware store. On a small island of grass between two palm trees, he displayed the fruits of his labor. He had some cypress knees with the bark still attached and others that had been stripped and polished. Thomas had cypress knee lamps and cypress knee tables. He had a full display of walking sticks and walking canes, many crafted of oak, sweet gum, dogwood, or tupelo, as well as a few from cypress,

Thomas was an Associate Pastor at a Holiness Church in McClellanville. The following Sunday he was to preach about a third of the three-hour service. The Lord who called him into the swamp also called him into the pulpit. He said God spoke to him nearly every single day.

"Just look at these cypress knees," he said, motioning toward a hundred or so spread out on the grass. "You can see the hand of God in every one of them. Each one is different. I've seen cypress knees that look like the Lord kneeling in prayer or the Mother Mary. I've seen cypress knees that look like angels. Each one is different, and each one is a sermon."

On that hot Saturday at Pawley's Island, I felt that I had been led to worship. The preacher was a man called Thomas. The text was cypress knees. The message was, if you pay close attention, you'll see a creative hand at work in the world around you, maybe in cypress knees, but especially in people like Thomas. The three cypress knees in my garden were purchased from Thomas.

These dislocated knobby knees are a reminder of my own aching joints. Any serious gardener knows that a primary posture in this endeavor is kneeling. Think about the simple act of kneeling. No wonder so many garden catalogues advertise kneeling pads or low carts suitable for sitting. I have appropriated an old Furman University stadium cushion for the purpose.

Habitual kneeling can make our knees calloused or cause them to pop and creak when we rise from our work. But kneeling is the most typical posture for a gardener.

High on my potting bench I have a small figure of Jesus praying in the Garden of Gethsemane. He is kneeling, making the most important decision of his life. "Not my will but Thine." To be reminded of Jesus kneeling in the garden somehow sanctifies my own bent posture. Kneeling to weed or kneeling to plant is an invitation. While down on my knees, I might as well use it as an opportunity to pray.

And I do.

Gardens are not made by singing 'Oh, how beautiful,' and sitting in the shade.
Rudyard Kipling

At the name of Jesus every knee should bow, in heaven and on earth and under the earth, and every tongue confess that Jesus Christ is Lord, to the glory of God the Father.
Philippians 2: 11 (RSV)

Drought

"...dry and thirsty land."
-Ezekiel 19:13, NIV

Miss Maude and her husband, known only by his last name, Creech, enjoyed a simple life. Miss Maude and Creech lived in an unpainted clapboard house in Barnwell County, South Carolina. The house was perched atop heart pine logs. The house had no running water. The bathroom was an outhouse at the end of a path that passed a beautiful flower garden. Their home was lighted with kerosene lamps. They cooked on a wood stove, which also served as their source of heat. In the summertime, they would sit together in matching rocking chairs on a shaded porch that wrapped around the house.

Miss Maude wore a sunbonnet and a faded calico dress. She cooled herself with a fan woven from a Palmetto palm. Creech wore a straw hat, a long-sleeved cotton shirt, and overalls. They drew water from a well.

They each took a bath once a week, usually on Saturday, whether they needed it or not. They took turns bathing in a galvanized tin tub in the kitchen. Miss Maude washed dishes in a blue enamel pan. The water left over from washing was taken to the garden. It was poured from a white porcelain pitcher around individual plants providing the moisture needed in the low country heat.

Their lifestyle was simple. Their flower garden was beautiful. Their vegetable garden was fruitful. Their conservation of water is to be admired and emulated.

The *Spartanburg Herald-Journal* reported that one year, the month of August set records for high temperatures and low rainfall. The state and local representatives from the Drought Response Committee reported that September that conditions had continued to deteriorate. The committee upgraded the drought level to severe for all counties in South Carolina except Beaufort and Jasper.

According to Hope Mizzell, State Climatologist, the drought impacted everything from agriculture to forestry, and water levels indicated an extreme drought for much of the Upstate.

In July and August, the SC Forestry Commission responded

to 518 wildfires that burned more than 2,730 acres. The high temperatures were hard for firefighters. Without widespread rainfall, the fall wildfire season had the potential to be severe.

State Hydrologist Bud Badr reported all lake levels below normal except Lake Murray. Fifteen water systems imposed water restrictions.

The Spartanburg Herald-Journal published an article by Janet S. Spencer about the problem in one rural Upstate community. Wells were drying up in Rock Springs in Cherokee County. Confronted with a lack of potable drinking water, about 110 residents of the community off Highway 18 north of Blacksburg rationed to conserve the scant supply of water. Residents were advised not to drink the water.

Coping with the declining water table is difficult. One resident said, "Many have to space out use of their water for washing clothes during the day, bathing at night. One family built a homemade holding tank with a timer on the well pump. It runs at intervals and fills up at night. That usually gets them through the next day."

Digging new wells was not always a solution. Some attempts to find a better source of water ended in disappointment with only a deep, dry hole. "Rock Springs has gone from desperate for water, to critical, to begging," said one man who had always lived in the area.

Though the situation was not nearly so critical for most of us, the drought that persisted in the southeastern United States through that summer was difficult for many of us who loved to garden. We had tried to stay ahead of the drought by watering regularly and by mulching deeply.

That summer, the drought was so severe that many gardeners lost prized trees and shrubs. Vegetable gardens and flower gardens suffered. I paid special attention to the plants in my garden that had survived. Some did well and flourished even through that hot, dry summer.

While I lost a number of plants, I learned what to plant next year and what not to plant. In the years after, there were more succulents like the always-reliable sedums; more heat tolerant annuals such as vinca, cosmos, cleome, and portulaca; and more drought tolerant perennials – Verbena, Black-eyed Susan, Yarrow, and Coneflowers. Even the miniature roses survived the drought well.

Clare and I also learned some important lessons about conserving water. It is not wise to leave a sprinkler running for several hours. It is impractical because of the loss of water due to evaporation.

Plastic pans in our kitchen sink conserve dishwater. Hanging baskets, flowerpots, flower boxes all get a daily drink of this recycled water. Shorter showers are in order. A three-gallon bucket placed in the shower conserves the water while we wait until it comes to the right temperature. Trees and shrubs that must be watered deeply love this recycled water.

Water shortages are at historic highs, especially in developing countries. As we deal with the growing effects of climate change, we are aware that conserving water is critical. Remember, the eight billion people who share this earth have a responsibility to care for each other and to care for the plant we inhabit.

We've learned from necessity the lessons that Miss Maude and Creech demonstrated so beautifully on their farm long ago. Coping with drought requires that we all conserve as much as possible. Most of all, pray for rain.

I will pour water on the thirsty land,
and streams on the dry ground;
I will pour my Spirit upon your descendants,
and my blessing on your offspring.
       Isaiah 44:3 (RSV)

Mockingbirds

"And when you pray, do not use vain repetition."
-Matthew 6:7, NKJV

Jesus was constantly teaching His disciples about prayer. When He cautions against piling up empty phrases, or vain repetition, He is speaking about prayer that has eroded into nonsense. His point, of course, is that prayer should be heartfelt, more like a love letter than an email.

While Jesus warns about frivolous prayer, He certainly was not talking about the mockingbird. As the state bird of Tennessee, the mockingbird was my grandfather's favorite bird. Appearing year round in Upstate South Carolina, mockingbirds make frequent appearances in many gardens around the state.

A lady in our church takes her newspaper and a cup of freshly brewed coffee to her back porch every morning. "I always have my cell phone with me," she explained. "I never know when one of my children might call."

Early one sunny day as she enjoyed her coffee, she heard the familiar ringtone of her cell phone. She took the phone from her pocket. "I thought that the call had been lost. Then I heard the sound again," she said. "It wasn't my phone at all! It was a mockingbird ringing from high up in a sweet gum tree. That bird had heard my ringtone so often that he memorized it!"

The scientific name for the mockingbird is *Mimus polyglottos*, which comes from the Greek *mimu*, to mimic, and *polyglottos*, for many-tongued. The mockingbird's song is a medley of the calls of other birds. The mockingbird imitates short units of sound, which it repeats several times before moving on to a new song.

Species with repetitive songs, such as the Carolina wren or the cardinal, are easily copied by the mockingbird. A mockingbird usually has 30 to 40 songs in its repertoire. These include other bird songs, insect, amphibian, and even the noise of a squeaky gate or a car alarm.

The mockingbird is not only a good mimic, but it is also a loud, vocal bird. Unmated males often sing through the night, especially when the moon is full. These bachelors are singing to woo any available female.

I enjoy sitting in my backyard at night. It is my favorite time to meditate. Eighteen-wheel petroleum trucks groan by on the four-lane in front of our home. Long freight trains rumble along the tracks in back. Dogs bark in the distance. An occasional siren pierces the night, prompting the dogs to howl. I breathe a prayer for whatever family is involved in the emergency.

When these sounds fade away, I am treated to the symphony of nature. Bullfrogs in the pond and tree frogs in the woods are joined by crickets and cicadas in a chorus. In the spring whippoorwills sing from the meadow near the railroad track. Once, beneath a bright moon, a mockingbird sang for hours from the top of a pecan tree.

The mockingbird is closely identified with the South, where it is a year-round resident. It is the state bird of Arkansas, Florida, Mississippi, Tennessee, and Texas. My grandfather, a Tennessee native, told me it was his favorite bird. From him I learned to identify the mockingbird by the distinctive white chevron markings on the wings and the long tail that constantly moves up and down.

Mockingbirds have an adaptable diet. They eat insects in summer but switch to a menu of berries and seeds in winter. Mockingbird males establish a nesting territory in early February. They tend to be monogamous. Both mates participate in the nest building. The male does most of the work while the female perches nearby to watch for predators. The nest is built 3 to 10 feet above the ground. The mother bird lays and incubates three to five eggs. Once the fledglings hatch, both the male and female feed them.

Mockingbirds aggressively defend their nest. I have seen a pair harass a red-tailed hawk until the encroacher left the territory. They have been known to peck bald spots on the rear end of a cat and inflict a wound on a dog that required stitches from a vet. Mockingbirds will even target humans, as my dear wife can attest. Clare walked through a gate into our backyard. Unbeknownst to her, she was too close to a nest. A mockingbird, diving like a kamikaze, struck her on the shoulder.

2010 marked the fiftieth anniversary of *To Kill a Mockingbird*, the Pulitzer Prize winning novel by Harper Lee. The story's hero, Atticus Finch, gives his children air rifles for Christmas, warning, "It's a sin to kill a mockingbird." A neighbor, Miss Maudie, explains to the children, "Mockingbirds don't do one thing but make music for us to enjoy. They don't eat up people's gardens, don't nest in corncribs, they don't do one thing but sing their hearts out for us."

Many know the song "Listen to the Mocking Bird," written by Alice Hawthorne in 1855. My favorite rendition is an instrumental guitar arrangement by Chet Atkins entitled "Hot Mockingbird." In his recording, Chet makes his Gretsch Country Gentleman sing like the gray and white bird.

Most parents have sung the "Mockingbird Lullaby" to their children. Carly Simon and James Taylor recorded a version that was a popular success in 1974. One of the joys of being a grandfather is singing to our grandchildren. They provide the only audience that will listen to my warbles without complaining. Recently, Clare and I were babysitting for one of our grandchildren. After supper and a bath, a fresh diaper, and clean pajamas, I took the little one upstairs to bed. We followed the usual routine, a sip of milk, a favorite book, a little rocking chair time, and a song. I started the lullaby.

"Hush, little baby, don't say a word.
Papa's going to buy you a mocking bird."

Outside of the bedroom window from the top of a sassafras tree, we heard the sweet music of a mockingbird. We listened together for a few minutes. I put the child to bed. Without a whimper, sleep came, brought on by the mockingbird's song.

Praying Mantis

"...guard with tenderness small things that have no words."
-Margaret Wise Brown, *A Child's Good Night Book*

Stagmomantis carolina

My garden is filled with many small things that have voices of their own. From katydids to crickets, from tree frogs to bullfrogs, the sound of the garden at night is a true symphony. However, also in my garden, there are many small things that have no words.

The blue tailed lizards (*Anolis gorgonae*) that hide in our geraniums and sun on our front porch never make a sound. The plodding box turtle (*Terrapene carolina*) and the slender ringneck snake (*Diadophis punctatus*) have no voice, at least as far as I can tell. There are countless insects that never make a sound. One of the most interesting among them is the preying mantis.

Mantises are an order of insects that have over 2,400 species. These are divided into fifteen families. The largest family, the mantids (*Mantidae*), is distributed worldwide. They have triangular heads, bulging eyes, elongated bodies, and greatly enlarged forelegs for catching and gripping their prey. Their posture, leaning with forelegs folded, has led to the common name "praying mantis." They are mostly ambush predators, camouflaged by their color and shape to resemble a twig. They usually live for about a year. In the autumn, the females lay eggs in hard capsules secured to a tree branch.

Mantises were considered to have supernatural powers by early civilizations, including the Greeks, Egyptians, and Assyrians. They were thought to have godlike qualities. The ancient Greek word "mantis" meant prophet, and one time they were given the name "mantis religiosa" because of their prayer-like posture as seen in the illustration below.

The earliest mantis fossils are about 135 million years old and were found in Siberia. While fossils are rare, some of the more interesting have been found in amber.

Mantises have stereo vision. They locate their prey by sight. Some species are nocturnal and are attracted to artificial light. Night flight is mostly by males who are locating fewer mobile females. They find them by detecting their pheromones. Mantises are predators; they feed upon live prey. Larger mantises will eat their own species as well as small lizards, frogs, birds, and fish. Mantises stalk their prey until it is close enough. Once it's in reach, mantises strike rapidly to grasp the prey in their spiked forelegs.

> The Carolina mantis (*Stagmomantis carolina*) is native to our area. It is considered a helpful insect, the state insect of South Carolina. Carolina mantis egg cases can be purchased from garden supply centers to promote biological control of pest insects. Only those labeled as "Carolina Mantis" should be released. The Chinese mantis is considered invasive in our area.

Ancient Chinese poetry reveres the mantis for its courage and fearlessness. Aldous Huxley made philosophical observations about death while two mantises mated in his 1962 novel *The Island*. The naturalist Gerald Durrell, in his 1956 book *My Family and Other Animals*, humorously reported on a battle between a mantis and a gecko.

The mantis has played a part in the martial arts; Chinese martial arts, in particular, have movements and fighting strategies based on the mantis. In southern African folklore, the mantis was a trickster deity.

Sexual cannibalism is common among most mantises. About one quarter of male-female encounters result in the male being eaten by the female. Think "Last Supper."

Madame Mantis

So trim and delicate
Might I ask one question more
About your sense of etiquette?
Your posture seems so pious
And menacing at once
Do you pray
Or do you prey
Before you eat your lunch?

Dogwoods And Redbuds

"The flowers appear on the earth; The time of singing has come,"
-Song of Solomon 2:12a, NKJV

Cornus florida

In the past, there was a magnificent weeping cherry tree that lived in our garden. In the spring, it would put on a glorious display with its full, vibrant blooms. There also used to be a weeping willow which painted a bright green backdrop for our garden. In early spring, we would be treated to a cheerful display of redbuds and dogwood flowers, showing off their blossoms to celebrate the Easter season. The garden would shout for joy and witness to our Lord's resurrection.

Stepping through our garden gate in early spring, we are greeted with an array of blossoms. Purple crocus, delicate grape hyacinths, nodding golden jonquils, spreading white and pink Lenten roses, and the spikes of pale blue scillia compose a companion carpet beneath the flowering trees. Yellow pollen is beginning to cover my truck and the porch furniture. My eyes are itching and my sinuses are congested. Spring has arrived.

The nonstop procession of blossoming trees in springtime is a wonder to behold. Flowering peach and apple trees across the Upstate promise abundant fruit at roadside stands in the summer months ahead. Some trees, like the sassafras that grows beside our home, have a less conspicuous green flower that adds its own subtle touch of grace to the glory of early spring.

Among the most eagerly awaited blossoms in our yard and throughout the Piedmont are those of the redbuds and the dogwoods. These two trees are closely connected in several ways. The redbuds burst forth into full bloom in March while the dogwoods flower in April. The redbuds are covered with a profusion of purplish pink flowers all along the branches. Heart shaped leaves follow the flowers. Old time herbalists report that the flowers have an agreeable acid taste and can be added to salads or used in the making of pickles. In the good old days, smaller redbud branches were boiled to make a pink dye for homespun yarn.

The dogwood is the most common flowering tree that dapples the woodlands of much of the United States in mid to late spring. It has been described as America's most beloved flowering tree and has been designated the official tree of several states. Pioneers learned from some of the indigenous people of the Americas that dogwood bark could be used to make remedies for various illnesses, including fever and headaches. The roots were boiled to make a scarlet dye.

The redbud and the dogwood have several things in common beyond their herbal use, their usefulness as sources of dye, and their sheer beauty. They are both small understory trees, that is, they grow beneath the canopy of larger woodland trees. Both are suitable as ornamental trees for home gardens and are generally quite hardy. Each tree will reseed readily, redbuds from distinctive seedpods, and dogwoods from bright red berries. More significant perhaps is that the redbud and the dogwood are connected by folklore.

The legend of the dogwood holds that until the time of the crucifixion of Christ, dogwoods grew to reach the size of mighty oaks. So strong and solid was the wood that it was chosen as the timber for the cross of Jesus. To be used for such a cruel death was distressing to the tree. In compassion, the Creator declared that the tree to which Jesus was nailed would never again have to be used as a cross. From that time forth, the dogwood has been slender, bent, and twisted, not as a punishment, but as a blessing. In sympathy to the suffering of Christ, the dogwood bore white blossoms in the shape of a cross, with two long and two short petals. Each petal bears, on its outer edge, the print of a rusty nail. At the center of each flower, red as if stained with blood, is a crown of thorns. The flowers themselves are a reminder to all who believe of the death of Jesus.

Even as the dogwood tree's blooming coincides with Good Friday, so the redbud tree flowers near the Ides of March, the date that lives in infamy as the day of the betrayal of Julius Caesar by Brutus. The redbud tree represents betrayal, not by Brutus, but by Judas Iscariot. People of the southern Appalachian Mountains have long referred to the redbud as the Judas tree.

An ancient woodcut, by the artist Castor Durante, depicts the figure of Judas hanging, as an act of suicide, from one of the branches of a redbud, illustrating the legend of the tree. Again, the tradition was so distressing that, rather than cursing the redbud as a symbol of betrayal, the Creator blessed the tree with heart-shaped leaves that are in full display by Good Friday. It is a reminder for those who believe that the tragedy of these events so long ago is evidence of the loving heart of God.

For me, these flowering trees of spring are evidence enough of the mystery and the majesty of a divine creative hand.

In our garden, there are three trees that stand close to each other. Beneath much taller oaks and walnut trees, these understory trees are sassafras (*Sassafras albidum*), dogwood (*Cornus florida*), and redbud (*Cercis canadensis*). In early spring, the first to bloom is the sassafras followed closely by redbud. Sassafras blooms unfold in a spectacular display of bright green. Redbud blooms create a deep pink purple. The dogwood blossoms are snow white. It is interesting that these trees often bloom during the season of Lent. The story behind each tree reminds me of the Passion of Christ. I don't know a specific story for sassafras, but the root was often used as a medicinal plant for those sick with a cold or chest congestion.

The Garden of Wisdom

"Blessed are those who hunger and thirst for righteousness, for they will be filled."
Matthew 5:6, NIV

Sage

"Cultivate poverty [of spirit] like the garden herb sage."
-Henry David Thoreau

Salvia officinalis

The word sage is defined in several ways. It is wisdom gained through reflection and experience. It is prudence, good judgement, and common sense, as in the phrase "sage advice." Sage is also a synonym for prophet. It's a mature or venerable person distinguished by their wisdom. Among these many definitions, sage is a culinary herb with a multitude of varieties.

In the Middle Ages, it was grown in many monastery gardens. The herb was said to ward off evil spirits, treat snake bites, and increase a woman's fertility. The Romans called it salvia and used it as a diuretic and anesthetic for the skin. The leaves of the plant were used to stop bleeding. Sage is considered an essential herb, along with parsley, rosemary, and thyme, as in the folk song "Scarborough Fair."

In the South, sage is used in the making of pork sausage. It gives the familiar breakfast meat its peppery flavor. In my garden, I enjoy growing several varieties of sage, not because I'm planning to make sausage but because the variations in foliage color add interest to the garden. The purple flowers attract pollinators of all kinds. If you have a hot, dry spot in your garden that you would like to neglect, try planting Mexican sage (*salvia luncantha*) and Mexican sunflowers (*tithonia*) together.

In 1994, I attended a National Order of the Arrow Conference at Purdue University in West Lafayette, Indiana. I was there as a chaplain for about 6,000 Boy Scouts. Three of our sons and two of our nephews participated in indigenous-centered learning activities that week.

At the conclusion of a large intertribal powwow at the end of the week, Abe Conklin, an honored guest at the event and head man of the Ponca tribe, invited me to a ceremony that night. He wanted me to bring my sons and nephews with me. About ten o'clock in the evening, we met Abe under the brush harbor constructed to protect the drum during the powwow. Abe introduced us to the ceremony called a "smudging."

A smudging ceremony is a ritual performed by some indigenous people. It is used to affirm positive traits and to cleanse and heal the human spirit. It is used to bestow a blessing of peace, harmony, and tranquility within a person's life. Abe had a ceramic pot in which he burned cedar shavings, sweet grass, and a bundle of wild sage gathered from the plains. He had an eagle wing fan used to direct the smoke from the burning incense.

Abe stood in front of me saying that he recognized my leadership qualities and my desire to have a spiritual influence on the young people in my family. As he fanned the smoke with the eagle wing, he prayed. His prayer was in the Ponca language. I could not understand any of it, but there was no mistaking the fervent sincerity in his words. He closed the prayer in the name of Jesus. Then, he moved to each of my sons and my nephews and bestowed on them a similar blessing.

Whenever I think of sage, I call to mind that smudging ceremony and I am grateful. Abe died the following year. He's buried at the Gray Horse Cemetery in Osage County, Oklahoma.

Garden sage (*Salvia officinalis*) is also called "common sage." It is a perennial shrub with wooden stems, silver-grey leaves, and blue to purple flowers. It's a native to the Mediterranean, though it has been naturalized in many places around the world. There are many varieties including golden sage, variegated sage, pineapple sage, and dalmatian sage.

Bullfrogs

"Greet one another with a holy kiss."
- Romans 16:16, NIV

The full moon in May is called the "Full Flower Moon" in the *Old Farmer's Almanac*. It is the name used by several indigenous tribes. May's full moon was also called "Mother's Moon," "Milk Moon," and "Corn Planting Moon." In May, the full moon marked a time of increasing fertility, with temperatures usually warm enough for safely bearing young, an end to late frosts, and plants in bloom.

The light of a silvery moon may provide the inspiration for a budding romance, but the full moon in May is the right time for bream fishing in our neck of the woods. After a long siege of health issues, I am now unable to go fishing, but I have an alternative. After a warm spring day followed by a cool evening, I enjoy sitting outside on our screened-in back porch. It is a marvelous time to sit in an old oak rocking chair and listen to the sounds of the night. The concert or the cacophony varies night to night, but there is always something interesting to hear in the darkness.

Chimney swifts put on a nocturnal aerial display, soaring and diving in the fading light, searching for insects. A lone male mockingbird sings a courting song from the top of a sweet gum tree. Tree frogs and crickets join in with their own melodies. Two feral cats confront each other with threats before darting across our lawn. A great horned owl gives a mournful hoot and waits for a response deeper in the woods. A big, fat possum ambles noisily out of the bushes and disappears quickly into the thicket beyond the chain-link fence. Dogs bark in the background. Two bullfrogs chime in with bass notes from our pond. All the activity is a prelude to an approaching thunderstorm. Our yard has been certified as a wildlife habitat. But, when the critters are stirred up, the place rivals the ancient Greek theatre with an ever-changing drama of comedy and tragedy.

A while ago, I heard a program on a local radio station. The talk show featured experts from the South Carolina Department of Natural Resources. Invited to call in questions, listeners kept the telephone lines humming throughout the hour. Most callers were concerned about fishing regulations. They wanted answers about licensing requirements, size and number limits, and information about stocking ponds and streams.

Finally, near the end of the program, a fellow named Ralph was on the line.

"Ralph, where are you calling from?"

"From my pickup truck."

"What's your question?"

"What about frog gigging?"

The Game Warden answered, "The laws of South Carolina are completely silent when it comes to frog gigging."

"You mean there ain't no rules?"

"That's right."

"Hot diggity-dog!"

"You must like to eat frog legs."

"Man, yes! Fried frog legs are the best thing ever with a good vegetable like macaroni and cheese and a cold beer!"

Our garden waterfall spills into a pond lined with creek rocks. The water is recycled back to the top of the hill by a pump, creating a continuous flow. On a visit to our garden, a friend sat by the pond watching the goldfish dart among the plants. "You need a couple of bullfrogs," he observed. I recalled the pleasant sound of bullfrogs from my boyhood fishing and camping adventures and agreed that a couple of bullfrogs would make a fine addition to our small pond. A few days later, a man from our church gave us six big croakers from the abundant population in his own pond. "I wanted to be sure you had at least one male and one female," he chuckled.

After our gift of frogs arrived, I learned several interesting bits of information: bullfrogs can live up to fifteen years, and female bullfrogs can actually lay as many as 20,000 eggs at one time. In a year or so more, I have no doubt that their croaks will be deafening. I have enjoyed hearing their deep, resonant voices singing after dark along with the symphony of tree frogs, crickets, and a persistent whippoorwill. The music conjures up thoughts of bullfrog tales.

In 1865, a budding journalist named Samuel Langhorne Clemens, better known by his pen name Mark Twain, was living in a cabin near Angels Camp, California. He frequented the bar at a local hotel, listening to yarns spun by prospectors from the nearby hills. It was there that he heard a tall tale, which he later crafted into a short story. Twain wrote about a bullfrog named Dan'l Webster, who fails to hop even once during a jumping contest. His dismayed owner, despondent over losing a bet of forty dollars, later discovers an opponent had filled the giant frog with lead quail shot. Twain's legendary amphibian helped make him famous. "The Celebrated Jumping Frog of Calaveras County" has become one of the best-known bullfrog stories.

Perhaps the most famous tale about frogs was written by the Brothers Grimm. "The Frog Prince," which has been told and retold, usually recounts how a princess finds a conversant frog. The frog asks that she kiss him in order to break an evil spell so he can change into the handsome prince he was prior to the curse. Though in the story's original form, the princess does not actually kiss the frog, it is most frequently told so that her kiss transforms the frog into a prince.

This theme has many variations, even one for liberated women. Once upon a time, a beautiful, independent, self-assured princess happened upon a frog in a pond. The frog explained, "I was once a handsome prince until an evil witch put a spell on me. One kiss from you, and I will turn back into a prince. Then we can marry and move into the castle with my parents. You can prepare my meals, clean my clothes, and bear my children. We'll live happily ever after."

That night, while the princess dined on frog legs, she laughed, "I don't think so."

A variation for senior adults places an old man on a log – wearing a tattered long-sleeve shirt, khaki pants, and a straw hat. Fishing with a cane pole from the riverbank was slow. As the late summer sun began to set, a bullfrog hopped up on the log next to the elderly gentleman and asked, "Are you married?"

"No, my wife died five years ago," the man answered, surprised to be speaking with a frog.

After a pause, the frog offered, "I am really a beautiful princess. If you kiss me, I will become a young woman and marry you."

"Did you hear what I said?" the frog asked. "I am really a beautiful woman. If you kiss me, I will become a princess and marry you."

The old gentleman considered the offer. Without a word, he gathered his fishing equipment, put the frog into his straw hat, and walked through the dark woods back to his pickup truck.

"Are you hard of hearing?" the frog demanded.

"No, not at all." Answered the old gentleman.

Annoyed at the man, the frog repeated, "I really am a beautiful princess. Kiss me, and I will become a gorgeous woman. I will marry you."

"I understand," the man answered.

The frustrated frog shrieked again, "I really am a beautiful woman! I'm offering to become your wife. Why won't you kiss me?"

The old man placed the straw hat containing the frog on the seat of his pickup truck and started the engine.

The frog screamed above the noise, "Please kiss me! Please! Don't you understand? I will be transformed into a lovely woman if you kiss me, and I will become your wife!"

The elderly gentleman paused a moment, then explained, "At my age, I can have a whole lot more fun with a talking frog than I can with a second wife."

Jeremiah was a bullfrog
Was a good friend of mine.
I never understood a single word he said
But I helped him drink his wine
     Three Dog Night

All creatures of our God and king
Lift up your voices and with us sing.
O praise Him.
Alleluia, alleluia.
     Saint Francis of Assisi

Trees

"…like a tree planted by streams of water…"
-Psalms 1:3, NIV

Quercus nigra

T he most beautiful wedding I have been a part of was for my nephew, Edward, and his bride, Jennifer, in October at Camp Greenville. Perched high above the Blue Ridge escarpment is Symmes Chapel owned by the YMCA of Greenville County, South Carolina. The views from the open-air chapel are spectacular. Known as Pretty Place, it is a popular site for weddings. While I have performed other weddings at Pretty Place, the one for Edward and Jennifer was special. They had gorgeous floral displays bursting forth everywhere you looked. The arrangements and bouquets were designed to blend with autumn colors. The sky was a clear deep blue, and the mountains were in their full autumn attire. Midway through the ceremony a pair of ravens soared up from the valley below and glided along the face of the mountains before disappearing over a ridge. For that wedding there was striking beauty that money cannot buy.

In the fall, the Blue Ridge Mountains and surrounding foothills are decked out for their annual autumn display. Peak fall colors in our area occur from mid-October through early November. Though the mountains are home to more than one hundred species of trees, the most colorful foliage comes courtesy of sugar maples, scarlet oaks, sweetgums, red maples, and hickory trees.

Those of us who live in the Piedmont are fortunate to enjoy a changing climate. As days shorten and night air becomes crisp, the soothing green canvas of summer foliage is transformed into a breathtaking autumn palette of color. Before settling down into winter's deep sleep, Mother Nature has one last fling, an amazing fashion show, when mountain foliage turns radiant shades of crimson, red, orange, yellow, and purple.

The Cherokee people have a legend that explains why the leaves change color. It is the tale of a mighty bear that roamed the countryside wreaking havoc. The beast would charge into their villages, eat all their food, destroy their homes, stampede their animals, and frighten the women and children.

Tribal elders held a council and selected the bravest hunters to put an end to the bear. The warriors set out with their dogs and weapons to stalk the marauder. The beast fled; the Cherokee gave chase. One hunter came close enough to shoot, and an arrow nicked the bear. The injury was not serious, but the culprit ran so fast he escaped up into the sky. The determined hunters, in their zeal, ran into the heavens in hot pursuit.

Use your imagination, and you can see the bear depicted in the four stars in the bowl of the Big Dipper. The three stars in the handle of the dipper represent the hunters chasing the bear. The stalkers and their prey go around and around in the northern night sky. Every autumn, the Big Dipper comes low to the horizon. It is then, according to the legend, that the bear's wound leaks a few drops of blood. According to the legend, the blood of the bear changes the colors of the leaves on the trees.

Four factors influence autumn leaf color: leaf pigments, length of daylight and darkness, rainfall, and temperatures. The timing of color change is primarily regulated by the increasing length of night hours. As days grow shorter and nights grow longer and cooler, chemical processes in the leaves begin to paint the autumn landscape.

During the growing season, chlorophyll makes leaves appear green. As night length increases in the autumn, chlorophyll production slows down and then stops. The pigments that are present in the leaf are then unmasked and the trees show their fall colors.

The timing of the color change also varies by species of trees. Sourwood and tulip poplars in southern forests can become a vivid yellow in late summer while all other species are still green. Oaks put on their colors long after other species have already shed their leaves.

The brilliance of the colors that develop in any particular autumn season are related to weather conditions that occur before and during the time the chlorophyll in the leaves is dwindling. Temperature and moisture are the main influences.

Mythical Jack Frost supposedly brings reds and purples to the forest by pinching the leaves with his icy fingers. The hues of yellow, gold, and brown are mixed in his paint box and applied with quick broad strokes of his brush as he silently moves among the trees decorating them.

But frost does not bring autumn hues; it actually turns the leaves brown. The most spectacular color displays are brought on by a succession of warm, sunny days and cool, but not freezing, nights. During these days, sugars are produced in the leaf. The cool nights and the gradual closing of veins going into the leaf prevent these sugars from moving out. The combination of sugar and light spurs production of brilliant pigments in the leaves.

The amount of moisture in the soil also affects autumn colors. Like the weather, soil moisture varies greatly from year to year. The countless combinations of these two highly variable factors assure that no two autumns will be exactly alike. A late spring, or a severe summer drought, can delay the onset of fall color. A warm, wet spring, favorable summer weather, and warm, sunny fall days with cool nights produce the most brilliant autumn colors.

The vivid change of color starts in late September in New England and moves southward, reaching the Blue Ridge Mountains by early November. The trees in cooler, higher elevations will change color before their relatives in the valleys.

A couple in the church I once served said, "We're skipping your sermon today. We are driving to the mountains to see the color."

You know, I really couldn't blame them. Clare and I enjoy cruising Highway 11 in any season, but especially in the fall of the year.

George Schrieffer, a minister friend, came up with a short rhyme for the fall season. He was concerned that folks would be tempted to skip church on Sunday to drive to the mountains to see the display. George's lines of poetry are dear to any pastor's heart.

"The leaves reach their peak
In the middle of the week!"

Fire

"For our God is a consuming fire."
-Hebrews 12:29, NIV

One of the garden features that I enjoy most is my chiminea. I bought it at the garden center in Commerce, Georgia. It is made of cast-iron. The original legs broke off, so I fitted the rounded bottom into an old wheel rim propped up on concrete blocks and spray-painted it flat black. It's the perfect size to build a small fire on a chilly night. For firewood, I use the dead limbs that have fallen off our many oak trees. Whenever I am there, seated in a rocking chair wearing a floppy felt hat before the fire on a cool night, Stormy the garden cat almost always hops up on my lap to enjoy the fire with me. There is something that is both mesmerizing and contemplative about staring into the flames of a small fire.

Some gardeners I know have a much larger fire pit in their yard. Others have elaborate grills with accommodating cooking surfaces. While I have roasted a few hot-dogs and toasted a few marshmallows in the chiminea, it is mostly for warmth and the tranquil effect it has on my soul. A fire that is contained can be quite pleasant. A fire that is not contained can be terrifying.

Years ago, I cleared a place for a vegetable garden at the back of this one acre of red clay. The plot was near the Southern Railway Track where it received full sun throughout the day. It was the most productive garden spot I ever had. Down one side of the plot, I had a strawberry bed planted with Ozark Beauties. Behind that was a bed of Mary Washington asparagus. On each end of the strawberry bed, I had a large rhubarb plant. These are plants that take a while to become established and then produce well year after year.

The remainder of the plot was divided into four quadrants with raised beds. I incorporated vertical gardening which allowed for sugar snap peas, Blue Lake green beans, and vining cucumbers. I planted crook-neck squash, patty pan squash, and zucchini squash. I even had a place for Silver Queen corn, russet potatoes, and several varieties of tomatoes. In the center of the garden, I had a pyramidal shaped structure planted with thirty-six varieties of herbs. It was a beautiful garden spot. Weed control was simplified by the raised beds and by gravel paths between the beds. Towering above the garden was a rack of plastic gourds designed to attract purple Martins.

One summer day, a neighbor decided to burn trash in an open field about a hundred yards from my garden. The fire was left unattended. A summer breeze carried the flames through dry grass. Before I realized what happened, my garden was in flames. The raised beds provided the necessary fuel. The strawberries, the rhubarb, the asparagus were all scorched to the ground. When the pyramid went up in flames, so did all the herbs. The flames were so high they melted the Martin's plastic gourds hanging twenty feet in the air.

Fire in the garden is a desirable feature unless it is out of control.

A house is not a home unless it contains food and fire for the mind as well as the body.
                                              Benjamin Franklin

The value of biodiversity is that it makes our ecosystems more resilient, which is a prerequisite for stable societies; its wanton destruction is akin to setting fire to our lifeboat.
                                              Johan Rockstrom

Heirloom Plants

"...surely I have a delightful inheritance."
-Psalms 16:6

One Saturday, I stopped by Bellew's Market to pick up some fresh fruits and vegetables. I was delighted to find the last fresh Spartanburg County strawberries of the season. I also found blackberries and red haven peaches. Clare and I enjoy sweet corn, and silver queen sweet was available. While picking out several good vine-ripe tomatoes, I noticed a display marked "heirloom tomatoes."

On the way home I wondered, *"What's all this fuss about antique vegetables?"*

Heirloom plants have become increasingly popular among home gardeners. Usually they are defined by their age. Some varieties are hundreds of years old, while others originated around the turn of the 20th century. Purists contend that in order to be an heirloom, the plant had to originate before the early 1950s when hybridization came into vogue.

Why the interest in planting older selections? Cultivating plants grown by previous generations offers greater variety. The Seed Savers Exchange, which deals solely in legacy plants, has seventy-seven kinds of tomatoes in their catalog.

Hybridizers have chosen to focus on properties like disease resistance and heavy yields rather than flavor. Fans of heirloom plants argue that the best tasting vegetables are those like your grandparents grew.

Growing heirlooms is a frugal way to have a bountiful garden. Each season, after sowing the seed, tending the crop, and harvesting the food, you can save some seeds for the next year's garden.

Two days after visiting Bellew's, I walked through my garden, paying special attention to the legacy plants.

As I walked in our garden, enjoying the morning air, I noticed a large outcropping of deep green shiny leaves. It was an unwelcomed heirloom: poison ivy!

Dragonflies

"He made their tiny wings"
-All Things Bright and Beautiful

Anax junius

I enjoy the writings of Will Campbell. He has authored numerous books. Two are favorites of mine, both are autobiographical. *Forty Acres and a Goat* was published in 1986. *Brother to a Dragonfly*, his best-known work, was a finalist for the National Book Award in 1978. In his book, *Brother to a Dragonfly*, he talks about an experiment his brother Joe conducted with a dragonfly. The two Mississippi farm boys followed a path across a field through the woods down to the river. Three days earlier, Joe had buried a dragonfly in an aspirin box.
In the soft mud Joe dug up the box. When he opened it, the dragonfly flew out.

Joe turned to Will and said, "He's just like Jesus. He was buried in the ground for three days. He's still alive."

Like the butterfly, the dragonfly is considered a symbol of immortality. The life cycle of the dragonfly leads to this assumption. Dragonflies mate in mid-air - quite a feat! Eggs are deposited in the water. Eventually a larva crawls out of the water and attaches to a reed. Its skin becomes hardened, creating a cocoon.

Then a transformation takes place. Before long, the chrysalis splits. A brand-new body emerges from the dead shell. The gauze-like wings unfold, and a colorful and sleek dragonfly takes to the air.

No wonder the dragonfly has become a sign of new life!

A few years ago, I conducted a graveside funeral service. The widow of the deceased wore on her black dress a silver pin crafted in the likeness of a dragonfly.

"My husband gave this to me. It is a symbol of hope."

This small insect is one of nature's most fascinating creatures. To any observer the dragonfly is an aviation marvel. The Boeing Corporation in Seattle, Washington, has filmed dragonflies in flight. After taking a close look at this small insect, engineers were amazed at their aerodynamics. They concluded that the dragonfly is a highly perfected flying machine.

Some dragonflies fly at speeds up to sixty miles an hour. The average cruising speed for a dragonfly is about ten miles an hour. They can fly backwards. They can dart from side to side. They can stop in mid-flight and hover.

The secret is the two pairs of wings that work independently of each other. The front two wings simply churn the air, creating disturbance. The back two wings provide the stability.

Researchers say that the dragonfly creates turbulence, whereas aircraft try to avoid it. Engineers acknowledge that it is impossible to approximate this mechanically. Their conclusion is that the flying ability of the dragonfly is superior to anything the Boeing Corporation can manufacture.

I saw a pair of blue dragonflies stalking prey above the pond in my garden. The predatory insects are always welcome guests in our yard. In half an hour's time, they can consume their own weight in mosquitoes.

Dragonflies have also been called horse stingers. People thought that they were doing the stinging. In fact, they were pursuing horseflies, the real pests. Sometimes they have been called mosquito hawks; a name that really fits because of their preference for the little bloodsuckers. It is the combination of their aerobatic maneuvers in flight combined with their voracious appetite that led to international acclaim.

The entire island of Japan was at one time called the Island of the Dragonfly. Legend has it that a pesky horsefly bit a Japanese emperor. No sooner had he been bitten than a dragonfly ate the horsefly. The emperor saw that a friend, the dragonfly, had attacked the one who accosted him. From that day forward, he decreed that the whole island of Japan be called the Island of the Dragonfly. Samurai warriors adopted the insect as their symbol. The dragonfly was such a ferocious fighter that they etched the symbol on the front of their leather helmets.

On the North American continent, the Lakota people of the northern Great Plains considered the dragonfly to be a fierce hunter. A dragonfly motif is common in indigenous peoples' beadwork. The Navajo people of the desert southwest regarded the presence of a dragonfly as an indication of pure water, something very important to people who live in arid conditions. They often incorporated the image of the dragonfly into their sand paintings.

There are six thousand varieties of dragonflies, each one unique. Sometimes they are called snake doctors and darners. People in Old England believed that falling asleep during the daytime was dangerous. They thought this insect with a body like a darning needle would sew your eyes shut as the penalty for laziness. It's enough to scare you out of an afternoon nap!

As a boy, I was fishing with my grandfather. I had not had even a nibble on my fishing line. Dragonflies were darting all around. One hovered close to me, and I was afraid. The thing looked like it had a killer stinger on its tail. Then, it disappeared from my sight.

My grandfather could still see it. "He is on the brim of your hat. Hold really still."

I did just as Pappy instructed. In a few minutes, the insect flew away.

"Don't worry. They don't sting," Pappy said, "Now, you'll catch fish."

Within just a short time, I had a bass on the bank. Before the afternoon was over, I had also caught several bream.

Appalachian folklore says that if dragonflies are about when you are fishing and one does not stop close by, you might as well pack up and go home. You are not going to catch any fish. But, if a dragonfly lights nearby while you are fishing, you are going to have good luck.

On that day, it was the truth.

A Garden Philosopher

"...a man of understanding walks uprightly."
-Proverbs 15:21b, NKJV

When Clare and I returned to Spartanburg in 1980, we moved into the home that my grandmother and grandfather built after The Great Depression in 1937. Soon afterwards, I met the man who would become my personal philosopher.

David lived on the King Line behind the old stockyard, located not far from our home. Though crippled with arthritis, he would walk from his home past our house on his way to the lumberyard. There he purchased his daily Coca-Cola.

David could barely walk. His feet were so gnarled that they hurt constantly. His gait was more like a shuffle.

In those days, in order to get to the lumberyard, he had to pass a mini-mart. I asked him why he didn't just go there to buy the Coke. He said, "At the mini-mart, it costs thirty-five cents. At the lumberyard, it costs a quarter. No need wasting money."
Though every step was painful, David walked twice as far just to save a dime.

Often David would stop at my house, sit in a rocking chair on my front porch to enjoy his Coca-Cola, and then shuffle on to his home. Many mornings I would take my mug of coffee and join David on the porch. Those were the times when I received my philosophy lesson.

In his starched and pressed khaki pants, David was always as neat as a pin. One February morning, his knees were covered with mud.

I asked, "David, what in the world have you been doing this early in the morning?"

"Yesterday, I put in my English peas."

David grew some of the best vegetables in some of the reddest clay in Spartanburg County. He planted according to the astrological signs.

"David, why are your pants so muddy?"

"Got up early. Dug up all the seeds."

"Why?"

"My daughter was readin' the Old Almanac. She told me I put in my peas on the wrong sign. So, I dug'em all up this morning before daylight."

"Did you find 'em all?"

"Found all but four."

He pulled a paper bag from his pocket with the seeds. He had planted three rows of English peas the day before.

"When's the right time to plant English peas?"

"Tomorrow."

"Will one day make a difference?"

"Yes sir. My daddy always planted by the signs, and he always made a crop. I do the same."

David was quite a gardener. David and I were standing in my garden late one summer day. My wife brought each of us a cup of ice water. At the time, Clare was pregnant with our daughter Betsy. As Clare walked toward the garden, obviously an expectant mother, David said to me, "Don't you let her come in this garden!"

"Why, David?"

"You let a woman with child come in the garden, and every watermelon and cantaloupe will bust wide open."

Clare had no intention of coming into the garden. She handed our ice water over the fence.

David always kept a saltshaker with him in the summertime. Occasionally, he removed his old stained hat and sprinkled a little salt in his hair. He said the application of salt kept him from passing out.

I do not know whether that works or not. David never passed out, and I saw him sprinkle a good bit of salt in his hair.

David was quite a churchman. He loved going to church. He especially enjoyed singing in the choir. On Monday mornings, he would give me a report from the Sunday services.

One Monday, we were having our early morning porch visit.

"Church was extra good yesterday."

"What was good about it?"

"We had good singing." David always bragged on the choir.

"How was the preaching?"

"Preaching was good."

"What'd the pastor preach about?"

"Well, he preached about sin."

"What did he have to say about sin?"

"He's agin' it!"

"What kind of sin did he talk about, David?"

"He talked about gambling. He talked about drinking. He talked about smoking."

"David, did he say that smoking is a sin?"

"Yes sir."

David dipped snuff. He almost always had tobacco tucked in his lower lip.

"David, did the preacher say anything about dipping snuff."

"No sir. He didn't say a thing about dipping."

"David, is it a sin to dip snuff?"

"No sir."

"It's a sin to smoke, but not a sin to dip snuff?"

"That's right."

"Why's that? How can smoking be a sin, but dipping snuff is not a sin?"

He said, "It's a sin to burn up anything that tastes that good!"

David's church built a new sanctuary. He invited me to come to the dedication. My dad and I went together to the Sunday afternoon service, all three hours of it.

David sang in the choir. Several preachers held forth. The building was thoroughly dedicated.

After the service, David showed us around the church he took so much pride in. He explained that the church didn't have stained glass windows. I will never forget the way that he expressed it.

"We don't have none of them windows with people on 'em that the light shines through."

What a phrase! "People that the light shines through."

When you know people like David, you don't need stained glass windows. David was the kind of person that the light shined through.

Hawks And Owls

"...the mountain birds of prey..."
-Isaiah 18:6, NIV

Buteo jamaicensis

R ecently, our granddaughter brought me a gift.

"PK! Look at what I found!" She exclaimed.

She handed me a small plastic bag. Inside, I could clearly see the tiny bones of a small bird. Along with the bones was a long slender mouse tail.

"Why don't you tell me about this?" I asked her.

"My teacher found an owl pellet! She said I could have it and cut it open and show the class what was inside!" she intoned excitedly.

"Well, you've learned something about what owls eat." I replied.

"Yes," she said, and added thoughtfully "And owls are good birds to have around."

My good friend, the late and very great Rudy Mancke, was the South Carolina State Naturalist. Rudy reported that as a teenager he used to venture to Greenlawn Memorial Garden. There, underneath the cover of the trees, he often found owl pellets. Rudy did as my granddaughter had, he cut them open to investigate what the owls had been eating. Naturalists have a knack for examining the waste of animals. Owl pellets are actually undigested and regurgitated small food pouches; think of them as owl vomit. Rudy can identify most animals by only their scat or, in the case of owls, by their vomit. I suppose my granddaughter is on the right track if she intends to be a naturalist.

On pleasant spring evenings, I often enjoy sitting in my yard after dark. I pay attention to the phases of the moon, the constellations in the stars, and the sounds of the season. It is a time when my mind can catch up with my body, an opportunity for my soul to be restored. On a recent night, a slight breeze gently moved the trees. A bullfrog croaked from the pond, crickets chirped from the flowerbeds, and a mockingbird sang his repertoire from high in the weeping willow tree. I was enveloped in solitude and deep in contemplation.

Suddenly, a massive bird swooped across my yard. I was startled by the dark form with broad wings. Its silent flight was so quick and the night so dark that I could not identify the creature. It was gone within seconds. The bird had launched from an oak tree in pursuit of something scurrying through a field behind my greenhouse. Though I could not identify the flying predator by sight, I suspected it might be an owl.

Two nights later, my suspicions were confirmed. I saw a great horned owl perched in the same oak tree. He is a welcome guest in our backyard. Great horned owls eat a variety of mammals. Rodents are like a blue plate special to them. Rats, mice, squirrels, chipmunks, and rabbits are all available in the open field behind our house.

I have often seen red-tailed hawks in our neck of the woods. Song birds fall silent when a hawk is around. Several years ago, I saw a red-tailed hawk nosedive out of a dead wild cherry tree into the field behind our house. The efficient hunter snagged a four-foot black snake in his talons and carried the wriggling reptile across the railroad tracks to another perch in a tall tulip poplar tree.

Birds of prey are important to the ecosystem. Raptor is a Latin word that means to carry away. This is precisely what birds of prey do. They order takeout every time. They always get their meals to go, whisking away their victim.

This group of aerial warriors is made up, not only of hawks and owls, but also of eagles and osprey. When I was a boy, these birds were scarce. The use of heavy-duty pesticides had decimated their populations. Thankfully, they have made a remarkable comeback. Raptors perform essential tasks of pest control in our world. They help maintain a vital balance in nature.

These birds are commonly used as symbols for athletic teams. Both Temple and Rice Universities have adopted the Owl. The University of North Florida alumni are proud Ospreys. Teams known as Hawks and Eagles prevail, dominating the world of mascot names. Individual birds in all of these raptor families call South Carolina home. I have seen osprey fishing in the Atlantic Ocean just off Pawley's Island and in a farm pond in Whitestone in Spartanburg County. I have seen bald eagles perched in pine trees on North Island along Winyah Bay near Georgetown. I have seen the national bird flying high above Lake Jocassee.

I look forward to seeing my night visitor again. It's good to know that a great horned owl is on duty. It makes for an effective Neighborhood Watch program.

I learned from my grandfather that owls and hawks are often paired, not as mates, but in sharing hunting areas. Such a relationship exists between the barred owl and its counterpart, the red-shouldered hawk. Both birds occupy the same range in the eastern United States, prefer moist woodland habitats, and eat similar diets. At different times, I have spotted both of these birds hunting the deep woods near Fairforest Creek in Camp Croft State Park, South Carolina. The barred owl pulls the night shift. The red-shouldered hawk works days.

Likewise, the red-tailed hawk and great horned owl frequently share the same area since the hawk hunts by day and the owl by night. Sometimes an owl will even occupy a hawk's abandoned nest as her own. So those two birds frequent my backyard. The red-tailed hawk is active in daylight. The great horned owl is, well, a night owl.

The second night that I saw the great horned owl I heard the familiar call, "who ho-hooo, hooo." Rumor has it that male great horned owls respond to human imitation of their hoot. I tried to have a conversation with my new neighbor. I got no response. Maybe she was a female.

I heard about a fellow who had a similar experience. He said the females did not respond to him either, but the males did. He said he tried it out at a place called Hooters.

I guess he was talking about owls.

The Garden of Peace

"Blessed are the peacemakers, for they will be called children of God."
Matthew 5:9, NIV

Garden Art

"For you have created my inmost being…"
-Psalms 139:13, NIV

A nyone who has visited a large botanical garden will understand the importance of garden art. Here in South Carolina, Brookgreen Gardens near Murrells Inlet, on Highway 17, is a 9,100-acre property. This elaborate garden includes a low country zoo, walking trails though several different ecosystems, and multiple theme gardens with American figurative art sculptures placed in them. If you're ever in low country South Carolina, I recommend spending a day in Brookgreen Gardens.

In my own garden, which is one acre of red clay, I too have incorporated art; we call it "yard art." Along the fence on one side of our property, I have three large mosaic panels. They have a concrete base with patterns of inlaid stained glass. These panels were originally windows in the sanctuary of First Presbyterian Church of Greenville, North Carolina. The windows were all changed to more traditional stained glass while my brother was pastor at the church. I donated to the church in return for these three panels and brought them to Spartanburg on the back of my pickup truck.

In that same area of the garden, a place that my grandchildren call "The Secret Garden" is a red ladder nailed to an oak tree, so the feet do not touch the ground. Our son Kris who paints guardian angels on found objects found the ladder in a dorm room at Wofford College abandoned by a student who had graduated. Kris painted it red and painted angels ascending and descending. He calls it "Jacob's Ladder."

In the shack in our garden, we have one old window sash. The panes were spray-painted with silver metallic paint, making it look like a mirror. On each pane, I painted colorful elephants. Hanging on the back wall of the shack are three old, wooden-framed window screens. I replaced the screen wire and then painted birds with acrylic paint.

Throughout our garden, we have other art forms; for example, there's a small section a brick wall that I recovered from the rubble of my old elementary school when it was demolished. It was the school where my dad and all eight of his brothers and sisters attended, where all seven of my brothers and sisters and I attended, and where our five children attended school. This section of brick wall serves as a retaining structure; above it is a low-growing purple catnip plant and a very tall, big, red, old-fashioned hollyhock. Other art within our garden includes wind screws, whirly-gigs, a windmill, numerous guardian angels, and several crosses. We even had a birdhouse built like a church, steeple and all. One feature of our garden is a gazing ball that reflects the moon and stars at night.

I have a collection of antique tools mounted on the wall of our barn, my grandfather's old cow barn. Several years ago, I accumulated four old wheelbarrows. I drilled drainage holes in the bottom of each one, filled them with planting soil, and used them as container gardens. I have done the same with two old iron pots, an old oak water barrel, and a galvanized tub.

If all of this seems somewhat tacky, so be it. It's my garden and all of these things add interest for me.

As I mentioned earlier, one of the features of our garden is a two-story play structure. I designed it and supervised the building in 1980 after we first moved into the old homeplace. At the time, we had four little boys. The play structure features a zip line, a fireman's pole, a sliding board, and monkey bars. Through the years, it has served as a hideout, a fort, a pirate ship, and whatever the imagination of children could make it. Is the play structure garden art? I can assure you, when we have entertained a church youth group, boy scout troop, and now our own grandchildren, there's no better piece of art in our garden than that play structure. The happy sound of children creates music that is truly art.

Let us not forget that the cultivation of the earth is the most important labor of humans. When tillage begins, other arts will follow. The farmers, therefore, are the founders of civilization.

Daniel Webster

Waterfalls

"Deep calls to deep at the roar of Your waterfalls..."
-Psalm 42:7, NKJV

Our son, Scott, and grandson, Ben, recently hiked the Foothills Trail. The secluded path stretches 77 miles between Table Rock and Oconee State Park in the northwest corner of South Carolina. The path winds through the wilderness area known as Jocassee Gorge. The trail follows the Blue Ridge escarpment called "The Blue Wall" by the Cherokee people. The Foothills Trail crosses several small creeks and larger rivers until it reaches the Chattooga River, which defines the boundary between South Carolina and Georgia. There are many waterfalls, small and large, all along the way. Whitewater Falls is the highest waterfall east of the Rocky Mountains; the drop is 811 feet. As our son and grandson approached the Whitewater River, they could hear the falls some distance away. When our grandson saw it for the first time, he shouted above the roar, "Look dad, can you believe that?!"

As I indicated earlier, the garden should appeal to all the senses: sight, sound, taste, touch, and smell. In our garden, all the senses are in play. To sample a fresh strawberry, or a cherry tomato plucked from the vine, is a tasty treat. To see five or six butterflies of various sorts clustered on a lantana is a sight to behold. To feel the texture of lamb's ear or a magnolia leaf, to feel raindrops or a cool breeze on our skin... these are all part of the garden experience.

Sometimes, I like to just close my eyes and listen to the sounds of the garden. Of course, I hear the train and the traffic; I hear the air handler kick on and off. Early in the morning, I can hear the sound of a rooster or a peacock; at night, I sometimes hear dogs barking or people talking. But beyond these extraneous sounds is the sound of an autumn wind rustling through foliage, a mother wren guarding her nest, blue-jays complaining about squirrels taking their pecans, or the buzzing of bees doing the necessary work of pollination. At night, there is a veritable chorus of crickets and cicadas, tree frogs and bullfrogs. Among my favorite sounds is that of falling water.

I made a serious attempt when we first came to live on this one acre of red clay. To one side of our house, there is a steep bank going into the side yard. I thought it would be the perfect place for a waterfall. I worked and worked all one summer digging a pond, installing a pump, placing rocks, trying to create what I hoped would be an approximation of a small mountain stream. There were many problems with both my homemade design and my amateur engineering. After several failed attempts, I hired a professional to do the work for me. He did a great job. We now enjoy a small pond, sometimes stocked with goldfish, often inhabited by bullfrogs. Recycled water flows down the hill over strategically placed rocks to create the gentle sound of a mountain stream. Plantings on both sides add to the natural look.

By far, the most soothing sound of falling water is not the product of human endeavor. It is the sound of rain provided by the creator to nourish the earth. It is one more reminder that it is hard to improve on the plan of God.

When we first had our water feature installed, I bought twenty young goldfish. As I recall, I paid a quarter apiece for them. I took all the precautions to be sure the pond water was dechlorinated and the right temperature before I introduced the goldfish. Goldfish are actually carp. They will eat algae, which is a good thing. I also stocked the little pond with small mosquito fish; they thrive on mosquito larvae. The pond was an absolute delight.

Early one morning I looked out of our upstairs window, and much to my surprise I saw a great blue heron standing at the edge of the pond having his breakfast. I called Clare and said, "We've got a visitor!" Clare said, "You've got to get rid of him; he'll eat all the fish!"

"I can buy more goldfish. I don't know where I would ever find a great blue heron to visit our pond."

Once again, some of the best things that happen in the garden are those that are unplanned by me. They come in small tender mercies and give some grace.

Rocking Chairs and Porch Swings

"Now when Jesus saw the crowds, He went up on a mountainside and sat down."
-Matthew 5:1, NIV

Early one morning, Clare and I took a few moments to enjoy a cup of coffee on our back porch. Sitting there, we were treated to an outdoor concert. In the fresh air and sunlight of a spring day, songs of birds filled the air. In a firethorn pyracantha at the corner of the house, a mockingbird sang a medley of at least fifteen different songs, all borrowed from her feathered friends.

A nuthatch made frequent trips to a suet feeder on the other side of the porch, busily feeding her young in her nest, hidden in an oak tree.

A black-capped chickadee darted back and forth between the seed feeder and a bluebird house she has rented for the season, a place to rear her brood.

A Carolina wren perched on a blooming rose, singing her clear song, and tending her nest deep inside a star jasmine vine.

Our backyard is a bird sanctuary. It is home to an amazing variety of songbirds. Cardinals and blue jays are regular visitors. Mourning doves flutter and coo. Tiny ruby-throated hummingbirds make occasional forays to the nectar feeders. A pair of eastern bluebirds has made a home in one of the cedar nesting boxes.

As I mentioned in the "Tree of Life" chapter earlier in this book, Stud was a tobacco farmer in the mountains of Kentucky. His beagle, Luther, was constantly by his side. Stud had a backyard that featured an old Ford pickup truck propped on concrete blocks. A bare dirt path meandered to his dilapidated barn. Along the way, a small vegetable garden flourished in the sunshine. Two dozen or so free-range chickens and a covey of Guinea hens skittered to and fro. Under a white pine tree that was oozing sap were two oak nail kegs, turned upside down, intended for sitting.

"When things become too burdensome," he explained, "I just sit here in the shade. I call this white pine the tree of life."

It was in that shady spot that Stud rested after he had worked his garden or stripped tobacco. There he swapped stories with his neighbors. A mason jar of cool well water and a place in the shade beneath the tree of life became, for Stud, a restorative.

As he put it, "This is where my tired body and my weary soul catch up with each other."

Every backyard, rustic or refined, needs a place to perch. Is anything more comforting than a cup of steaming coffee, savored as you sit in a rocking chair on the back porch? Is anything more refreshing than iced tea, sipped from a frosty tumbler, as you rest in a favorite chair on the patio?

Our yard features a Charleston bench tucked away in a secluded corner of the garden. A double swing provides a place where sweethearts of any age can enjoy the transition from sunset to moonlight.

Gathering on the porch or in the yard is a Southern tradition. We have several areas for sitting; within a grove of oak trees, beneath an arbor, or on our screened porch. Before the advent of air conditioning and television, sitting outside was relief from the accumulated stress and heat of the day.

Many yards and porches featured clusters of chairs, homemade or store-bought, arranged as an outdoor room. In pleasant weather, the outdoor room was always open and could accommodate extra guests.

Sunday was a day of rest. Sunday afternoon was a time for visiting family and friends. Visitors were welcomed with a greeting, "Sit down and stay awhile!"

Outdoor hospitality, Southern style, should include a few amenities. My resident hostess, Clare, keeps a basket positioned near our outdoor living area. The basket is stocked with insect repellent and a citronella candle. A bottle of homemade bubble mixture is available for visiting children. Several fans, the non-electric kind, some fashioned from palmetto fronds and some obtained from funeral parlors, are within easy reach. Of course, Clare offers our guests something cold to drink.

Hospitality is not the only function of a backyard sitting area. In a gentle rain, a shed with a tin roof becomes a musical instrument. It also provides shelter for an artist to set up an easel or sit down with a sketchpad. A writer finds there an old table and ladder-back chair; a place to work on a laptop, crafting words in peace and quiet. A poet kicks back in a hammock until the muse visits and thoughts become verse scribbled in a journal. The artist, the writer, and the poet are not the only ones who need privacy. All of us need some solitude.

The backyard can become a sanctuary, not only for the birds, but also for the weary in body, mind, and spirit. Most of us need some time alone, to meditate, to pray, or to ponder. Sitting outside may give us a ringside seat to a sunrise or a sunset. We may be treated to a concert of singing birds or to the graceful ballet of hummingbirds and butterflies.

This is not a waste of time. Far from it! It is more valuable than many of the other things we might choose to do.

Our yard is a sanctuary indeed.

Maybe Stud put it best, "This is where my tired body and my weary soul catch up with each other." Wherever that spot is for you, you will surely find your own "place of quiet rest near to the Heart of God."

Setting alone in an old rocking chair
I saw an old mother with silvery hair.
She seemed so neglected by those who still care
Rocking alone in an old rocking chair.

Her hands were all callused wrinkled and old
A life of hard work was the story they told.
And I thought of angels as I saw her there
Rocking alone in an old rocking chair.

Bless her old heart do you think she'd complain?
Life has been bitter tho' she'd live it again,
And carry the cross that is more than her share
Rocking alone in an old rocking chair.

It wouldn't take much to gladden her heart
Just some small remembrance on somebody's part.
A letter would brighten her empty life there
Rocking alone in an old rocking chair.
                                    Traditional Bluegrass

Violas

"Each little flower that opens"
-For the Beauty of the Earth

Viola cornuta

What is a viola? There are two definitions. Musically speaking, a viola is a stringed instrument slightly larger than a violin that is bowed or plucked. Since the 18th century, it has been the alto voice of the violin family, between the violin and the cello. Botanically speaking, a viola (*Viola cornuta*) is a flowering plant that is a member of the violet family.

My mother told a story about a time when I was two years old. She had picked pansies of various colors and floated them in a bowl of water as a simple centerpiece on our table. While she was cooking a meal, I climbed up in a chair and saw the delightful bowl of pansies. I did only what was normal; I ate most of them.

Mama was horrified. She called Dr. Lesesne Smith, our wonderful family doctor. His only suggestion was that, next time, my mother might provide some salad dressing. Years later, when I served a church in Winston-Salem, North Carolina, one of our members, Jean Kirk, made the most delicious lemon soufflé; and she always decorated the special dessert with candied, purple wild violets. Even at age two, I was on the right track in finding something good to eat.

While Clare and I often identify red geraniums as our signature plant, violas and pansies are our go-to plants for the winter months. I usually plant them by Halloween. By December, they are absolutely prancing. They offer color and fragrance through the winter, blooming even in the snow. By the middle of April, they begin to grow leggy and disheveled. That is when I replace them, usually with a mixture of bronze-leafed begonias and petunias. Those two plants thrive in the hot summer months, the way pansies and violas thrive in the cold.

In our neck of the woods, violas and pansies are usually treated as annuals. They are perfect for fall, winter, and spring bloom. Most violas thrive in sun or partial shade; the smaller ones are tougher than pansies, tolerating heat and cold much better. Both violas and pansies do well as bedding plants, but they really sparkle in containers, like flower boxes, hanging baskets, or flower pots. Though pansies' bright faces offer a cheery display, I am more partial to the smaller violas. They have a wonderful fragrance and last much longer in warmer weather here in South Carolina.

Shade

"...the Lord is your shade at your right hand;"
-Psalm 121:5b, NIV

O ne day, when I was in the seventh grade, I came into the lumberyard warehouse after working all morning to unload a boxcar full of bagged cement. I was tired and soaked with sweat. I stopped in front of a huge exhaust fan, spread out my arms, and stood, letting the moving air cool me off. My pappy walked in behind me, puffing on a cigar, and as he passed me on his way to the door, said, "You know Kirk, if you get enough education, you'll be able to work in the shade." I have never forgotten his advice.

Oystein Sveumn Moen raised an interesting point:

> With my English friends, I constantly wind up in the discussion of whether something is in the "shade" or the "shadow." Is that a clear definition of the difference between these two? Where I come from (Norway) we have a single word covering all forms of light blocking darkness."

Both shade and shadow come from the same Old English word "sceadu," meaning shade, shadow, or darkness. The general definitions given for both words are almost identical in the Oxford English dictionary. The shade is what we seek on a hot, sunny day. Plants that thrive in the shade, like hosta, astilbe, and coleus are grown for their beautiful foliage. While shade usually has a pleasant and soothing association, shadow is evocative of something mysterious or threatening. Shadow usually refers to a shape cast by an object blocking the sun.

"The Shadow Side" is a term used by Carl Jung for the aspects of human personality formed by fears and unhappy experiences. He picked this name as a reference to the concept of dark shadows and what can be concealed within them.

"The Shadow" was a radio program broadcast from the mid-1930s until 1954. Narrated by Orson Wells, the program was about Lamont Cranston, a wealthy man who used hypnotic powers to fight crime as an invisible avenger known only as The Shadow. The opening line of every program was, "Who knows what evil lurks in the hearts of men? The Shadow knows."

In the garden, both shade and shadows are important. In *Modern English Usage*, H.W. Fowler concludes that shade is to shadow what pool is to water. Shade is a general blocking of the sun. Trees, clouds, buildings can all block the sun, rendering shade, but shadow implies a shape, as when a child tries to catch his or her own shadow.

A fun thing to do with children is to hang a sheet in the garden against a barn wall or suspended on a rope between two trees, then fix a light source so that children and adults can make shadow puppets with their hands. It is a creative use of shadow, and not at all frightening.

A person has made at least a start on discovering the meaning of human life when he plants shade trees under which he knows full well he will never sit.
Elton Trueblood

Someone is sitting in the shade today because someone planted a tree a long time ago.
Warren Buffett

Mourning Doves

"...the cooing of doves is heard in our land."
-Song of Solomon 2:12b, NIV

Zenaida macroura

Found in a huge portion of North America, Doves are often hunted for sport and for food. Doves are notoriously slow in flight, making them easy targets for bird hunters. Doves are monogamous. Mating partners are together for a lifetime; they are good parents, rearing their offspring with devotion and protecting them.

Mourning Doves get their name because of their melancholy sound. It is the same as the sound of grief and misery, following the loss of a loved one. Though the sound is sorrowful, the bird itself is a symbol of peace and hope.

A dove was the bird that descended upon Jesus, when he emerged from the waters of baptism. Therefore, it has become a symbol of the Holy Spirit.

In the story of Noah's ark, a dove released by Noah returned with a sprig from a tree, conveying hope following the flood. That sprig was one of hope and reassurance.

While the name "Hawk" has been used to describe people who are aggressive and even war-like, the name "Dove" is applied to people who are peaceable and honorable.

Doves can be trained and domesticated. The ancient Egyptians identified them with innocence. The Chinese felt that doves symbolize long life as well as peace. For Greeks and Romans, the dove symbolized devotion and care for family. According to legend, Aphrodite, or Venus, regarded the dove as a sacred bird.

In my garden, doves are welcome guest unless they become too numerous. I am usually able to control their numbers by limiting their food supply.

The black oil sunflower seeds that fill our birdfeeders beckon a variety of feathered friends. Bright red cardinals and brilliant goldfinch join perky black-capped chickadees, tufted titmice, and Carolina wrens for a quick snack. The nutritious morsels also attract other birds considered by some to be less desirable. Some backyard birdwatchers would prefer not to have blue jays and mockingbirds. These larger birds consume more food. Grackles and starlings are the most objectionable because they are messy and wasteful.

Mourning doves also have their critics. Clare, who makes no claim to being an ornithologist, refers to the large brownish-grey birds as "doofus birds that eat all the food." The birds we usually call doves are rock doves. They come in several varieties: turtlenecks, mourning doves, ring-necks, diamond doves, and homing pigeons.

Mourning doves are the ones we see in our backyard. As Clare and I sip our morning coffee on the back porch, we enjoy hearing the cooing of doves. It is that plaintive call that gives the bird its name. The mourning dove's wings create a distinctive whistling sound during takeoff and landing.

Mourning doves are almost exclusive seedeaters. Because they devour many weed seeds, they are called the farmer's best friends. Also known as the turtledove, the Carolina pigeon, or Carolina turtledove, they are one of the most abundant and widespread of all North American birds. They are the leading game birds hunted in the fall of the year in the United States.

Doves are generally monogamous. The courtship begins when the male brings the female nesting material. She will either accept or reject his gift, thereby indicating her intentions. Mated pairs develop nuanced songs to communicate only with each other. This mating for life gives doves the reputation for being love birds.

As romantic as this may seem, the death of one bird does not cause the mate to pine away and die of loneliness. Quite the contrary! The single dove seeks a new mate almost immediately. They are not solitary birds. They need companionship. A single dove does not fare very well.

The dove is one of the most storied of all birds.

In some cultures, doves are symbols of sensuality. As the fertility goddess Aphrodite's constant companions, they represented sexuality and lust. In both Indian and Syrian mythology, the dove was a totem of passion. In Greek mythology, the bird was associated with the goddess Athena. It represented marriage and the renewal of life.

Perhaps this sensual connotation led Mars, Incorporated, to select Dove as the brand name for chocolate candy and for chocolate-covered ice cream bars. Dove is also a Unilever brand of soap and other personal care products.

According to Genesis, Noah stood at a window in the ark when the rain finally stopped, gazing upon an endless sea. Through watery eyes, he hunted for some glimpse of hope.

He dispatched a raven that flew to and fro, searching for dry land. Then Noah sent forth a dove, but it returned with nothing. After seven more days, Noah released a second dove, which returned with an olive leaf in its beak. Noah received the dove carrying in its beak a sprig of hope.

A dove also symbolizes the Holy Spirit at the baptism of Jesus, according to the Gospels. In Christian iconography, the image became prominent. Often accompanied by the word peace, the design of a dove carrying an olive branch was incorporated into the funerary art of the Roman catacombs.

The dull brownish-grey birds at our feeders have a noble heritage. Archeologists have uncovered terra-cotta representations of doves dating back to Old Testament times in Mesopotamia and Egypt.

In a second-century writing known as the Gospel of Thomas, Jesus is presented as a divine child with miraculous power. The story is told of him, as a boy, molding clay pigeons on the Sabbath. When criticized for making images on the holy day, Jesus clapped his hands. The doves received life and flew away.

In our day, the discs launched in trap or skeet shooting are called clay pigeons. Those who participate in this competition, called sporting clays, sometimes feel as though the discs take on a life of their own.

The dove has been a symbol of peace throughout history. Doves are usually featured in the opening ceremonies of the Olympic Games. Pablo Picasso's lithograph "The Dove" was chosen as the emblem for the World Peace Congress in Paris in 1949. He explained why he presented the bird in his art "I stand for life against death; I stand for peace against war."

Homing pigeons are rock doves that have been selectively bred for their ability to return home over long distances. These birds fly at speeds up to eighty miles per hour and cover distances of thousands of miles.

Doves have served in times of war and even been awarded medals. Three honored birds deserve mention. Cher Ami, enshrined in the Smithsonian Institution, was awarded the French Cross. G.I. Joe received a citation for preventing the bombing of an Italian village, saving the lives of more than 1,000 people. On Guadalcanal, Blackie Holligan was dispatched into a barrage of enemy fire. He showed up long overdue, bloody from shrapnel. He still delivered his message.

White homing pigeons – symbols of love, hope, and peace – are sometimes released at weddings. They fly back to their dove cotes after leaving the marriage ceremony.

White doves are also used at funerals. Three birds representing the Father, the Son, and the Holy Spirit are generally released first. They are trained to circle the cemetery. Then a single bird, symbolizing the spirit of the dearly departed, is released to join the other three as they fly over the grave. This reunion of birds indicates that the spirit of the deceased has joined the Holy Trinity as they rise toward the heavens.

A funeral director had planned such a dove release for the bereaved family at a service at Putnam Baptist Church in West Springs in Union County, South Carolina. The doves were from Gaffney, South Carolina. The release did not go as planned. The director did not realize that he had scheduled the funeral on the same day that dove season opened. Hunters beyond the treelined field near the graveyard were not aware of the funeral.

At the conclusion of the graveside service, the funeral director took a large double-sided basket carrying the doves outside the funeral tent. He explained the meaning of the dove release.

Soon after the funeral director opened the lid on one side of the basket, and the first three birds were released. The people gathered at the cemetery heard shotgun blasts.

Instead of circling as they had been trained to do, the three doves representing the trinity took off like darts back to their owner in Gaffney.

The funeral director hurriedly released the fourth bird ahead of schedule. The pretty white dove representing the spirit of the deceased flew directly over the trees and the killing field below. More blasts were heard.

The following day the owner of the birds called the funeral director and said, "Three of my birds came home, but I haven't seen the fourth one. Any idea what happened?"

"No, not really."

"Maybe he'll show up. Sometimes the males get a romantic urge and venture off."

Sure enough, two days later, the stray bird returned home, no worse for the wear. Fortunately, there was no mourning for that dove.

On the wings of a snow-white dove
He sends His pure sweet love
A sign from above
On the wings of a dove

When troubles surround us
When evils come
The body grows weak
The spirit grows numb
When these things beset us
He doesn't forget us
He sends down His love
On the wings of a dove.

Ferlin Husky

Stargazing

"He is the Maker of the Bear and Orion, the Pleiades and the constellations..."
-Job 9:9, NIV

I traveled with a group of Boy Scouts to the high mountains on the border between North Carolina and Tennessee. Troop leaders had planned the trip to help younger scouts learn camping and cooking skills. One young scout was overjoyed with the prospect of grilling over an open fire and baking in a cast iron Dutch oven. He was so eager to prepare food that he forgot to pack one essential item for the trip.

At bedtime, I knew that something was troubling him. As darkness settled over the mountains the night air turned cold. The young scout huddled near the campfire and became very quiet.

"You need to get some sleep if you're going to do all of that cooking tomorrow," I advised.

"I forgot my sleeping bag," he said sheepishly.

This was not my first experience with young scouts. As a grizzled old scout leader, I was prepared. I offered the lad my sleeping bag which he accepted gladly. I retired to my pickup truck only two hundred yards walk away.

I grabbed a foam pad and a couple of tattered fleece blankets from a stash behind the driver's seat in the truck cab. I made a comfortable pallet in the bed of the truck and stretched out for the night. There in the parking area at the trailhead on top of a mountain, I had a magnificent view of the night sky. There was no moon. Neither were there any ground lights to dim my view of the heavens. I was perfectly oriented beneath Polaris, the North Star.

Throughout the night, I woke occasionally, tracking the procession of constellations around the pole star. The Big Bear, the Little Bear, Queen Cassiopeia reclining on her couch, King Cepheus, and Draco the Dragon move in a close circle at the top of the sky. Further down the heavens, other constellations rise into view and then dip out of sight. On this spring night, I saw Bootes the Kite, Orion and his dog, Taurus the Bull, Cygnus the Swan, and the Gemini Twins.

The stars have always fascinated me. Last August I thought would have been the perfect time for me to witness the impressive display of lights from a meteor shower. I was at the beach. I would have a clear view of the night sky. The moon was in the first phase. On Sunday night, I walked to the end of a long boardwalk to gaze into the sky. There were no clouds. The moon was faint. The stars were bright, but few meteors streaked across the sky. As it turned out that was the last clear night for viewing the stars while we were at the coast.

I remember standing on the tailgate of a truck with a pair of binoculars on a cold February night in 1986 straining to see Halley's Comet on its last pass of earth. Two nights later, I took my children out in the middle of the night to see the comet. If you missed it, don't worry. Halley's Comet will return in July 2061.

Just eleven years after Halley's Comet, Comet Hale-Bopp made a grand appearance. I saw the comet clearly from the church parking lot during the daytime in the spring of 1997. If you missed Hale-Bopp, I am sorry. It will be back again in 4385.

These celestial sights pale in comparison to what the ancient Magi must have seen. They were probably members of the Zoroastrian religion. They believed the heavens mirrored the events on earth. When these wise men from ancient Persia gazed into the sky and saw an unusually bright star, it was a sign that a royal person had been born. Following the star, they traveled to Bethlehem to honor the child and to offer tribute. This is the event that we remember on Epiphany.

The stars fascinated a young man named Edward. Born in Marshfield, Missouri, in 1889, Edward majored in math and astronomy in college. He graduated from law school and became a practicing attorney. He got bored after just a couple of years and decided to pursue a Ph.D. in astronomy. He focused his research on nebulae, distant objects in the sky that couldn't be categorized as stars. He moved to Pasadena, California, to work with the world's largest telescope.

Edward made discoveries that revolutionized the field of astronomy. He identified a pulsating star in Andromeda. At the time, scientists believed that the Earth's galaxy, the Milky Way, was the only galaxy in the universe. The Milky Way, they thought, was only about 100,000 light years across. Edward's discovery proved that the universe was billions of times larger than scientists had thought.

Edward devised a system to classify galaxies based on their shapes. In 1929, he made what is considered his most important discovery when he formulated a mathematical relationship that explained the correlation of a galaxy's radial velocity to its distance from Earth. He determined that "the farther a galaxy is from Earth, the faster it appears to move away." This led to the conclusion that the universe is expanding.

In 1990, four decades after Edward's death, NASA launched the Hubble Telescope, the first telescope based in outer space. It was named for Edward – Edward Hubble. The telescope captures accurate images of faint, distant objects. Photographs taken from the telescope have expanded scientific knowledge of the universe. Even more, the Hubble Telescope has increased the sense of wonder about the stars.

The shepherd boy David spent long hours through the night protecting the flock and watching the constellations circle Polaris. David was also the sweet singer of Israel and a song writer. Psalm 8 is among his best known, especially among star gazers.

> "O Lord, our Lord,
> How excellent is Your name in all the earth,
> Who have set Your glory above the heavens!
> When I consider Your heavens, the work of Your fingers,
> The moon and the stars, which You have ordained,
> What is man that You are mindful of him,
> And the son of man that You visit him?
> For You have made him a little lower than the angels,
> And You have crowned him with glory and honor.
> O Lord, our Lord,
> How excellent is Your name in all the Earth!"
> -Psalm 8, NIV

The Beauty of Autumn

"God has made everything beautiful in its time."
- Ecclesiastes 3:11, NIV

In the aftermath of a September hurricane, I sat on our screened porch, an eyewitness as the back edge of summer was yielding to the front side of fall. Our back porch is a sanctuary. I prayed for the many people sick and bereaved, those living in fear and uncertainty from the wildfires in the western United States, for those affected by many tropical storms, and for those suffering from oppression and injustice around the globe.

Purple finches, blackcap chickadees, gray titmice, and bright red cardinals took turns feasting on the black oil sunflower seeds in the feeder suspended over the barn door. A procession of butterflies, including two orange monarchs, fluttered above pink begonias, pausing to sip nectar from the blue flower spikes of yellow and crimson coleus plants. Across the yard, a large yellow tiger swallowtail feasted on late-blooming purple hyssop. A few pale yellow and pink roses were putting on their final display. The Japanese maple was cloaked in deep red while the redbud trees dropped their first golden leaves in a gentle breeze. So much color! And may I remind you, I am color blind!

Fall is one of my four favorite times of the year. Sitting on the porch, I feel peacefully energized. My soul is best restored in quiet solitude. The Southern Appalachian Mountains and surrounding foothills will soon be decked out for their annual autumn display. Peak fall colors in our area usually occur from mid-October through early November. Though the mountains are home to more than one hundred species of trees, the most colorful foliage comes courtesy of sugar maples, scarlet oaks, sweet gums, red maples, and hickory trees.

Before settling down into winter's deep sleep, Mother Nature has one last fling, an amazing fashion show, when mountain foliage turns radiant shades of crimson, orange, and purple.

The English poet, Samuel Taylor Coleridge, celebrated autumn with a rhyme.

The one red leaf, the last of its clan,
That dances as often as dance it can.

As I mentioned earlier, the Cherokee people have a legend that explains why the leaves change color. It is the tale of a mighty bear that roamed the countryside wreaking havoc. The beast would charge into their villages, eat all their food, destroy their homes, chase away their animals, and frighten the women and children.

Tribal elders held a council and selected the bravest hunters to put an end to the bear. The warriors set out with their dogs and weapons to stalk the marauder. The beast fled; the Cherokee gave chase. One hunter came close enough to shoot, and an arrow nicked the bear. The injury was not serious, but the culprit ran so fast he escaped up into the sky. The hunters, determined in their chase, ran into the heavens in hot pursuit.

Use your imagination, and you can see the bear depicted in the four stars in the bowl of the Big Dipper. The three stars in the handle of the dipper represent the hunters chasing the bear. The stalkers and their prey go around and around in the northern night sky. Every autumn, the Big Dipper comes low to the horizon. It is then, according to the legend, that the bear's wound leaks a few drops of blood. According to the legend, the blood of the bear changes the colors of the leaves on the trees.

Those of us who live in the SC Piedmont are fortunate to enjoy a changing climate. As days shorten and night air becomes crisp, the soothing green canvas of summer foliage is transformed into the breathtaking autumn palette of reds, oranges, yellows, and browns.

Four factors influence autumn leaf color – leaf pigments, length of daylight and darkness, rainfall, and temperatures. The timing of the color change is primarily regulated by the increasing length of night hours. As days grow shorter and nights grow longer and cooler, the chemical processes in leaves begin to paint the autumn landscape.

During the growing season, chlorophyll makes leaves appear green. As the length of night increases in the autumn, chlorophyll production slows down and then stops. The pigments that are present in the leaf are then unmasked, and the trees show their fall colors.

The timing of the color change also varies by the kinds of trees. Sourwood and tulip poplars in southern forests can become a vivid yellow in late summer while all others are still green. Oaks put on their colors long after other species have already shed their leaves.

The brilliance of the colors that develop in any particular autumn season is related to weather conditions that occur before and during the time the chlorophyll in the leaves is dwindling. Temperature and moisture are the main influences.

Mythical Jack Frost supposedly brings reds and purples to the forest by pinching the leaves with his icy fingers. The hues of yellow, gold, and brown are mixed in his paint box and applied with quick, broad strokes of his brush as he silently moves among the trees decorating them.

As I mentioned earlier in the chapter on trees, frost does not bring autumn hues. It turns the leaves brown. The most spectacular color displays are brought on by a succession of warm, sunny days and cold, but not freezing, nights. During these days, sugars are produced in the leaf. The cool nights and the gradual closing of veins going into the leaf prevent these sugars from moving out. The combination of sugar and light spurs the production of brilliant pigments in the leaves.

The amount of dampness in the soil also affects autumn colors. Like the weather, soil moisture varies greatly from year to year. The countless combinations of these two highly variable factors assure that no two autumns will be exactly alike. A late spring, or a severe summer drought, can delay the onset of fall color. A warm, wet spring, favorable summer weather, and mild sunny fall days with cool nights produce the most brilliant autumn colors.

Our son, Mike, lives in Concord, New Hampshire. The good folks of the Granite State celebrate the changing of the autumn leaves, usually before the autumnal equinox. The vivid change of color starts in late September in New England and moves southward, reaching the Blue Ridge Mountains by early November. The cooler, higher elevations will change color before the valleys.

I wonder. What must autumn be like in heaven? Do the leaves change colors? Do the butterflies and the birds migrate? I am not sure, but, for now, the beauty of this season is a brief foretaste of the glory to be experienced on the other side. It must be, well, just glorious.

Yes, glorious!

When thru the woods and forest glades I wander
And hear the birds sing sweetly in the trees,

When I look down from lofty mountain grandeur
And hear the brook and feel the gentle breeze,

Then sings my soul, my Savior God, to Thee;
How great Thou art, how great Thou art!
Then sings my soul, my Savior God, to Thee;
How great Thou art, how great Thou art!

Carl Boberg

The Garden of Grace

"Blessed are those who mourn, for they will be comforted."
Matthew 5:4, NIV

Sanctuary

"The Lord is in His holy temple;"
-Psalms 11:4, NIV

After we moved into the old homeplace, it was two and a half years before we finally bought the house. My Uncle Asbury had rented the house to us while we waited for our house in Winston- Salem to sell. In 1980, interest rates were above 18%; so, we waited. When the house in Winston-Salem finally sold and we were able to buy this house, we were certain this was going to be our home for several years. It was then that I started the long process of developing a garden. The old barn was here and was quite suitable for storage. It only needed a fresh coat of paint and a new roof to be given the chance at a new life, a new purpose.

I built a crude arbor around an old muscadine vine that my grandmother had planted. It was huge, but it had no support, so I built the arbor. It held until the third year we were here, when the winter temperatures dropped below zero and the sap in the muscadine vine froze. When the thaw came, the vine split apart. Down came the muscadine vine, and down came the arbor.

Another structure I built in our yard was the play structure. I built it very early on.

One of the companies that had occupied this old house was an enterprise that made paving stones. Against the fence on the side yard was a large, open concrete bin with a concrete floor where river sand had been stored, to be used in the making of the stones. At first, I converted that large bin into a sandbox for the children to play in. Problems occurred when that large sandbox attracted feral cats, making it an unsanitary place to play.

Matt Crosland was a member of the church I pastored. I knew Matt to be a skilled carpenter, so I asked him to build a shack using the old concrete sand pit as the foundation. Matt put a tin roof on the shack so when I was working in the garden and a sudden shower came up, I could sit in a rocking chair under the shack and enjoy the rain. We had several attempts at constructing a covered gate at the back of the property. When we got around to rebuilding Mammy's arbor, we also built a "lych-gate" as one of our English friends called it. The two matching structures provide good shade from the hot summer sun.

Clare asked if we could have a gazebo in the side yard. It was an architectural feature that she remembered from her childhood, especially when she visited her grandparents in Leesville, South Carolina. We looked in magazines, gathering ideas. We occasionally saw gazebos for sale, but their construction seemed inferior to the construction I knew we wanted. One day, I was talking about the idea with a group of other clergymen. Two days later, I got a phone call from Mike McGee, my friend and the pastor who preceded me at Morningside Baptist. Mike said, "Kirk, I've built three of these, and I have the plans. If you'll provide the lumber and be my carpenter's helper, we can build a gazebo in your yard." The deal was done.

Within a few weeks, Mike had his table saw set up in our side yard and the construction was underway. Unlike the pre-fab gazebos that Clare and I had found, this one was anchored by eight four-by-four, treated posts set in concrete. That was the first thing we did, was set up those eight posts. It's a traditional octagonal design, with a bench on seven sides and one side as the opening.

Initially, gazebos were not garden structures. They were derived from the biblical concept of a guard tower. In numerous places in the Bible, towers were placed in vineyards and in olive groves. They were a place where watchmen could be on the lookout for thieves, the two-legged kind and the four-legged kind. Jesus told a parable about "a man who planted a vineyard and set a hedge around it and dug a pit for the wine-press and built a watch tower" (Mark 12:1, NIV).

Later, structures were built on rooftops overlooking the gardens of ancient Egypt, Persia, Greece, and Rome. It was not until the Victorian era that these structures came down from their lofty perch and were placed in the garden. It gave homeowners a private place to relax. Chinese and Japanese cultures use gazebos for more formal ceremonies and as places for meditation. The word "gazebo" wasn't used until the mid-1700s, when two architects, William and John Halfpenny, coined the term. It seems to be a mixture of Latin and English, though some have speculated that the Halfpenny brothers borrowed the word while traveling through Asia.

A gazebo has many uses. It can be a delightful place to write or create art. A gazebo gives an opportunity to enjoy fresh air and sunshine. One advantage is that it is a covered structure where children can play or adults can gather, even during a summer shower.

Clare and I have found that it's a good place to enjoy a cup of coffee. From our gazebo, we have a clear view of our waterfall and small pond. I have planted a Japanese maple in the side yard near our gazebo; it is the beginning of what I hope will one day become a small Zen Garden.

Perhaps the best use of our gazebo was on May 25th of 2013, when our daughter, Betsy, and her wonderful husband, Jay, were married in it.

Every year, at the beginning of Advent, I put a small Fraser fir inside the gazebo decorated with white lights and topped with a small Moravian star. There could hardly be a better Christmas decoration for our garden.

I come to the garden alone,
While the dew is still on the roses, And the
voice I hear falling on my ear The Son of God
discloses.

Refrain:
And He walks with me, and He talks with me, And He
tells me I am His own;
And the joy we share as we tarry there, None other
has ever known.

He speaks, and the sound of His voice Is so
sweet the birds hush their singing, And the
melody that He gave to me Within my heart is
ringing.

Refrain

I'd stay in the garden with Him,
Though the night around me be falling,
But He bids me go; through the voice of woe His voice
to me is calling.

Refrain

Charles A. Miles

221

Unexpected Blooms

"Consider how the wildflowers grow."
-Luke 12:27, NIV

Viola sororia

O ne of the fascinating aspects about gardening is that it is so much like life. There are times when the plants we enjoy are quite predictable. They seem to thrive and bloom as if they had an internal calendar. At other times, the garden is full of surprises. Pansies and violas carry us through the winter with their bright happy faces. Pink and white Lenten roses begin blooming in January. They are closely followed by yellow jonquils and multicolored crocus. Border plants like blue, purple, and pink creeping phlox (*Phlox stolonifera*) and lacy white candytuft (*Iberis sempervirens*) take their turn in a predictable succession. "To everything there is a season" (Ecclesiastes 3:1, NIV).

It is also true that gardening sometimes presents to us the unexpected. I was pleasantly surprised when the potted red geraniums on our front porch were able to dodge killing frost until the week after Christmas. Their red blooms and green leaves were a counterpoint to the Christmas decoration on the front door of our home – a green Fraser fir wreath (*Abies fraseri*) with streamers of red velvet ribbon.

Two plants in the garden startled me last winter. On December 21, the shortest day of the year, I found a single, stately tuberose (*Polianthes tuberosa*) blooming. I cut it and put it in a vase in our home. The perfumed fragrance lasted until after the New Year. Then, on a cold, sunny afternoon in late January, I found a bright lavender anemone (*Anemone coronaria*) nestled beneath our redbud tree. These plants, blooming out of season, were special unexpected gifts from the garden.

The writer of Ecclesiastes reminds us that life itself moves in predictable patterns. There is "a time to be born, and a time to die; a time to plant, and a time to pull up what is planted; a time to weep and a time to laugh; a time to mourn, and a time to dance" (3:2, 3:4, NIV).

A young couple expecting their first child delights in the predicable joyous event of childbirth that occurs on or near the due date set by the physician. A family says goodbye to an aging loved one following a long illness. Though we weep, we may also rejoice. Through our tears, we experience a blessing. When life is predictable, it is more manageable. It is easier to affirm that God is in His heaven, and all is right with the world.

But, sometimes, life startles us. We are called upon to stand gazing at a tiny casket by an open grave with young parents who weep in shocked disbelief at the untimely death of their baby. We find ourselves struggling to know how best to react to a forty-three-year-old woman who ponders the best way to tell her teenagers that they are going to have a new brother or sister. Birth and death, like many experiences of life, are usually predictable. Often, however, the unexpected happens: the news of an impending birth startles us, or death comes as a harsh intruder. These events remind us that for all of our attention and care and our tending of life, we are not in control.

The beauty of nature can be a gentle reminder that even in life's most difficult moments, God is in control. A snowfall surprised us here in the South on the Sunday before Thanksgiving many years ago. It was the day of the funeral for our twenty-seven-year-old son, Erik. The snow, we have since felt, was a special gift of God's grace to make the day a little easier.

In the gathering dusk after the funeral on that day, I walked through our garden. In a melting patch of snow under an oak tree, I saw through teary eyes the nodding purple blossoms of a violet

(*Viola sororia*), blooming entirely out of season, but at just the right time for me. God is great, and God is good. The timing of His grace is amazing.

All things bright and beautiful
All creatures great and small
All things wise and wonderful
'Twas God that made them all

Each little flower that opens
Each little bird that sings
He made their glowing colors
And made their tiny wings.

All things bright and beautiful
All creatures great and small
All things wise and wonderful
'Twas God that made them all

He gave us eyes to see them
And lips that we might tell
How great is the Almighty
Who has made all things well.
Cecil Francis Alexander / Edwin George Monk /
George Mcbeth McPhee

Wind Chimes

"...you do not know what is the way of the wind..."
-Ecclesiastes 11:5, NKJV

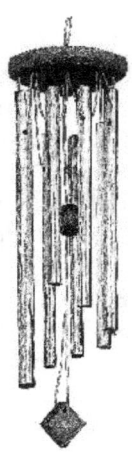

On a recent trip to the South Carolina coast, Clare and I stopped for breakfast at a place that has become a familiar landmark along interstate highways. We put our names on a waiting list. Tables for two in the non-smoking section are in high demand. Fortunately, this particular establishment has an array of rocking chairs on the front porch for those who prefer to sit outside and wait. The rocking chairs, by the way, are for sale. Inside the building, those who wish to eat must make their way through a maze of merchandise on display. As Clare and I waited for our name to be called, we chose
to browse. I discovered a rack of wind chimes.

Wind chimes are a favorite at our house. Clare's father, who made the first ones I ever saw, fashioned them from conduit pipe and small gauge chain. The entire assembly was fastened to a piece of square wood with screw eyes and S hooks. Though he died in 1984, we still enjoy the sound of those chimes whenever a breeze blows.

The art of making wind chimes has gone high tech. Chimes have been tuned to sound like Gregorian chants or eastern temple bells. Chimes have been tuned to the first few notes of Vivaldi's *Four*

Seasons. I found wind chimes on the rack at the restaurant tuned to the first few notes of "Amazing Grace."

I showed the "Amazing Grace" wind chimes to Clare. She suggested we buy several sets.

We gave one set of the "Amazing Grace" wind chimes to my sister and brother-in-law who live in Mount Pleasant, South Carolina. My brother-in-law, Terry has given us a report: "If I sit on my screened porch with a cup of coffee and listen carefully while a gentle breeze is blowing, I really can hear a suggestion of 'Amazing Grace.'" He smiled and continued, "The other night we had a big storm. The 'Amazing Grace' wind chimes rang like crazy, and twenty-five people in our neighborhood came to our door looking for the revival meeting."

John Newton wrote "Amazing Grace." His father was a sea captain, and John became a sailor as a teenager. By the time he was twenty years old, he was the captain of his own slave ship. For nine years, he bought and transported people from Africa in the slave trade.

On March 21, 1748 in the midst of a storm, Newton prayed to God for deliverance. The experience changed his life. John Newton left the sea and eventually entered the ministry. His memory of that night at sea later led him to pen the words of the hymn "Amazing Grace."

Newton's words were put to the melody of an African slave song, a song Newton had heard many times rising from the hold of his slave ship. For generations, "Amazing Grace" has been sung in rural churches and in city cathedrals. Shape-note singers in southern revivals have harmonized it. The Harlem Boys Choir has performed it. Cherokee Tribe members sang it on the Trail of Tears. Johnny Cash included "Amazing Grace" in nearly all of his prison performances. It never failed to move hardened criminals to tears.

In 1970, folksinger Judy Collins released her version of the song. Her clear, beautiful voice carried the song to the top of the pop music charts. Since that time, it has become the world's most popular religious tune. Judy Collins credits the song with helping her overcome her own problems with alcohol.

On June 11, 1988, in Wembley Stadium, London, England, various musical groups, mostly rock bands, gathered in celebration of the political changes in South Africa. For twelve hours, rock bands like Guns N' Roses blasted away. The crowd was loud and rowdy. The promoters of the event had asked Jessye Norman, an opera singer, to perform the final number. A single spotlight followed her onto the stage. With no musical accompaniment, alone and acapella, Jessye Norman began singing.

> Amazing grace! How sweet the sound,
> That saved a wretch like me!
> I once was lost, but now am found,
> Was blind, but now I see.

Seventy thousand people fell silent. Jessye Norman began the second verse.

> 'Twas grace that taught my heart to fear,
> And grace my fears relieved;

By the end of the verse, the crowd was entranced. By the time she got to the third verse, several thousand people were singing with her.

> 'Tis grace hath bro't me safe thus far,
> And grace will lead me home.

Remembering words they had heard in the past, the crowd was transformed into a congregation as they sang the final verse.

> When we've been there ten thousand years,
> Bright shining as the sun,
> We've no less days to sing God's praise
> Then when we first begun.

Jessye Norman later said that she felt an unseen power descend on Wembley Stadium that night.

Whether "Amazing Grace" is played on Scottish bagpipes or on a blues harmonica, whether it is sung by the untrained voice of a cotton mill worker or by the Mormon Tabernacle Choir, whether it is played on a pipe organ in a great cathedral or on wind chimes in a summer breeze, the hymn is a reminder of God's love.

When grace descends, the world falls silent, and human lives are changed.

Weeping Willow

"We wept when we remembered Zion. We hung our harps upon the willows."
- Psalms 137:1-2

After Erik died, I planted a weeping willow tree
near the railroad tracks behind our house.

One brisk November morning, I dug a hole in the soggy earth,
eyes brimming in the chilly wind.

Bending against the cold, I loosened the burlap around the ball,
eyes overflowing with tears.

Down on my knees, I packed composted cow manure around the
roots, streams running down my cheeks.

With icy fingers, I hauled a bucket of water to the tree,
pouring from the bucket, pouring from my eyes.

After I mulched, I sat on a bale of straw,
weeping with the willow.

Being a planter, being a grave digger,
being a father are all the same.

With a sharp shovel you dig a hole to plant something so alive,
hoping for new life.

I sat on the bale pawing at the red dirt with my boot
sobbing quietly for my son.

For eleven years
I found comfort in the weeping willow as it grew.

For eleven winters
it survived ice and wind and snow and it grew.

For eleven springs hanging green branches
danced in the breeze and it grew.

228

For eleven summers in drought and heat
it sent roots deep and it grew.

For ten autumns I stood draped beneath golden branches
weeping with the tree.

Last spring, a lonely mockingbird sang through the night,
and I listened.

For eleven years the tree grew tall and strong
weeping every season.

Then, a new property owner moved in next door
to start a landscape business.

Chainsaw in hand, he cut the weeping willow down.
My eyes filled again.

Standing over the stump, he said he didn't know,
"Sorry for the misunderstanding."

And I wept for the weeping willow.

> *I think that I shall never see*
> *A poem lovely as a tree.*
> *A tree whose hungry mouth is prest*
> *Against the earth's sweet flowing breast;*
> *A tree that looks at God all day,*
> *And lifts her leafy arms to pray;*
> *A tree that may in summer wear*
> *A nest of robins in her hair;*
> *Upon whose bosom snow has lain;*
> *Who intimately lives with rain.*
> *Poems are made by fools like me,*
> *But only God can make a tree.*
> *Joyce Kilmer*

Daffodils

"...their faithfulness is like the flowers of the field."
-Isaiah 40:6, NIV

Narcissus 'Fergie'

A dear friend of mine, Helen Babb, lived in the country between Greer and Gowansville. Mrs. Babb loved beautiful flowers. In the late summer, wild flowers covered an area near the old barn. They reseeded each year, multiplying in number and in beauty. In the early spring, Helen Babb's yard featured bright yellow jonquils (*Narcissus jonquilla*), the petite relatives of daffodils (*Narcissus pseudonarcissus*). They, too, spread each year flowing like a graceful yellow ribbon down a gentle slope.

After Mrs. Babb's death several years ago, her daughter knew that she would have to sell the home place. She wanted to save some of the heirloom flowers for her own yard in Spartanburg. In the fall, she dug up a box full of the jonquil bulbs, many more than she needed. She shared some with me. On a rainy cold November afternoon, I planted the bulbs on an embankment near the waterfall in my garden. In late February each year, the tiny flowers put on a magnificent display.

Daffodils and their smaller Spanish cousins, jonquils, dance in the wind. Once the daffodils bloom, there can be no doubt that the seasons are changing. It is as if the nodding trumpet-shaped flowers herald the arrival of spring.

When I think of daffodils, Gene comes to mind. Gene was a dear friend who grew up on a farm in Cherokee County, South Carolina. His success with the family business enabled him to build a comfortable home on the family farm within a stone's throw of the old home place. The beautiful new house had a wraparound porch, graced with big rocking chairs. Visitors approached the home by a long driveway, flanked on the left by a horse pasture and a weathered barn. Up a hill to the right was the foundation of the former home. In the early spring, this hill was covered with bright yellow daffodils. Originally planted by Gene's mother around the old farmhouse, the daffodils naturalized, spreading helter-skelter down the hillside. Each year the flowers still bloom from late February through March. The yellow-splotched hill is a sight to behold.

A few years ago, after several months of increasingly serious health problems, it became clear that Gene was quite ill. The diagnosis was a rapidly growing, rare form of cancer. In mid-March, Gene went home from the hospital. On a bright, warm Sunday afternoon, Gene asked if he could see the daffodils. Surrounded by his loving wife, children, and several grandchildren, Gene was transported by wheelchair down the driveway near the barn. He sat quietly for a few moments, taking in the sight of the hillside covered in delicate yellow blooms dancing in the breeze. Three days later, Gene died.

At the graveside in a country churchyard, the children and grandchildren each placed a daffodil, picked from the hillside, atop the polished wooden casket. Jesus taught His followers how to deal with worry and anxiety. His counsel was to pay attention to birds and flowers.

For Gene's family, those flowers will always be daffodils. Even though the yellow blossoms bring to mind bittersweet memories, for that family, the flowers will be a perennial symbol of hope.

Treasures of Snow

"Have you entered the treasury of snow…"
-Job 38:22, NKJV

Meteorologists know that forecasting weather for Upstate SC is always a challenge. Winter accuracy in their work becomes high risk. With advanced technology at their fingertips, and instruments of their trade close at hand, most weather professionals would agree with our local weatherman, Jack Roper. The tool that would be most helpful to them is the one that is usually absent in their weather room. They would probably be more accurate in their predictions if they only had a window. They could at least look outside to see for themselves what the weather was actually doing.

Country folks have their time-honored ways of determining the long-range forecast. The length of hair on a horse's back or the colors of the fuzz on a wooly worm are indicators of the winter ahead. The relative scarcity or plenty of acorns, pecans, hickory nuts, and beechnuts are portents of the severity of winter.

In our part of the world, ice is the most dreaded winter weather event. A forecast of sleet and freezing rain is reason for concern. While ice covered trees have a crystalline beauty, the popping of breaking limbs and the cracking of splitting trunks are sounds of nature's agony. Frozen roads and sidewalks, ice-laden power lines, contribute to human agony of broken limbs and splitting headaches. During an especially severe ice storm two years ago, electric power at our house was out for several days. A friend called to add his unique brand of humor to the cold and dark. "This is the devil," he announced. "It's frozen over down here, too."

On the other hand, many people in the South, especially school children and teachers, greet the prospect of snow with wild excitement. When the seven-day forecast held the promise of snow last winter, I asked a school principal, "Is it supposed to snow?" "It's always supposed to snow!" came the ready reply. A snow that sticks, that is, a snowfall with accumulation, creates a delightful playground. Snow angels, snowmen, snowballs, snow ice cream, and sledding are all fun, though fleeting, possibilities.

Some of our Northern transplants are baffled by our enthusiastic reaction to snow. Enough is enough for them. Snow is a detestable nuisance. They are annoyed that a few inches of snow can bring life to a screeching halt for so many of us.

The truth is that people of the South do behave in strange ways when snow is impending. Grocery store shelves are quickly depleted of milk and bread. It was always difficult for me to understand why. Did hundreds of people sit in their homes eating bread and drinking milk because we had snow? I posed the question while standing in the express line at a grocery store several years ago. Snow was in the forecast.

The woman ahead of me made sense out of what seemed like nonsense. "If my power goes out, I can give my three children peanut butter and jelly sandwiches and a glass of milk. The peanut butter and milk give them complete protein." I was glad to have a reasonable answer as I stepped forward to purchase my own bread and milk.

Dr. Alastair Walker, long time pastor of First Baptist Church Spartanburg, had a favorite sermon for just such an occasion. His text was Job 38:22 where the Lord asked Job, "Have you entered the treasury of snow?" (NKJV).

As I recall, Dr. Walker had three points to his sermon. (1) No two snowflakes are alike. As the Creator fashioned each snowflake uniquely, so, too, has He created us. (2) Snowflakes are small and delicate, inconsequential as individuals. When many snowflakes accumulate, the world is altered by their combined power. So, too, can individual Christians, ineffective when acting alone, do marvelous things for God when working together. (3) Snow is instant urban renewal. A blanket of snow makes a dark, drab landscape bright and beautiful. Lives that are darkened by sin can become whiter than snow through God's forgiveness. These are treasures of the snow.

My experience is that for children and adults alike, winter weather provides for many of us a day of grace, the unexpected blessing of a day off. It can be a day to enjoy our families. My mother always fixed a big pot of vegetable soup on snow days. Though the roads were too bad to go to school, her grandchildren found a way to go "over the river and through the woods to grandmother's house." Even if the power goes out, this day of grace can be a time to sit by a hearth and read a book.

This day of grace is a time to think of others. As winter weather approaches, I try to remind our members to check on family and friends, especially those who live alone.

Last year, a man in our church made a special gift to our benevolent fund. "When I served in World War II, I was so cold I didn't think I would ever be warm again," he explained. His gift was used that very week to provide heating oil for a family of five, including three small children.

Two years ago, I was visiting the hospital during an ice storm when I came upon a homeless man sleeping in the stairwell. Winter weather is not a delight for everybody. It can be a reminder to those of us who have food and warmth to share. Organizations such as Miracle Hill Ministries, The Haven, the Soup Kitchen, Mobile Meals, and TOTAL Ministries provide service to our most needy citizens.

Winter weather can be a call to prayer for people of faith. If we receive a day of grace, some of that time can be spent in prayer. Remember those who are working while others have the day off. Medical personnel, paramedics, firefighters, law enforcement officers, utility employees, road crews, and tow truck drivers are but a few examples of those who labor long hours in the cold and damp. To remember them in prayer with petitions for their safety and gratitude for their service is our privilege.

These treasures of the snow come to all of us as gifts. When our twenty-seven-year-old son, Erik, died in November 2000, our grief was profound. Spartanburg received a surprise snowfall with slight accumulation on the day of Erik's funeral. Some attendees expressed sadness that we had to have his burial in the snow. We felt differently.

When we first saw the flakes falling gently from heaven, Clare said, "Maybe Erik asked God for a favor: 'Lord, you know this will be a difficult day for my family. Could you please surprise them?'"

Like every good and perfect gift, snow comes from above. The snow has become, for us in South Carolina, a blessing, a symbol of God's grace.

The Garden In Winter

"As long as the earth endures, seedtime and harvest, cold and heat, summer and winter, day and night will never cease."
- Genesis 8:22, NIV

One mild winter day, I took a bag lunch to the gazebo at Hatcher Garden and Woodland Preserve. The ten-acre public space within the city limits of our town was quiet. The conifer planting near the gazebo displayed a stunning collection of small trees and shrubs of various shapes and colors. I took a deep breath, offered a silent prayer of thanksgiving, and allowed the peace and calm of the garden to enfold my soul.

Two men were busily working near the entrance to the garden. They quickly finished their task and disappeared. As far as I could tell, I had the place to myself, except for a large red-tailed hawk perched on a tree limb above a pond. I thought he, too, must have had food on his mind.

There was evidence that work was being done in several areas of the garden. The staff and volunteers are always busy with one project after another. After lunch, I strolled through the beautiful landscape, a gift to our community from Harold and Josephine Hatcher. This public area is open year-round. It features a series of ponds and an impressive waterfall. The main attractions are the plants – trees, shrubs, and perennial flowers. Birds and insects add interest to this public treasure.

The peaceful solitude and quiet beauty of Hatcher Garden in winter is quite a contrast to the happy sounds and active people that fill the space in the warmer months. I have officiated at weddings and conducted memorial services in this space. But on this winter day, I felt as if I were in a secluded sanctuary. Along one of the paths, I found a bench in the sun. I paused there, listening to the birds and the breeze in the trees. In that moment, the garden became a place of contemplation and prayer for me.

I told a friend who has a passing interest in gardening about my winter afternoon visit to the public preserve. She commented, "I've never thought of going there in the winter. What is there to see?"

"Try it sometime," I said. "I'll bet you find plenty to see, to hear, and to enjoy."

One of my friends does not like gardening at all. Yard work for him is just one more thing on his honey-do list, usually the last thing. The only plants he admires are the grasses on fairways and putting greens. His philosophy regarding his yard is: if it is green and growing, leave it alone. He knows that I do not play golf, but he also knows how much I enjoy tending my plants. He commented, "I play the links all year long, but I guess there's not much for a gardener to do in the winter."

Nothing could be further from the truth. There is never an off-season for a gardener. In fact, gardening in winter is one of the delights of those of us who love tending plants. Here is a list of a few things that winter gardeners might consider.

1. Study your garden. Now you can see the bare bones of the landscape. Winter provides an opportunity to see where the gaps are that need to be filled. You will also notice branches and limbs that overhang paths or crowd other plants.

2. Pruning is a winter chore. However, some plants, such as azaleas, should not be cut back until after they bloom in spring. If in doubt, check with the Clemson Extension Service or your local garden shop.

3. Plan now for new garden projects in the spring. Much to the dismay of my wife, I have a stack of gardening magazines and nursery catalogs piled next to my favorite chair. Whenever I have a few minutes, I read and make notes about interesting plants that I would like to add to my garden.

4. Visit your local full-service garden center. Browse through the shrubs and trees. Look for plants that have colorful berries, pleasing shapes, or attractive bark. Consider adding some of these to your own winter landscape.

5. Keep a garden calendar that can also serve as a journal and a notebook. Take note of when certain things bloom in your garden. On my visit to Hatcher Garden, I not only enjoyed the solitude, but I also recorded which plants and features I would like to add to my own yard.

6. Compost organic matter. I have a tumbler bin that receives vegetable and fruit scraps, dead leaves, and grass clippings. When these materials decompose, they yield rich soil that can be used to mulch plants or amend the flower beds. Making compost is one of the smartest things a gardener can do in any season.

7. After a heavy rainfall, weed a flowerbed and turn the soil. Mix in some compost to get a head start on spring.

8. Repair arbors, trellises, fences, and other structures while nearby plants are dormant and can be pruned or trained without disturbing the roots.

9. Cold weather is the time to try your hand at propagating hardwood cuttings. This method of creating additional plants for your garden is both useful and enjoyable. The extension service can provide detailed information.

10. Buy some year-end bulbs for half price. Don't worry that it's a bit late in the year to plant them; they'll do just fine.

11. Cool weather is the best time to add hardscape to the garden. Place rocks, sculptures, and garden whimsies in aesthetically pleasing locations. Prepare raised beds, walkways, and other features so you'll be ready to plant at the first hint of spring.

12. Take a day to clean and sharpen all your garden tools. An old-fashioned grinding wheel is just the thing for the task.

13. Transplant shrubs. They will resettle best in winter. The relocated shrubs will awaken in spring far less shocked, barely realizing they're in a new spot.

14. Feed the birds. Clean and repair birdhouses. Once, I saw a pair of bluebirds flitting around one of the cedar boxes that are ready and waiting for spring occupancy.

15. Most important of all is to enjoy your winter garden. Look at the night sky through bare tree limbs. Take time to appreciate the simple beauty of mosses and lichens. Winter-blooming perennials are a special delight. Lenten roses are in full flower now. Crocus and early jonquils will soon be dazzling.

A few winters ago, late in the season, we were graced with a light snowfall overnight. In the early morning, I walked through my garden. The last few flakes were drifting from the sky. Hungry birds crowded the feeders. Bright berries of holly, pyracantha, and woodbine were touched with white frosting. Rising above the snow, happy faces of pansies and violas danced in the cold breeze. Then I saw a bright red cardinal chirping a winter greeting from his snowy perch.

The garden is a joyful, calming retreat for all seasons!

Saints in the Garden

"Blessed are those who are persecuted because of righteousness, for theirs is the kingdom of heaven."
Matthew 5:10, NIV

Garden Statues

When a person has difficulty falling asleep at night, I often recommend they read the book of Leviticus. It will put you right to sleep. That is to say, Leviticus can be pretty tedious reading. However, there are some very important passages in this book. The heart of the holiness code lies in Leviticus. One is the second commandment from Jesus – to love your neighbor as you love yourself – which is found in Leviticus 19:18.

Additionally, perhaps the most significant verse, one worth memorizing, is "Be holy because I, the Lord your God, am holy" (Leviticus 19:2, NIV). Holiness is a concept that is unquantifiable, it is elusive. Yet clearly God expects us to be holy. Perhaps Jesus was referring to this same passage when He said in Matthew 5:48 in the Sermon on the Mount "Be perfect, therefore, as your heavenly Father is perfect" (NIV).

The Greek word used in that scripture is *teleios* which translates to "fully complete." Jesus is saying to His disciples there on the mountain side, you are to be complete as your Father. Being godlike is something we will never achieve, but there are some individuals who seem to exemplify a Christlikeness in ways that others do not. These people are often called "saints."

Stick with me here as we travel down a brief tangent. At this writing, the final Star Wars movie was "The Last Jedi." In that film, Luke Skywalker, the perennial star of that series, has gone into isolation. The place depicted in that segment is known as Skellig Michael. It is a small stone island with twin peaks located off the coast of Ireland. It is located off the coast of Kerry in the Atlantic Ocean. The stone beehive shaped structure depicted in the movie were built by Celtic Christian monks in the sixth century.

When I watch the movie, viewing that old monastic site, I was reminded of how long and how wide is the Christian tradition of people striving to be holy. Skellig Michael was just one among many such places that testified to this.

Perhaps the most famous of the Celtic monasteries is the one located on Iona off the coast of Scotland. Founded by St. Columba, an Irish Monk, it too featured beehive shaped stone dwellings. Living ascetic lives in isolation, the monks of Iona created the Book of Kells. Completed in the eighth century, this book is considered one of the greatest works of medieval time. As far as I know, St. Columba is unique among the people who lived in these remote monasteries. He was the only one canonized as a saint.

Now for the question I'm sure you've been asking yourself: Why in a book about gardening should the final chapter be about saints? Well, good question, thank you for asking.

My mother-in-law, who I call Miz Lib, was a devoted gardener. She worked in her garden daily. My father-in-law, Mr. Jack, also loved to garden. He had a Troy-built tiller, which I knew as "The Pony." He used this machine to cultivate one half acre of rich sandy loam in Leesville, South Carolina.

You have already read about Mr. Jack's vegetable garden, but Miz Lib focused on flowers. Azaleas and daylilies were her pride and joy. Before her death, she insisted that I take cuttings off her azalea bushes. I propagated those plants by burying the lowest branches in that rich soil and holding them down with brick and stone. The following year, they were well rooted and I could plant them in the amended red clay of Spartanburg County. They put on a show every spring.

Miz Lib also insisted that I dig and divide some of her daylilies. They too still bloom every year. After Miz Lib died, I went back to her garden hoping to get more plants for my garden. However, in a very brief time, her beautiful garden had been taken over by weeds and fire ants. The garden cannot stand neglect for very long. It must be carefully tended.

One of the things I retrieved from Miz Lib's garden was a statue of Saint Francis feeding birds. The statue is made of molded concrete and, when I got it back to Spartanburg, I painted it with flat black acrylic paint to seal the pores of the concrete. That statue of Saint Francis still stands in our garden behind a bird bath.

Over time, I added more statues of saints to our garden. I continued the practice of sealing them with paint to preserve the integrity of the sculpture. These statues are reminders of saints in the garden. There are also other saints not canonized by the church, but saints nonetheless, because they are striving for righteous lives.

In our study of church history, we learn that in the early monastic period, almost every monastery had large acreage devoted to farming. This was a way that the Christian Church dealt with the perennial problem of hunger. These agricultural endeavors were started to provide nutritious food for hungry people.

This tradition has been continued by churches of various denominations and faiths. Many churches have a crisis closet or a food pantry, designed to serve those in need, just as those early monastic monks served through their farming. At the church I served, before retirement, we started a vegetable garden on an unused patch of ground on the church property. Volunteers from the congregation amended the soil, tilled the ground, planted the rows, and harvested the crops. The food grown in the garden was given to a soup kitchen, a homeless shelter, and a children's shelter to be used in their meal services. In our community, TOTAL Ministries was started by a minister's wife as a way to encourage congregations of all faiths to join together to sustain this ministry to those experiencing food insecurity in our community.

By the late monastic period, in addition to the gardens used for food, most monasteries and abbeys had a garden dedicated to prayer known, unsurprisingly, as a prayer garden. It was a place for those of the religious life and visitors alike to meditate and pray.

A large part of my Master Gardener course was to develop a project in a public place. I chose to design a prayer garden in a barren courtyard. Many volunteers participated in the planting and care of this garden. Most of the people in my church seemed to enjoy visits to this sacred space.

In my own garden, I also have a prayer garden with many plants given by our dear friends. I think of these cherished people I mentioned in Pass Along Plants. Many of those people visited our garden and their plants have found a place, not only in our garden, but also in memories in our hearts.

Throughout this book, I have tried to make the point that a garden is holy ground. It is God's turf and it is our great privilege to join with Him in cultivating the plants and cultivating our spirit through that work. With that in mind, I would like to identify seven qualities of the saints. I found these online in an article written by Lucy Fuchs which was written for the *Saint Anthony Messenger*. She mentioned many points which ring true in this chapter.

243

The Eight Characteristics of Saints

1. Saints are filled with the love of God.

- They have chosen God above all others and made a definite commitment to God.

- In her book, *Saint Watching* (Viking Press), Phyllis McGinley writes that saints are human beings with an added dimension. "They are obsessed by goodness and by God as Michelangelo was obsessed by line and form, as Shakespeare was bewitched by language, Beethoven by sound."

- St Bernard of Clairvaux's book, *On Loving God*, identifies four stages in learning to love God. These four steps will require deep meditation to understand the importance of this process.
    - a) The love of self for self's sake
    - b) The love of self for God's sake
    - c) The love of God for self's sake
    - d) The love of God for God's sake

2. Saints love other human beings.

- It cannot be any other way. In the First Letter of John (4:20), we read: "If anyone says, 'I love God,' but hates his brother, he is a liar; for whoever does not love a brother whom he has seen cannot love God whom he has not seen."

- St. Clare was a woman who was a companion and colleague of St. Francis of Assisi. She founded The Poor Clares, originally called The Poor Ladies, which is an order to serve those in need, as a way of expressing her compassion for all people.

- St. Martin of Tours was a Roman soldier. When he encountered a poor beggar shivering in the cold, Martin drew his sword and cut his own woolen cloak in half and wrapped the man against the frigid weather. My son Kris and I attended a service of Holy Communion at St. Martin's Cathedral in Trafalgar Square in London. The sanctuary was packed with homeless people. St Martin's is often remembered for its beautiful music, but its ministry to those in need is the true hallmark of this cathedral. In the narthex of the church, there is a small statue depicting the kindness of St. Martin to the beggar. By the way, communion on that Wednesday was served by the priest from a common cup. Kris and I were near the end of the line. We took the bread and dipped it in the wine, receiving by intinction, affirming the common connection we share with all.

- McGinley also says that, although saints may be different in many ways, they are always generous. You will never find a stingy saint.

3. Saints are risk-takers.
- When God called, they answered. For some, it was taking a chance on a new way of life in a new place. In the Old Testament, we have the example of Abraham, called at an old age to leave his country and to go to the place God had selected for him. Even today, it is difficult for older people to leave their level of comfort and to face the new and unknown.
- St. Patrick asked to become a missionary to Ireland, a place where he had been enslaved by a druid priest as a teenager. It is said that Patrick was responsible for the conversion of the entire country of Ireland. Tradition holds that his mission was accomplished in a mere 30 years. Even today, he stands as an example of how best to do mission work. There are very few Irish martyrs because so few people lost their lives in the reforming work of St. Patrick. He took a risk to return to his homeland and founded an incredible Christian legacy through it.
- St. Brendan, another Irish Christian, built a leather boat and set out to cross the Atlantic Ocean to explore and witness throughout the world. In the journal that he kept, we know that he got at least as far as Iceland before returning to Ireland.
- Abraham's story is a marvelous example of trust in God, but even more so of a decision to plunge into the unknown. Like Abraham, saints responded to the graces that were given to them. Some were called to be popes, bishops, abbots, or abbesses. Others found their calling in a quiet, reserved life, far away from the center of activity.

245

- St. Julian of Norwich, a well-known anchoress, lived in a small room attached to a church. She was fully walled in with only a small window, but that did not keep people away; they came to her and asked for her spiritual advice.

4. Saints are humble - willingly and lovingly attributing to God all that they have and all that they will ever be.

- Humility has always had a poor press; many people think that humility means saying derogatory things about oneself. Far from it! The saints showed their humility by using whatever gifts they had to perfection, but never attributing these gifts to themselves.
- St. Augustine and St. Thomas Aquinas were brilliant men and they did not go around saying how stupid they were. They did acknowledge, however, that all they knew was as nothing compared to the infinite wisdom of God.
- Thomas Merton and Henri Nouwen were people of wisdom and humble. I had the privilege of meeting Thomas Merton in the Abbey of Gethsemane in Bardstown, Kentucky. I went there with a small group from seminary with two of my professors, Dr. Dale Moody, a professor of Systemic Theology, and Dr. Glenn Henson, a professor of Church History. We met with Thomas Merton for about an hour. In the monastery, he was known as Brother Louis. Merton was a man of quiet humility and he was a prolific writer of devotional literature, especially about contemplative prayer. His book, *Confessions of a Guilty Bystander*, reveals that even as a monk, he spent long hours in a cabin in the woods of Kentucky and yet was still engaged with the world through a life of prayer.
- Henri Nouwen taught at both Yale and Harvard. He gave up a distinguished academic career near the end of his life. At a home for the mentally challenged in Toronto, Canada, Nouwen became a companion and caregiver to a man who needed daily help. He dedicated a vast number of years to taking care of this man, giving up his career in favor of serving others.
- St. Catherine of Siena lived at home, not in a convent, as a person dedicated to God. People flocked to her, but not

because she wanted them to. She spent her time pointing her many visitors to God through prayer and spiritual advice.

- Others, whose names are not well-known, lived simple lives among their families and friends, serving God with all their hearts, but never making a splash in the world.

5. Saints are people of prayer.

- Some, especially members of religious orders, had entire days of prayer. Others found their time with God in other ways.

- Dorothy Day—not canonized but recognized by many as a truly holy person—started her day with prayer but said that she met God daily in the crowds of the poor who came to her hospitality house. None of the saints saw prayer as a waste of time or as an activity for only the weak or naive.

- One of my favorite devotional classics is entitled *The Practice of the Presence of God*. The book is attributed to Brother Lawrence, who was illiterate. An unknown person transcribed the book of the elderly monk who was more than 80 years of age. Brother Lawrence says that he learned to pray washing pots and pans in the monastery kitchen or while he was cleaning out the monastery stables. These times of prayer were no less important than the appointed times of prayer in the monastery chapel.

- St Francis de Sales taught that all Christians should pray at least one hour every day. It seemed to him a sweet hour of prayer, but few of us have ever learned to pray for that length of time. Prayer does not begin by talking, prayer begins by listening. Prayer is not a monologue telling God things He already knows. We often say prayer changes things, but if we pray, the thing most likely to change is us. Prayer is a kind of spiritual alignment, meant to realign our will with God's Will. Perhaps that is the reason St. Francis taught one hour of prayer a day, unless that person is especially busy, then they should pray for two hours a day.

6. Saints are not perfect.

- Each of the saints had human flaws and faults. They made mistakes. Even at the end of their lives, they still found themselves in need of contrition, pardon, and reconciliation.
- St. Jerome, it is said, had a fearful temper. When another scholar of his time, a former friend, Rufinus, questioned his conclusions, St. Jerome wrote pamphlet after pamphlet blasting him.
- St. Aloysius apparently had bad timing in his spiritual quest; the other novices were just as happy when he was not there. He was the kind of saint who did not seem to know how to enjoy the things of this life.
- Some saints misunderstood their own visions. When St. Francis was told to rebuild the Church, he thought it meant the local church building. It is interesting and amusing to note that Jesus did not clarify the request for him until after he had exerted a lot of sweat and energy repairing an old church.
- St. Joan of Arc was coerced into signing a retraction of her visions, although she later retracted that retraction.
- St. John Vianney, "the Curé of Ars," did not believe the children of La Salette concerning their visions of the Virgin Mary.
- During the time of the Babylonian Captivity of the Papacy at the end of the 14th century and beginning of the 15th, when one pope resided in Avignon and another pope in Rome, saints found themselves on opposite sides of the rival popes, as confused as many of the common people were.

7. Saints are people of their times.

- One wonders how anyone escapes being of his or her time. There were injustices around the saints that they did not speak out against. St. Paul did not condemn slavery but encouraged slaves to obey their masters. St. Thomas Aquinas considered women unequal to men. He believed their only task in life was to bear children. Since we are just as prone as they were to be wrong in our views and perpetuate harm, let's be very clear: racism, sexism, and enslavement are sins. Each of us bears the image of God, every one of us equally. To remember Jesus's teaching of the Golden Rule in Matthew 7, how would you want to be treated?

- If we look at the lives of all the saints, we can certainly find faults. Far from discouraging us, this can give us courage.

Perfection is not what we are striving for, unless it is as perfect a love as possible.

Along with the seven characteristics put forth by Lucy Fuchs, I would like to add one more characteristic to this list which will help us to better understand the saints.

8. Saints are people who have walked through the dark valleys of life.

- The apostle Paul writes that after his conversion, he went to Arabia. He writes of his experience in 2 Corinthians "We do not want you to be uninformed, brothers and sisters, about the troubles we experienced in the province of Asia. We were under great pressure, far beyond our ability to endure, so that we despaired of life itself" (NIV).

- The Spanish priest, St John of the Cross, wrote about his own troubles in life in *The Dark Night of the Soul*. It was through his experience in darkness that he found the true light. He joined Saint Therese of Avila in her attempts to reform the Carmelite Order. Arrested, imprisoned, and tortured for his attempts, John underwent a spiritual awakening. Inspired by this awakening, he penned *The Dark Night of the Soul*. He was canonized on December 27, 1726.

- English Baptist preacher John Bunyan was imprisoned for preaching a gospel that was contrary to the teachings of the Church of England. In his book, *Pilgrim's Progress*, Bunyan writes an allegory about the life of a Christian. He says that on our way to the Heavenly City, we must first pass through the Slough of Despond.

- Her journal published after her death, Mother Teresa's *Come Be My Light: The Private Writings of the "Saint of Calcutta"* is a collection of her private letters. The publication of this journal was a surprise to many who revered the simple nun as an icon of compassion. Her journal shows she spent almost fifty years without sensing the presence of God in her life. She had multiple periods of deep depression and despair, but never lost faith in God. Her focus remained fixed on Him even through the darkest times.

Sainthood does not inoculate a person against the wear and tear of life. We all have our ups and downs.

The apostle Paul, in one of his earliest letters to the Galatians, identifies the fruit of the spirit. They are "love, joy, peace, patience, kindness, goodness, faithfulness, gentleness and self-control" (5:22-23). Please note that many beautiful Christmas cards contain these words, except for the last of the fruit of the spirit. I think that one, most of all, should be on Christmas cards. May God grant us self-control at Christmas time. Jesus Himself said "by their fruit you will know them." In the lives of saints, it is this visible fruit that is most revealing about their inner nature. This is fruit that should be evident in the lives of every Christian.

The path to sainthood in the Roman Catholic Church must pass through several checkpoints. One of those points is beatification, which comes just before canonization. To be blessed calls to mind the beatitudes of Jesus. These beatitudes describe people who have found a deep joy that goes beyond fame and fortune. It is the spiritual state of contentment. The sections of this book have each been based around one beatitude. We look at them again here as a guide to the life of holiness.

Do not be afraid of holiness. It will take away none of your energy, vitality or joy. On the contrary, you will become what the Father had in mind when he created you, and you will be faithful to your deepest self.

Pope Francis

Saints have bees in their halos.

Elbert Hubbard

The Beatitudes: Eight Traits of Saintliness

Matthew 5:1-10

The First Beatitude

"Blessed are the poor in spirit, for theirs is the kingdom of heaven."

The meaning of the word, ptōchoi, "poor" in the Greek language means "one who has nothing and is completely empty." Was Jesus saying that the economically poor are blessed? No. Economic poverty is not something to be desired. Many world religions advocate an ascetic lifestyle, including some forms of Christian monasticism. Poverty in and of itself is not blessed, because the poor can be as arrogant, as ungodly, and as separated from God as are many of the rich. So, what does it mean to be "poor in spirit"? It means those who realize that they can never achieve salvation on their own merit. Instead, they must put their faith and trust in Christ Jesus.

The poor in spirit are those who are not self-assertive, self-reliant, self-confident, self-centered, or self-sufficient. The poor in spirit are not baptized in the mirky water of self-esteem. They do not boast in their God-given advantages, such as their birth, their heritage, their nationality, their education, their race, their wealth, or their physical appearance. None of those things matter. The poor in spirit are those who are conscious of their sin. The Apostle Paul writes, "For it is by grace you have been saved, through faith—and this is not from yourselves, it is the gift of God— not by works, so that no one can boast" (Ephesians 2:8-9). The poor in spirit realize that their righteousness is, as Isaiah said, "like filthy rags" before a holy God (Isaiah 64:6).

The parable of the Prodigal Son is the story of a young man who went from self-confident arrogance to poverty of spirit. It was then that he could return to his father, confess his wrong-doing, and be restored to a loving relationship.

I have found that this one acre of red clay will absolutely humble me. Gardening requires poverty of spirit so that the beauty of the garden is never something we can take credit for. Instead, the garden itself is a gracious gift from a loving God.

"Truly, I say to you, unless you turn and become as little children, you will by no means enter the kingdom of heaven. Therefore, whoever humbles himself as this little child, will be the greatest in the kingdom of heaven."
   - Matthew 18:3-4, NIV

The key isn't whether you have money or have it not, but whether you have God or have Him not. As St. Francis de Sales put it in his "Introduction to the Devout Life,"

"Woe then to those who are rich in spirit, for their portion will be hell. He is rich in spirit whose heart is in his riches, and whose riches fill his heart... if you possess them, preserve your heart from loving them. Do not, then, complain of your poverty (if you are poor), for we complain only of that which displeases us; and if poverty displeases you, you are no longer poor in spirit, for your heart would rather be otherwise."

So, blessed are those who realize their constant need for God over, above and beyond everything else. Blessed are those not chained to the material and passing pleasures and luxuries of this finite world. Blessed are those free from anything and everything that would interfere with an ever-growing awe of God's mercy and love. Blessed are those who recognize that no matter how their life is going in the eyes of the world, they are successful in heaven when they are faithful on earth. Blessed are those who need nothing more than God's love and want nothing more than to share that love with all they encounter.

A soul with nothing to lose on earth is a wonderfully dangerous soul, a soul that will lead many to heaven.

Mark Hart, Teen Life

The Second Beatitude

"Blessed are they who mourn, for they shall be comforted."

After the death of our son, Erik, in the year 2000, I found refuge in my garden. Erik died in November. The following spring, I asked the personnel committee of the church I served if I could use my conference allowance to do something personally enriching to me. They graciously granted my request, and I enrolled in the Master Gardener program offered by our local extension service. That experience restored my soul as I traveled through one of the most difficult periods of my life.

Several sections of this book reveal the way grief guided me. I devoted a section of the garden to Erik's memory. I planted a weeping willow and a weeping maple. Rather than regarding mourning doves as intruders, I saw them as companions who, with their mournful song, brought comfort to me.

The mourning of Christians referred to in this Beatitude is not necessarily because of financial loss, terminal illness, the death of a loved one, divorce, loneliness, or rejection. Paul wrote about one purpose of Godly sorrow in 2 Corinthians 7:10: "For sadness in a Godly way makes for repentance that leads to salvation." Jesus said that he had come "to seek and save those who are lost." I have several crosses in my garden, most of them rustic, as a reminder of the old rugged cross. When we look to the cross of Jesus Christ and realize that Christ died for our sins, we quite naturally grieve. The words of a hymn by Isaac Watts written in 1707 put into verse this kind of sorrow.

> When I survey the wondrous cross
> On which the Prince of Glory died,
> My richest gain I count but loss,
> And pour contempt on all my pride.
>
> Forbid it, Lord, that I should boast,
> Save in the death of Christ my God!
> All the vain things that charm me most,
> I sacrifice them to His blood.

See from His head, His hands, His feet,
Sorrow and love flow mingled down!
Did e'er such love and sorrow meet,
Or thorns compose so rich a crown?

Were the whole realm of nature mine,
That were a present far too small;
Love so amazing, so divine,
Demands my soul, my life, my all.

Christians also mourn because we live in a broken world. I used to wish that my children could grow up and be happy. Then, I changed my mind. I wanted my children to be aware of the suffering of others. In the same way that Siddhartha Gautama left the palace grounds and witnessed the suffering of others before he became the enlightened Buddha, Christians mourn the suffering in our world.

The garden provides a place of solitude where, through prayer, fasting, and quiet reflection, we can enter the divine sorrow of a good Creator for the world God loves very much.

The second beatitude builds on our mental recognition of our poverty of spirit by adding an emotional response of sorrow. When we face the evil in our own lives, it saddens us; when we face the evil in the world. The evil may come from ourselves, from others, or from sources unknown. In any case, when we honestly mourn evil words, evil deeds, evil policies on the job, God sees our sorrow and comforts us with the knowledge that it will not always be this way.

Those blessed with mourning about their own failings can receive comfort by admitting their errors. If we make a mistake, we admit it and pray for pardon. This takes courage! Without the emotional blessing of sadness over our actions, we would probably never muster the guts to admit our mistakes. But if we do, we may be surprised how often people are ready to forgive us.

Pat McLeod, Crosswalk.com.

The Third Beatitude

"Blessed are the meek, for they shall inherit the earth."

T he Greek word for meek, *praus*, refers to a domesticated animal. It does not refer to a wild, unruly animal but to a strong, powerful horse that has been well-trained. It can refer to a team of oxen, disciplined and obedient to a human master. In this Beatitude, the word "meek" refers to a strong, capable person, obedient to a sovereign Lord. A meek person is a man or a woman who is controlled by God in thought, word, and action. In the Garden of Gethsemane, Jesus made the most important decision of His life, "... not my will, but yours be done." (Luke 22:42, NIV) The garden was for Jesus, and is for us, a place for spiritual, front-end alignment. Our will becomes aligned with God's will.

A meek person is not wishy-washy. They are not timid. Neither is a meek person a doormat to be walked over. A meek person is not passive or spineless; they are just the opposite. What makes a person meek? They see God as almighty, all-powerful, all-knowing, and all-wise. A meek person experiences God and is humbled in God's presence. They can say with the Apostle Paul, "I can do all this through him who gives me strength." (Philippians 4:13, NIV)

Humility is a prerequisite for enjoying the garden. To be down on our knees up to our elbows in the dirt.

To be meek is to be gentle, humble, lowly. The meek are the 'gentle'... those who do not assert themselves over others in order to further their own agendas in their own strength, but who will nonetheless inherit the earth because they trust in God to direct the outcome of events.

ESV Study Bible

The Fourth Beatitude

"Blessed are those who hunger and thirst for righteousness, for they shall be satisfied."

To help us understand this Beatitude, we must ask ourselves, "What does it mean to be a righteous person?" Psalm 1:1-3 gives insight into the meaning of righteousness:

> Blessed is the one
> who does not walk in step with the wicked
> or stand in the way that sinners take
> or sit in the company of mockers,
> but whose delight is in the law of the Lord,
> and who meditates on His Law day and night.
> That person is like a tree planted by streams of water,
> which yields its fruit in season
> and whose leaf does not wither—
> whatever they do prospers (NIV).

According to the Psalmist, the person who is righteous does not keep company with the unrighteous, as tempting as that might be. Rather, the righteous person is rooted and grounded in the Word of God. They practice *Lectio Divina*, much like those of the Benedictine order.

In modern Christianity, this is sometimes called "praying the scriptures." In Islamic Sufism, a similar practice is known as *Dhikr* or *Du'a*, where the practitioner prays parts of the Quran, the Hadiths, or original Muslim prose in an act of supplication to or remembrance of Allah.

Lectio Divina simply means reading the scriptures until some verse or even just a few words hit a nerve. Then we stop and meditate on those words, transitioning then into prayer using those same words. In this way, we may satisfy the hunger, quench the thirst for righteousness, and provide nourishment for our soul. This path of righteousness enables us to become like fruit-bearing trees well into old age.

Righteousness is a lifestyle in which we strive to be upright and ethically sound. Our decisions are guided by what Jesus called the two greatest commandments, "Love the Lord your God with all your heart and with all your soul and with all your mind and with all your strength…" and "Love your neighbor as yourself" (Mark 12:30-31, NIV).

"My Father gives you the true bread from heaven. For the bread of God is that which comes down from heaven, and gives life to the world." They said to him, "Lord, give us this bread always." Jesus said to them, "I am the bread of life; he who comes to me shall not hunger, and he who believes in me shall never thirst."

John 6: 32-32 (RSV)

"Whoever drinks of the water that I shall give him will never thirst; the water that I shall give him will become in him a spring of water welling up to eternal life."

John 4: 14

"Therefore are they before the throne of God,
* and serve him day and night within his temple;*
* and he who sits upon the throne will shelter them with his presence.*
They shall hunger no more, neither thirst any more;
* the sun shall not strike them, nor any scorching heat.*
For the Lamb in the midst of the throne will be their shepherd,
* and he will guide them to springs of living water;*
* and God will wipe away every tear from their eyes."*

Revelation 7:15-17 (RSV)

The Fifth Beatitude

"Blessed are the merciful, for they shall obtain mercy."

Mercy is love toward those that are miserable, those that are wretched, and those that need some type of help or assistance.

The merciful are those that are tender hearted and who truly feel in the deepest parts of their being the pain and the suffering of those who need mercy. But most important is the fact that the merciful are those special individuals who go out of their way and make the effort to help. Having compassion on those that are in any way hurting is only the first part of having mercy. Doing something about it is the all-important second part.

This beatitude is also very concerned with mercy through the act of daily forgiveness. Of forgiving offenses that have been inflicted upon you, and in which you show mercy towards everyone who wrongs you regardless of the reasons and regardless of the circumstances. Our Lord demands that we forgive one another just as he is constantly forgiving you. Matthew 6: 14-15 points this out so very clearly. "For if you forgive men their trespasses, your heavenly Father will also forgive you. But if you do not forgive men their trespasses, neither will your Father forgive your trespasses."

He has shown you what is good;
and what does the Lord require of you
but to do justice, and to love kindness,
and to walk humbly with your God?
Micah 6:8 (RSV)

Grace is getting something we do not deserve.
Mercy is not getting something we do deserve.
Sparky Anderson

The Sixth Beatitude

"Blessed are the pure of heart, for they shall see God."

"How can a believer keep his heart pure? By keeping it according to The Word of God."
-Psalms 119:9, NIV

The truth is we can't do any of these things on our own. We can't reform ourselves. We can't cleanse ourselves. Many people have tried to clean themselves. Some have tried to do this through asceticism or leading a life of complete self-denial, or by other methods such as by going away from the world and living in solitude, or permanent silence, or by beating their bodies with whips and clubs. They have tried to cleanse themselves through celibacy, fasting, and prayers. But such asceticism is not biblical, and it will not result in purity of heart.

This beatitude tells us if we are pure in heart then we will see God. The reward for this beatitude is truly marvelous because when the believer becomes pure in heart, not only will they see God as they pass into heaven immediately upon their death, but they will see God right now, not with their natural eye, but through their spiritual vision, through their faith in Jesus Christ.

Who may ascend into the hill of the Lord?
Or who may stand in His holy place?
He who has clean hands and a pure heart,
Who has not lifted up his soul to an idol,
Nor sworn deceitfully.
He shall receive blessing from the Lord,
And righteousness from the God of his salvation.
Psalm 24:3-5 (NKJV)

Purity of heart is to will one thing.
Soren Kierkegaard

The Seventh Beatitude

"Blessed are the peacemakers, for they shall be called sons of God."

The peacemakers are those children of God who not only have great love for God, but also have love for all of h u mankind and they attempt to do everything possible for the advancement of peace everywhere. The term "peacemakers" includes all who make peace between people, whether as individuals or as communities. It includes those who endeavor to make peace even though they fail.

The peacemakers are those who have a peaceful disposition because to make peace is to have a strong and hearty affection for peace. Romans 14:19 tells us, "So then let us pursue the things which make for peace and the building up of one another."

However, peacemaking does not mean seeking peace at any cost, for the peacemaker realizes that peace at any price will usually end up in complete and total destruction. So, a peacemaker is not an appeaser. They are not one who smiles a lot and don't take a position on anything. They are not one who has an easygoing personality and who is nice and sweet. A peacemaker is one who through strength and Godly knowledge endeavors to establish a right relationship between estranged parties based on truth and righteousness.

The apostle Paul speaks about what he calls the "ministry of reconciliation." It is the process of setting things right between people and God. 2 Corinthians 5 says "Therefore, if anyone is in Christ, the new creation has come: The old has gone, the new is here! All this is from God, who reconciled us to himself through Christ and gave us the ministry of reconciliation: that God was reconciling the world to himself in Christ, not counting people's sins against them. And he has committed to us the message of reconciliation" (5:17-19, NIV).

The word peace in the Hebrew language is *"Shalom."* It may mean peace between people, races, communities, or nations, but most of all, it means peace within oneself. Peacemakers live a peaceful life for they have discovered the peace of heart and mind which extends past human understanding. It is centeredness of interior peace that they are able to make peace with those around them. It is the message of the angels hovering over the shepherds' field near Bethlehem. Peace on earth, goodwill to all humankind.

The Eighth Beatitude

"Blessed are those who are persecuted because of righteousness, for theirs is the kingdom of heaven."

In this beatitude, Christ pronounces a blessing on those who are being persecuted. But the persecution that they are suffering is not for misdeeds or evil acts. Their persecution is for doing righteousness. They are those who suffer and use that suffering in a redemptive way.

In the Greek language there is a word: *"marturios."* It is the word from which we get our word "martyr". A martyr is a witness. They witness to the love of God. They witness to the truth of God. They do all this in a self-sacrificing way.

Stephen was a deacon and one of the first Christian martyrs. He was put to death because of his witness by stoning. Acts 6:8-8:2 tells the story of Stephen's martyrdom. James the Apostle was the first of the twelve disciples to be martyred. This account takes place in Acts 12:1-3. King Herod of Agrippa had James put to death by sword during the Passover, the Festival of Unleavened Bread.

James, the brother of Jesus, sometimes called James the Just, was the leader of the church in Jerusalem following the resurrection. He earned this "Just" title because of his piety and clear sense of justice. He was the author of the letter of James, often called the Proverbs of the New Testament. James the Just was stoned in 62 CE when he was accused of blasphemy. According to Jewish and Christian history, James was put to death when priestly authorities had him thrown from a temple tower being crushed on the rocks below, another type of stoning. This is what they threatened to do to Jesus of Nazareth when they threatened to push Him from the cliff.

In 64 CE, Nero, the emperor of Rome, conducted his own plan of urban renewal for The Eternal City. He ordered that the slums of Rome should be set ablaze. The legend, that Nero fiddled while Rome burned, is false. The fiddle had not yet been invented. The truth is that he was responsible for having the fire set. The citizens of Rome were outraged. However, Nero found a convenient excuse – he blamed the Christians. This ignited one of the first and most horrific persecutions of the Christians. At this time, Peter and Paul were both in Rome with their younger protégé, John Mark.

In the same year of the fires, Nero ordered Peter to be crucified. At his own request, Peter was crucified upside down because he said he was unworthy to die in the same way that Jesus Himself had died. At this time, Paul was already imprisoned in Rome. Nero ordered for the great missionary to be beheaded. Young John Mark escaped, most likely to Antioch, where there was a large Christian community already established. Realizing that the first generation of Christians was gone, he knew it was time to write what he could. He penned the gospel, Mark. Ten years later, that document was used by both Matthew and Luke to construct their writings.

Polycarp, another well-known martyr, was a Christian bishop of Smyrna and a Roman citizen. He died a martyr's death because he refused to renounce his Christian beliefs. He was bound and burned at the stake in 155 CE at the age of eighty-six. As the fire was lit, he prayed, "I bless you Father for judging me worthy of this moment so in the company of martyrs I may share the cup of Christ." However, when the fire failed to kill him, he was stabbed to death.

Joan of Arc was a young French peasant woman born in 1412 into a pious Catholic family. She started having visions of angels when she was only 13 years old. She became a military leader, acting under divine guidance. She became known as "The Maid of Orleans" because she defended the French city against the English armies. She is said to be the person who turned the tide in of the Hundred Years war. She also turned a territorial war into one over religion. She was found guilty of crossdressing and heresy and was burned at the stake. She died at the age of nineteen. After her death, she was found innocent and canonized by the Catholic Church.

There are many others up until our present time who have been persecuted because of righteousness. Simon Peter gave one of the earliest confessions of faith: "You are the Christ the son of living God" in Matthew 16:16 (NIV). This was a turning point in the life of Jesus. From then on, He began to teach the disciples that He would have to go to Jerusalem and be a witness for God's love, dying the death of a criminal on that cross.

Those of us that are Christians profess Christ as our Savior and Lord. Somewhere in each of our gardens, there should be a cross, a simple reminder that we too must bear the cross of Christ. Our mission is clear; according to Matthew's gospel, the final words of Jesus were a great commission to go into all the world and make disciples of all people.

I often ask myself the question, "When is the last time I made a disciple?" I pray for the opportunity to disciple others and, I find that when I pray that prayer, I am often presented with that opportunity. I have even had the privilege of praying the sinner's prayer with people in my own garden. It is, after all, a place for the Master Gardener, Jesus Himself. I have a bed of regal blooming iris. One of them is named resurrection, another immortality; both recall the majesty of Jesus' sacrifice.

The question, "Who can be a saint?" lingers. Who can be a saint? We all can. We are all called to a life of holiness. Several years ago, my brother-in-law bought a Jeep. He ordered a special license plate with the Greek word *"hagios"* which translates to holiness. He was driving from the hospital to his home, merging into oncoming traffic on one of my hometown's busiest streets in the proper line. This is when another car sideswiped him. It dented the back fender and scraped the vehicle all the way to the front fender. I later saw the Jeep with that license plate "holiness" and all the dents and scratches. With our flaws and dented fenders, we are called to be saints – *hagios* – the ones who are different.

There were those who, under torture, refused to give in and go free, preferring something better: resurrection. Others braved abuse and whips, and, yes, chains and dungeons. We have stories of those who were stoned, sawed in two, murdered in cold blood; stories of vagrants wandering the earth in animal skins, homeless, friendless, powerless—the world didn't deserve them! —making their way as best they could on the cruel edges of the world.

Hebrews 11:35-40 (MSG)

Seven Paths of Spiritual Growth

Represented by the statuary in my garden, these seven saints each represent a different path of spiritual growth.

1. St. Ignatius of Loyola (1491 – 1556 CE), was the founder of the Society of Jesus.

The Path of Prayer
- The compiler of the *Spiritual Exercises* and a gifted spiritual director, Ignatius has been described as, above all, a man of God, who gave the first place of his life to God and was a man of profound prayer.

2. St. Anthony of Padua (1195 – 1231 CE) was born in Lisbon, Portugal.

The Path of Compassion
- In his abbey, Anthony was responsible for hospitality. He was a gentle and quiet man of prayer given to great compassion, especially for children.
- He is especially invoked for the recovery of things lost ("Saint Anthony, Saint Anthony, please come around. Something is lost and cannot be found.").

3. St. Joseph, surrogate father of Jesus.
The Path of Faithfulness
- Joseph's profession is described in the Gospels as a τεκτων, a Greek word for a variety of skilled craftsmen, but Christian tradition has him as a carpenter, although stonemason might fit the sense of the Greek better.
- Joseph is the patron saint of workers, homes, and families.

4. St. Francis of Assisi, (1181 – 1226 CE) was a Roman Catholic monk.
The Path of Service
- The founder of the mendicant Order known as the Franciscans.

- He is known as the patron saint of animals, birds, and the environment.

5. St. Patrick, (378-493 CE) was a Roman Britain-born Christian missionary
The Path of Witness
- The patron saint of Ireland. Legend also credits Patrick with teaching the Irish about the concept of the Trinity by showing people the shamrock.

6. St. Augustine of Hippo, (354 – 430 CE), Bishop of Hippo.
The Path of Bible Study
- The *Confessions*, which is often called the first Western autobiography—are still read around the world.
- "Thou hast made us for Thyself and our hearts are restless till they rest in Thee."

7. St. Benedict of Nursia (480 – 547 CE) was the founder of Western Christian monastic communities.
The Path of Discipleship
- A rule-giver for cenobite monks. *The Rule of St Benedict* became one of the most influential religious rules in Western Christendom. For this reason, Benedict is often called "the founder of western Christian monasticism."

For the beauty of the earth,
For the glory of the skies,
For the love which from our birth
Over and around us lies,

[Chorus]

Lord of all, to thee we raise
This our hymn of grateful praise.

Folliott S. Pierpoint

Resurrection

When we think of winter, we may think of endings. It is natural and appropriate, when contemplating the end of things, to reckon with our own end. We are born and we will die. This old body will one day be placed in the ground.

Many religions, not only Christianity, encourage us to face our mortality, and in doing so to gaze beyond the horizon of our lives. We can see so little, what lies beyond is a mystery. But in the most practical and earthy terms, even this human body can be recycled. And the garden bears witness to our hope. After winter comes spring. That which seemed dead awakens to new life.

And with every spring comes Easter.

Faithfully,

Kirk

Acknowledgements

My mother, known to me and my family as Mama, often placed a bowl of water with floating flowers on the coffee table in our home. The blooms I remember most were camellias, roses, and pansies. When I was a toddler just beginning to gain my footing, I would pull up on the coffee table to gain a better view of the world around me. One of those times, I spied a beautiful bowl of floating pansies. Fascinated by their bright blossoms, I ate the entire bowl of blooms.

Mama was horrified until she learned from our family doctor that pansies and violas were safely edible and that his wife used them to garnish summer salads and desserts. We had a good friend when we loved in Winston-Salem who made a delightful lemon souffle which she decorated with purple violets. When Mama told the story about my eating the pansies, she said that from the time I was knee high to a duck, I had a taste for gardening.

Gardening is the most popular hobby in the United States. Nearly one half of all Americans enjoy gardening as a pastime. Some folks have extensive land devoted to the hobby. Others may have a small patio garden, a rooftop garden, a few spring annuals in a window box, or a single geranium in a clay pot. Gardening is an enjoyable and relaxing way to get in touch with nature, but it also has plenty of health benefits. Gardening is an activity that's good for the mind, the body, and the spirit. It can be enjoyed by people of all ages from the youngest toddler to the oldest senior adult.

I have found joy in gardening for most of my life. I am indebted to the people mentioned on the dedication page of this book for planting the fertile seeds of the pleasure of watching things grow within my heart. I remember fondly walking the freshly plowed furrows following my grandfather's hand tiller. By the age of twelve, I was driving an old Ford tractor cultivating our family's large garden. When my father-in-law died, I inherited his Troy-Bilt tiller.

I was the Senior Pastor of Morningside Baptist Church when our twenty-seven-year-old son, Erik, died in November 2000. I was still grieving the following spring. I asked the Personnel Committee if I could use my annual conference allowance to do something that would not necessarily make me a better pastor but would be personally enriching for me. They agreed. I enrolled in the South Carolina Master Gardener Class.

My project at the conclusion of the course was to design and lead the construction of a Prayer Garden in a courtyard that was muddy red clay. Many volunteers from the congregation helped with the project. The group became the Gethsemane Garden Club. Together we maintained the Prayer Garden and replanted each spring.

I am grateful to the members of Morningside for supporting that effort.

I am thankful to Winston Hardigree and Joe Maple who were the lead teachers of the Master Gardner Class.

I appreciate the friendship and encouragement of other Master Gardeners. To Everett Lindberger, the iris and daylily king. To Betty Montgomery, a garden columnist and the hydrangea queen. To Linda Cobb, garden writer and expert on cottage gardens. To Linda McHam, English Garden aficionado. To Dr. Clay Turner, my colleague in ministry, classmate in the Master Gardner Class, and avid fly fisherman.

I have learned much from the people who have owned and operated garden shops in our area. To Jay Moore, a reputable horticulturist and teacher. To George Gunter who has more knowledge about growing plants that anyone else I know. To the fine folks at Piedmont Farm and Garden who are always helpful. To Carolina Garden World for all of their help through the years. I have often stopped to browse in other garden shops and greenhouses across the Upstate. Thanks to all.

I have had good help, especially as my health declined. In the first years we lived in the old home place, David Tanner helped me with my early efforts to tame this one acre of red clay. Roger Young has been a good friend and a beloved garden companion for many years. Rick Garett and his crew take good care of our lawn. Todd Kuri of Upstate Arborists helps keep our trees fit and trim. Steve Young, Roger's brother, spent hours here beating back encroaching weeds and invasive plants that did not belong in our garden. Johnny Fowler gave invaluable help with landscaping work. David Pizor helped me plan and execute the waterfall and pond design. Brandon Schafer has since helped me maintain the water feature.

This book has been a long time in the making. I have tried to combine my awareness of Christian Theology and spiritual practice with my gardening observations.

Krista Redding did all the beautiful artwork using her color pencils. Many are featured on the cover of the book. Krista's husband, Nathan, labeled all her drawings with correct biological nomenclature. Holly Barnett was most helpful in getting the project off the ground. Abby Ledford helped me move it across the finish line. Abby urged me to us my own paintings as the section divisions in the book. Holly and Abby are two young women with a bright future ahead because they are both gifted, intelligent, diligent, and cheerful workers. I have truly enjoyed working with them. Thank you very much.

David Tullock of Parson's Porch Publishing has been a patient encourager and friend. I am grateful.

My family has encouraged me throughout the project My children and grandchildren have delighted in my stories and my grandfather humor.

My wife Clare has been constantly by my side. I could not do this writing without her. She is my first and final reader. But so much more. Clare is my best friend, my wife, my companion in all things, my lover for fifty-nine years. She enjoys the garden mostly from the kitchen window or from a rocking chair on the back porch.

Kirk H. Neely
Spring 2023

About the Author

K irk H. Neely and his wife, Clare, have been married since 1966. They are parents of five children and have thirteen grandchildren. Since 1980, Kirk and Clare have lived in the home built by his grandparents in 1937. Additionally, Kirk is a Master Gardener and enjoys working in his own garden. The National Wildlife Federation has certified the Neelys' backyard as a wildlife refuge.

Kirk was born in Spartanburg, South Carolina. Kirk went on to receive a Bachelor's of Science degree in Biology and Chemistry from Furman University, Greenville, South Carolina (1966). He was licensed in ministry by First Baptist Church, Taylors, South Carolina, in 1966. He was ordained in Pastoral Ministry by Crescent Hill Baptist Church, Louisville, Kentucky, in 1970. He received the Master of Divinity Degree (1970) and the Doctor of Ministry Degree in Pastoral Counseling (1973) from The Southern Baptist Theological Seminary, Louisville, Kentucky. He was named a Merrill Fellow at The Divinity School of Harvard University (1980), where he did postdoctoral study.

Kirk was coauthor with Wayne E. Oates of *Where to Go for Help*, Westminster Press, 1972. He has written two books of devotions, both published through Christian Supply Company (1996) *By the Sea* and *Unto the Hills*. *When Grief Comes: Finding Strength for Today and Hope for Tomorrow* was published in July 2007 by Baker Books. *A Good Mule Is Hard to Find and Other Tales from Red Clay Country* was published by Hub City Writers Project in 2009. This book was selected as a finalist for the 2010 SIBA Awards, presented annually by the Southern Independent Booksellers Alliance for the best in Southern literature. *Banjos, Barbecue, and Boiled Peanuts and Other Tales from the South* was published by Hub City Writers Project in 2011.

Kirk frequently wrote for The Spartanburg-Herald Journal. Kirk has had a life-long interest in promoting ecumenical and interfaith relationships. For eighteen years he was a leader in the annual community Thanksgiving service as well as an ongoing interreligious dialogue within the Spartanburg faith community. Kirk continues fostering his passions for ministry, gardening, and family both within his own home and throughout his community.